Mary Louisa Boyle

Biographical Catalogue of the Portraits at Longleat

Mary Louisa Boyle

Biographical Catalogue of the Portraits at Longleat

ISBN/EAN: 9783744679381

Printed in Europe, USA, Canada, Australia, Japan

Cover: Foto ©ninafisch / pixelio.de

More available books at **www.hansebooks.com**

BIOGRAPHICAL CATALOGUE

OF THE PORTRAITS

AT LONGLEAT

IN THE COUNTY

OF WILTS

THE SEAT OF

THE MARQUIS OF BATH

'*A true delineation, even of the smallest man, and his scene of pilgrimage through life, is capable of interesting the greatest man; for all men are to an unspeakable degree brothers, each man's life a strange emblem of every man's, and human portraits faithfully drawn are, of all pictures, the welcomest on human walls.*' CARLYLE.

LONDON: ELLIOT STOCK
1881.

DEDICATION

TO THE OWNERS OF THAT BEAUTIFUL HOME,

ENDEARED TO ME BY THE KINDNESS AND FRIENDSHIP
OF THREE GENERATIONS,

THESE PAGES ARE INSCRIBED

BY THEIR FAITHFUL KINSWOMAN

MARY LOUISA BOYLE.

LONDON, *September* 1881.

 FEEL it incumbent upon me to offer a few words of apology for the shortcomings and inequalities of this small work, and the disproportion of the length of some notices, and that of others; but I have had many difficulties to contend with since I began my pleasant labours,—the absence, for instance, of books of reference when travelling, and still more, the failure of sight, which has rendered me more than usually dependent on the kind help of

others for description of pictures, details of dress, and the like.

Being essentially a family record, I have given more especial attention to the notices of such personages as were connected, even remotely, with the owners of Longleat, making, as a rule, the records of public, subservient to those of private, and domestic life, excepting, as in many cases, where they were closely intertwined. To Kings and Queens I have usually apportioned but a few lines, deviating from this rule, however, when treating of the King and Queen of Bohemia, whose lives read as a romance.

I have consulted history by many hands, and memoirs of all kinds,—Clarendon, Burnet, Strype, Aubrey, Conway, Granger, Lodge, etc. etc., and only refrained from quoting my authorities in footnotes from the fear of swelling a volume already, I fear, too bulky.

To Canon Jackson, for whose invaluable help I can offer no adequate thanks, I am indebted for stores of information, which his well-known local knowledge, and love, and power of research, could alone supply. Neither am I ashamed to own (since I had his permission) how largely I have helped myself to gifts so freely bestowed.

Mr. Ernest Law kindly came to my assistance in the vexed question of the portrait of Francis I. and his Queen, for so many years improperly named, by allowing me to make use of a note belonging to his forthcoming interesting work on Hampton Court Palace. The picture in question has been attributed to different painters, —Sir Antonio More, Janet, and a French artist, Maître Amboise, little known to fame. A similar portrait was painted, and has been engraved, of Charles Brandon, Duke of Suffolk, and his wife, Mary, widow of Louis XII., King of France, but the position of the figures is transposed, the Queen (doubtless in deference to her rank) being on the right hand.

Many delightful hours, both at Longleat itself, and in manifold, and devious wanderings, have been passed, in compiling this brief memorial of the portraits in 'the most august house in England.'

ENTRANCE HALL

Contains large pictures by John Wootton, representing the second Lord Weymouth, several gentlemen, members of the hunt, attendants, horses, hounds, etc. etc.

LIBRARY.

LIBRARY.

No. 1.

FIRST VISCOUNT WEYMOUTH.

Oval. Brown coat. Wig.

No. 2.

BISHOP KEN.

BY SIR PETER LELY.

BORN 1637, DIED 1711.

Oval. In Canonicals. Black skull-cap.

E was the youngest son of Thomas Ken, of Furnival's Inn. Born at Berkhampstead, county Herts. The Kens were a family of great antiquity in Somersetshire. The future Bishop was educated at Winchester and New College, Oxford, and entered the University, about the year 1656, at the same time as Mr. Thynne (afterwards Lord Weymouth), who became the faithful friend of his whole (subsequent) life.

Oxford was at that time in a state of great disorder;—the Book of Common Prayer forbidden; 'the Proctor a boisterous fellow at cudgelling, and foot-ball playing; the Vice-Chancellor in Spanish leather boots, huge ribbons at the knee, and his hat mostly cocked.'

But such examples were lost on Ken. He pursued his studies with sobriety, and diligence, and took his Degree. In 1666 he became a Fellow of Winchester College, and was made chaplain to Morley, Bishop of the diocese, who gave him a living in the Isle of Wight.

Here he was most zealous in his duties, allowing himself but little sleep, and (in the words of a near relation and friend) 'so lively and cheerful was his temper that he would be very facetious to his friends of an evening, though he could scarce keep his eyes open, and he used to sing his morning hymn to his lute before he dressed.' In 1669 he was appointed Prebendary of Winchester, and travelled to Italy with his nephew, who was also the nephew and namesake of the celebrated Izaak Walton; and in 1682 we hear of him on board the Tangiers fleet, with Lord Dartmouth.

The Princess of Orange (afterwards Queen Mary of England), whose chaplain he became, appreciated Ken's straightforward and uncompromising character. But the Prince was very wroth with him on one occasion, when the Englishman stood forward as champion of a young lady, at the Dutch Court, who had been wronged.

Ken insisted that her seducer should marry her, and he carried his point, but William (with whom he had not been on friendly terms, before this event) resented the interference, and threatened to deprive his wife's chaplain of his post.

The Princess was in despair when she found her favourite on the eve of departure, and endeavoured to compromise matters; but Ken would brook no half measures, and told his royal mistress roundly, that he would not remain in Holland unless requested to do so by the Prince, and that in person.

The matter was soon settled according to Ken's own stipulations; but shortly afterwards he was back in England, and appointed to a royal chaplaincy by Charles II.

It seemed his fate, however, to fall out with his royal patrons, for the Court repairing to Winchester for the summer, Ken's prebendal house was pitched on as a suitable residence for Madam Eleanor Gwynne; but the merry monarch had reckoned without his host, in every sense of the word, and no power on earth could persuade the Churchman to admit the siren.

It speaks well for Charles that he bore Ken no ill-will for his resistance, as he preferred him not long after to the See of Bath and Wells. But before the new Bishop entered on his Episcopal duties, the King fell sick, and Burnet bears testimony to the zeal with which Ken attended Charles's death-bed, striving 'to awaken his conscience, and speaking with great elevation, as of a man inspired.'

On the King's death, the Bishop devoted himself to his Episcopal duties; he published several works, chiefly on divinity, and, disgusted with the ignorance of the people in his diocese, he founded several schools, trying, as he said, 'to lay a foundation to make the next generation better.'

He was invariably courteous in his demeanour to all men, so much so, as to give some members of the Roman Catholic faith, a hope of his conversion; but he was a staunch Protestant, and withstood and denounced Popery, regardless of Court favour. Indeed, he spoke boldly from his own pulpit, but, more daring still, he admonished the Court on the subject, calling on them to hold fast by the reformed religion, and rebuking them for unmanly policy. James II. bore with Ken for a time, and was said to have done all in his power to gain over one, who was indeed a staunch champion of the creed, or opinion he professed; but Bath and Wells would listen to no overtures, and took his way to the Tower with the six other prelates. In spite of all these religious differences, Ken was loyal to the house of Stuart, and when William and the Revolution appeared, he refused to take the oath of allegiance, and was in consequence deprived of his bishopric—William perhaps not unwilling to pay off old scores.

Ken was much beloved in his diocese, and when he took his departure he was followed by the prayers and good wishes of all men; and now that the horizon had clouded over for him, there rose up a noble and faithful friend, 'even like unto a brother, who was born for adversity.'

Lord Weymouth, who had been his fellow-collegian at Oxford, gladly availed himself of the plea that Longleat was in the diocese, and cordially bade the outcast welcome. In that beautiful home did the ex-Bishop reside for twenty years, treated with the greatest kindness and consideration, his own apartments assigned him (near the old library), allowed to come and go at his own free will, to enjoy perfect leisure, to choose and receive his friends, and pursue his literary labours in peace. Lord Weymouth's only son, who died before his father, was of a studious and scholarly turn of mind, and he and Ken had friends in common, among others the celebrated Elizabeth Rowe, daughter of a Nonconformist minister at Frome of the name of Singer. She showed great talent at an early age, and Mr. Thynne took much pleasure in giving her lessons in Latin and French, when she came over to Longleat.

Dr. Harbin, Lord Weymouth's chaplain, and the Rev. Izaak Walton of Poulshot, Ken's nephew, were also members of this pleasant society. Had it not been for the failure of his health, the learned divine might have spent the evening of his days in peace and rest.

Perhaps we may say he did so, in spite of his sufferings, for he accepted every trial in a truly Christian spirit, and in a collection of hymns he called 'Anodynes' (seeing that their composition afforded him solace when unable to prosecute works which required more research and continuity of work), there is a most pathetic poem on pain, in which he blesses the pangs that bring him nearer his God. He says—

> 'One day of pain improves me more
> Than years of ease could do before.
> By pain God me instructs;
> By pain to endless bliss conducts.'

And many such passages indicating his entire submission to the Divine will. His descriptions also of his sleepless nights show us, we were indebted to that very sleeplessness for his hymns for morning, evening, and midnight.

There is a tradition that he composed one of these sacred songs at least while reposing on the beautiful hill which overlooks the house, and is familiarly and fondly called 'Heaven's Gate.' In truth, it is a spot to inspire a poet as well as a painter, more especially when radiant with autumnal tints.

Ken had had enough to do with political troubles, and wisely abstained from interference in public affairs, from the moment of his retirement. He refused to acknowledge his first successor to the see, Dr. Kidder; but on that prelate's death in 1703, he requested Dr. Hooper to accept his congratulations, signing himself 'Late Bishop of Bath and Wells.'

The Queen had a great admiration for Ken's intellectual and moral reputation, and made him an allowance. But his bodily infirmities increased; he went to the hot wells at Bristol, and afterwards to pay a visit to Mrs. Thynne, near Sherbourne, where he had a stroke; and wishing to go to Bath, he set forward, but halted at Longleat, where he died. Surely no one could be better prepared to meet death, which he called his final friend. The day before he breathed his last, he told his friends to look in his portmanteau and they would find his shroud, which he always carried with him, saying it might as soon be wanted, as any other of his habiliments.

He was buried, by his own desire, in the nearest parish within his diocese; and there, in Frome churchyard, under the east window of the chancel of St. John's, a quaint tomb covers the mortal remains of Thomas Ken. Many are the pilgrims who still visit that stone coffin, surmounted by a mitre and pastoral staff.

Some years after his death, four volumes of miscellaneous works were published—theological, devotional, secular, in prose and verse. In consequence of the rumours which had been circulated of a leaning towards Roman Catholicism, an extract from his will was made public :—' I die in the Holy Catholic and Apostolic faith; more particularly, I die in the communion of the Church of England, as it stands distinguished from all Papal and Puritanical denominations, as it adheres to the doctrines of the Cross.'

Professor Keble, in speaking of his forerunner in sacred lyrical composition, pays a graceful tribute to Thomas Ken when he says :—' We shall scarcely find in all ecclesiastical history a greener spot than the latter years of this courageous and affectionate pastor, persecuted alternately by both parties, and driven from his station in his declining age, yet singing on with unabated cheerfulness to the last.'

From all we hear and read indeed of Ken, it would seem as if he had reached nearer his own ideal than is the lot of most men. In his description of what a poet should be, he says—

> ' Prophets and poets were of old
> Made in the same celestial mould ;
> True poets are a saint-like race,
> And with the gift receive the grace,
> Of their own songs the virtue feel, etc.
>
> A poet should have heat and light,
> Of all things a capacious sight,
> Serenity with rapture joined,
> Aims noble, eloquence refined,
> Strong, modest, sweetness to endear,
> Expressions lively, lofty, clear.

Such graces can nowhere be found
Except on consecrated ground,
Where poets fix on God their thought,
By sacred inspiration taught,
Where each poetic votary sings
In heavenly tones of heavenly things.'

No. 3.

ANTHONY ASHLEY COOPER, FIRST EARL OF SHAFTESBURY.

BY SIR PETER LELY.

BORN 1621, DIED 1683.

In coloured Chancellor's robes.

SON of Sir John Cooper of Rockbourne, county Hants, by Anne, daughter and sole heir of Sir Anthony Ashley, Bart., of Wimborne St. Giles, county Dorset, where the future Chancellor was born.

In his autobiography, he describes his mother of 'low stature,' as was also the aforesaid Sir Anthony, 'a large mind but his person of the lowest,' while his own father was 'lovely and graceful in mind and person, neither too high nor too low,' therefore the pigmy body of which Dryden speaks must have been inherited from the maternal side.

Sir Anthony was delighted with his grandson, and although at the time of the infant's birth, the septuagenarian was on the point of espousing a young wife, his affection was in no wise diminished for his daughter, or her boy.

Lady Cooper and her father died within six months of each other. Sir John married again, a daughter of Sir Charles

Morrison, of Cassiobury, county Herts, by whom he had several children. He died in 1631, leaving the little Anthony bereft of both parents, with large but much encumbered estates, and law-suits pending.

Many of his own relations being most inimical to his interests, Anthony went with his brother and sister to reside with Sir Daniel Norton, one of his trustees, who—we once more quote the autobiography—'took me to London, thinking my presence might work some compassion, on those who ought to have been my friends.'

He refers to the suit in which they were now engaged. The boy must have had a winning way with him (as the old saying goes), for when only thirteen, he went of his own accord to Noy, the Solicitor-General, and entreated his assistance as the friend of his grandfather. Noy was deeply touched, took up the case warmly, and gained one suit in the Court of wards, stoutly refusing to take any fee whatever.

After Sir Daniel Norton's death, Anthony went to live with an uncle, Mr. Tooker, near Salisbury, though it was supposed Lady Norton would gladly have kept him under her roof, with a view to a match with one of her daughters. He says himself,—' Had it not been for the state of my litigious fortune, the young lady's sweet disposition had made me look no farther for a wife.'

In 1637 he went to Exeter College, Oxford, where he 'made such rapid strides in learning as to be accounted the most prodigious youth in the whole University.' By his own showing, he was popular with his companions and well satisfied with himself, indeed a general spirit of self-complacency pervades these pages. In little more than a year he went to Lincoln's Inn, where he appears to have found the theatres, fencing galleries, and the like, more to his taste than the study of the law.

An astrologer who was in old Sir Anthony's house at the

time of the grandson's birth, cast the horoscope, and to the fulfilment of these predictions, may probably be attributed young Anthony's own predilection for the study of astrology in later days. The horoscope in question foreboded feuds and trouble at an early age, and some years afterwards the same magician, foreseeing through the medium of the planets that a certain Miss Roberts (a neighbour without any apparent prospects of wealth) would become a great heiress, he endeavoured to persuade his pupil to marry her. The lady did eventually come into a considerable fortune; but Mr. Tooker, who was not over-credulous, had other views at the time for his nephew; and accordingly, at eighteen, Ashley Cooper became the husband of Margaret, the daughter of my Lord-Keeper Coventry, 'a woman of excellent beauty and incomparable gifts.'

The young couple resided with the bride's father in London, Anthony paying flying visits to Dorsetshire. He was subject to fits, but even this infirmity redounded to his advantage according to his own version; how that being in Gloucestershire on one occasion, and taken suddenly ill, 'the women admired his courage and patience under suffering,' and he contrived to ingratiate himself with the electors of Tewkesbury to some purpose.

He gives us an amusing and characteristic description of how he won the favour of the electors and bailiffs of this town by his conduct at a public dinner, where he and a certain Sir Henry Spiller were guests, and sat opposite each other. The knight, a crafty, perverse, rich man, a Privy Councillor, had rendered himself very obnoxious in the hunting-field, and at the banquet aforementioned, began the dinner with all the affronts and dislikes he could possibly put on the bailiffs and their entertainment, which enraged and disgusted them, and this rough raillery he continued. 'At length I thought it my duty to defend the cause of those whose bread I was eating, which I did with so good success, sparing not the bitterest retorts, that I had a complete victory. This gained the townsmen's hearts, and their wives' to boot. I was made free of the town, and at the next Parliament (though absent at the time), was chosen burgess by an unanimous vote, and that without a penny charge.'

Sir Anthony had strange humours: he loved a frolic dearly. He had a confidential servant who resembled him so much that, when dressed in his master's left-offs, the lackey was often mistaken for his better. This worthy was a clever man-milliner, and had many small accomplishments which made him popular in country houses, and his master confesses that he often listened to the valet's gossip, and made use of it, in the exercise of palmistry and fortune-telling, which produced great jollity, and 'of which I did not make so bad a use as many would have done.' With this account he finishes the record of his youth. A time of business followed, 'and the rest of my life is not without great mixture of public concerns, and intermingled with the history of the times.'

Sir Anthony sat for Tewkesbury in 1639, but that Parliament was hastily dissolved. He raised a regiment of horse for the king's service, and occupied places of trust in his own county; but believing himself unjustly treated and slighted by the Court, he listened to the overtures of the Parliament, and returned to Dorsetshire as colonel of a regiment in their army.

In 1649 he lost the wife he dearly loved, to whose memory he pays a most touching tribute in his diary. But she left no living child, and before the expiration of the year the widower had espoused Lady Frances Cecil, daughter of the Earl of Exeter, a royalist.

The friendship of the Protector and Sir Anthony was of a most fitful and spasmodic nature,—now fast allies, now at daggers drawn. Some writers affirm that, on the death of his second wife, he asked the hand of one of Cromwell's daughters;

others, that he advised the Protector to assume the Crown, who offered it to him in turn!

He held many appointments under the reigning Government, and continued to sit in Parliament; but having, with many other Members, withstood the encroachments of the great man, Oliver endeavoured to prevent his return, and not being able to do so, forbade him to enter the House of Commons. (See the history of the times.) The Members, with Ashley Cooper at their head, insisted on readmittance. Again ousted, again readmitted; nothing but quarrels and reconciliations. The fact was, that Sir Anthony was too great a card to lose hold of, entirely. He had still a commission in the Parliamentary army, and a seat at the Privy Council, circumstances that in no wise prevented him carrying on a correspondence with the King 'over the water.' Indeed, he was accused of levying men for the Royal service; arrested, acquitted, sat again in Parliament under Richard Cromwell, joined the Presbyterian party to bring back Charles, and when the Parliament declared for the King, Sir Anthony was one of the twelve Members sent over to Breda, to invite his return. When in Holland Ashley Cooper had a fall from his carriage, and a narrow escape of being killed. Clarendon (there was no love lost between them) says it was hoped that by his alliance (as his third wife) with a daughter of Lord Spencer of Wormleighton, a niece of the Earl of Southampton, 'his slippery humour would be restrained by his uncle.'

He now took a leading part in politics, was appointed one of the Judges of the Regicides, created Baron Ashley at the coronation, and afterwards became Chancellor of the Exchequer, Under-Treasurer, and further high offices, and in 1672 Lord Cooper of Pawlett, county Somerset, and Earl of Shaftesbury; and so quickly did honours rain on him, that the same year saw him Lord High Chancellor of England. He appears to have given great umbrage to many of the law officers, by his haughty bearing. We are told 'he was the gloriousest man alive; he said he would teach the bar that a man of sense was above all their forms; and that he was impatient to show them he was a superior judge to all who had ever sat before on the marble chair.'

He maddened the gentlemen of the long robe by his vagaries, and innovations, and defiance of precedents. He wore an ash-coloured gown instead of the regulation black, assigning as his reason, that black was distinctive of the barrister-at-law, and he had never been called to the bar.

He went to keep Hilary term 'on a horse richly caparisoned, his grooms walking beside him,' all his officers ordered to ride on horseback, 'as in the olden time.'

No doubt the good Dorsetshire country gentleman, the lover of sport and of horse-flesh, who had been accused of regaling his four-footed favourites on wine and cheese-cakes, had a mischievous pleasure in seeing the uneasy and scared looks of his worshipful brethren, some of whom perhaps had never sat on a saddle till that day.

At all events, poor Judge Twisden was laid in the dust, and he swore roundly no Lord Chancellor should ever reduce him to such a plight again. Shaftesbury lived at this time in great pomp at Exeter House, in the Strand, and was in high favour with his royal master, who visited him at Wimborne St. Giles during the Plague, when the Court was at Salisbury.

At Oxford, when Parliament sat, he made acquaintance with the celebrated John Locke, who afterwards became an inmate of his patron's house, his tried friend, and medical adviser.

The situations of public employment which Shaftesbury obtained for this eminent man were, unfortunately, in the end, the source of difficulty, and distress rather than advantage. The history of the Cabal, of which he was the mainspring, and of which he formed the fourth letter (Clifford, Arlington, Buckingham, Ashley, Lauderdale), would suffice for his biography, during the five years of its life. But it must never be forgotten that to Shaftesbury England owes the passing of the Habeas Corpus Bill, as likewise one for making judges independent of the Crown.

The reader must seek elsewhere, and elect for himself, whether Shaftesbury was or was not guilty of all the plots and conspiracies against King and country of which he has been accused. To the Duke of York he made himself most obnoxious. He was instrumental in establishing the Test Act, which made Roman Catholics ineligible for public offices; he was, moreover, the champion of the Exclusion Bill, and opposed James's marriage with Mary of Modena; and there is little doubt that the Duke did all to undermine Shaftesbury's favour with the King.

There was always an element of humour mixed up with his doings, even when fortune frowned on him. Finding that the King meant to unseat him from the Woolsack, and that his successor was already named, he sought the royal presence; the King was about to proceed to chapel. The fallen favourite told Charles he knew what his intentions were, but he trusted he was not to be dismissed with contempt. 'Cod's fish, my lord,' replied the easy-going monarch, 'I will not do it with any circumstances that may look like a slight,' upon which the ex-Minister asked permission to carry the Great Seals of Office for the last time before the King into chapel, and then to his own house till the evening.

Granted permission, Shaftesbury, with a smiling countenance, entered the sacred building, and spoiled the devotions of all his enemies, during that service at least. Lord Keeper Finch, who was to succeed him, was at his wit's end, believing Shaftesbury reinstated, and all (and there were many) who wished his downfall were in despair.

The whole account is most amusing and characteristic, including the manner in which the Seals were actually resigned, but we have not space to say more. Shaftesbury was indeed now 'out of suits with fortune.' In 1677 he, with other noblemen, was committed to the Tower for contempt of the authority of Parliament, and although other prisoners were soon liberated, he was kept in confinement thirteen months. On regaining his freedom he was made Lord President of the Council, but opposing the Duke of York's succession, was dismissed from that post in a few months. In 1681 he was again apprehended, on false testimony, and once more sent to the Tower on charge of treason, and that without a trial.

His papers were searched, but nothing could be found against him except one document, 'neither writ nor signed by his hand.' The jurors brought in the bill 'Ignoramus,' which pleased the Protestant portion of the community, who believed the Earl suffered in the cause of religion.

Bonfires were kindled in his honour; one of the witnesses against him narrowly escaped from the fury of the mob; a medal was struck in his honour to commemorate his enlargement. Hence the poem of that name from the pen of Dryden, suggested by the King. On regaining his liberty, Shaftesbury went to reside at his house in Aldersgate Street, when, finding his enemies were still working against him, he took the friendly advice of Lord Mordaunt, and after lying *perdu* in another part of London, for a night or two, he set off for Harwich *en route* for Holland with a young relative, both disguised as Presbyterian ministers, with long black perukes. Adverse winds detained them at a small inn, when one day the landlady entered the elder gentleman's room, and carefully shutting the door, told him that the chambermaid had just been into his companion's apartment, and instead of a swarthy sour-faced dominie, had found a beautiful fair-haired youth. 'Be assured, sir,' said the good woman, 'that I will neither ask questions, nor tell tales, but I cannot answer for a young girl's discretion.'

The man who had been so hunted of late, was touched, thanked the good soul, and bade his handsome young friend make love to the maid, till the wind changed.

The fugitives, however, had an extra run for it, as it was, for the hounds were on their track. Fortunately the capture of one of Shaftesbury's servants, dressed like his master, gave them time to embark.

They arrived at Amsterdam after a stormy passage, where Shaftesbury hired a large house, with the intention of remaining some time, and all the more that he found himself treated with great respect, by all the principal inhabitants. But misfortune pursued him. He was seized with gout in the stomach, and expired on the 1st of January 1683. His body was conveyed to England, and landed at Poole, whither the gentlemen of his native county flocked, uninvited, to pay a tribute to his memory, by attending the remains to Wimborne St. Giles.

We leave the sentence to be pronounced on the first Earl of Shaftesbury to wiser heads than ours, but one remark we feel authorised to make,—that we are not called on to believe him as black as Dryden has painted him, since we cannot but question the justice of the pen that described Charles the Second as the God-like David, in the far-famed poem of 'Absalom (the Duke of Monmouth) and Achitophel' (Shaftesbury). He loads the latter with invective :—

> 'A man to all succeeding nations curst,
> For close designs and crooked councils fit,
> Sagacious, bold, and turbulent of wit.
> Restless, unfixed in principles and place,
> In power unpleased, impatient of disgrace,
> A fiery soul, which working out its way,
> Fretted the pigmy body to decay.

> Great wits are sure to madness close allied;
> Oh, had he been content to serve the Crown
> With virtues only proper to the gown,' etc. etc.

There spoke the Poet-Laureate, and woe indeed to the man who had such a poet as Dryden for his censor! Yet for all this abuse which he had written to order, Dryden could not help bearing testimony as follows:—

> 'Yet fame deserved, no memory can grudge,
> The Statesman we abhor, but praise the Judge;
> In Israel's court ne'er sate an Abithin
> With more discerning eyes or **hands more clean**,
> Unbribed, unsought, the wretched to redress,
> Swift of despatch, and easy of access.'

Lord Shaftesbury was kind and charitable to the poor in his neighbourhood, and was very hospitable. In 1669, Cosimo de' Medici, being in England, went to St. Giles's, and was so much pleased with his reception, that he kept up a correspondence with his English friend, and sent him annually a present of Tuscan wine. It has been adduced by some, in evidence of his immorality, that on one occasion, while still in favour with Charles, the King said to him, 'I believe, Shaftesbury, you are the greatest profligate in England.' The Earl bowed low, and replied, 'For a subject, sire, I believe I am.' It would be hard to condemn a man on the testimony of a repartee.

No. 4.

EDWARD SEYMOUR, FIRST DUKE OF SOMERSET, THE PROTECTOR.

By Holbein.

EXECUTED IN 1552.

Black gown, with fur.   Black cap, and jewel.   Collar of Garter, and George.

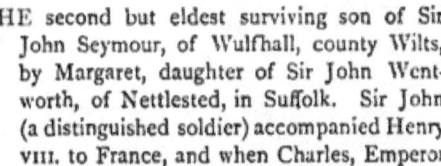HE second but eldest surviving son of Sir John Seymour, of Wulfhall, county Wilts, by Margaret, daughter of Sir John Wentworth, of Nettlested, in Suffolk. Sir John (a distinguished soldier) accompanied Henry VIII. to France, and when Charles, Emperor of Germany, came over to England, he was selected to attend on that monarch.

He was in high favour with the King, who appointed him to many places even before the royal marriage with Jane Seymour, 'the fairest and most discreet of his wives.' The ceremony took place at her paternal home of Wulfhall in 1536. The old barn, the scene of great festivities, may still be seen, with hooks dangling from the rafters where the hangings were attached; Sir John Seymour died the same year.

Many interesting papers relating to this and other subsequent royal visits, and the domestic economy of Wulfhall, are treasured among the archives of Longleat, Sir John Thynne having been the Protector's confidential agent and secretary, and having conducted the whole of his private, and personal business when the Duke was occupied in public matters.

But we are anticipating, and must return to the early years of Edward Seymour. He was educated both at Oxford and Cambridge; and afterwards joining his father at Court, entered the army, and also distinguished himself greatly in France, and was knighted for his services in 1525. On his return to England he was appointed Esquire to the King, and was one of the challengers in the tilt-yard of Greenwich, when Henry kept his Christmas there. On the King's marriage with his sister Jane, Edward Seymour was created Viscount Beauchamp, with other grants and honours, and in 1537, Earl of Hertford. He was sent to France on a mission of importance, and, returning, was made Knight Companion of the Garter at Hampton Court.

From this time Seymour's life became most eventful, he went twice to Scotland, high in command, likewise again to France, where he did good service, and was instrumental in concluding peace with that country. Honours and distinctions too numerous to relate were heaped on the King's brother-in-law, even after the death of poor Queen Jane. Nor must we omit to mention that Henry, shortly before his marriage with Anne of Cleves, revisited Wulfhall, where he was sumptuously entertained (with an enormous retinue) for three days, which pleased him so much, that he returned thither a third time in 1543.

The papers and bills at Longleat testify to the grandeur of these receptions, showing at the same time how all the family took up their quarters in the long barn (once used for the ill-fated Jane's wedding dance), leaving the rest of the house to the royal party. Could they have given the King credit for any over-sensibility on the occasion?

Lord Hertford was a gallant soldier; but in some of his expeditions against the Scots he has been reproached for his 'heavy hand.'

When Henry VIII. felt his end approaching, he took his brother-in-law into his confidence, and spent a long time in conferring with him, and Sir William Paget, on the state of the country, his hopes and fears for young Prince Edward, etc. They were both with him at his death, and there were rumours to Hertford's disadvantage, respecting the royal will. He was one of the many executors, but he agitated so successfully, that, as the King's uncle, he was granted precedency, and appointed his guardian with many conditions, from which he soon emancipated himself. He hurried his royal ward to London, where the nephew was proclaimed King, and the uncle Protector of the realm.

The latter already bore the title of Earl and Viscount, and the King further bestowed on him that of Baron, and next day the ducal coronet was awarded him, with the title of Somerset, the royal patent setting forth 'that the name of that family, from which our most beloved mother, Jane, late Queen of England, drew her beginning, might not be clouded by any higher title, or colour of dignity.' On the Duke of Norfolk being attainted, the Duke of Somerset was made Earl Marshal for life. His power seemed almost absolute, and Edward, who delighted to do him honour, both publicly and privately, appointed him to sit on the right hand of the throne. Nor was the Duke any way loath to enjoy such dignities; the first years of the reign of Edward the King contain the biography of Edward the Protector, and are recorded elsewhere. But he climbed too fast; he was King in all but name. He surrounded himself with regal pomp, and his enemies accused him of aspiring to the throne in good earnest, in proof of which it was adduced that he used the royal pronoun 'we,' and signed himself, 'Protector, by the grace of God.' True it is that he wrote in former times to his well-beloved Mr. Thynne, 'I bid you heartily farewell,' while later documents, amid Longleat's varied stores, are couched in grander terms, such as 'we greet you well,' 'it is our intention,' and the like.

For all the vicissitudes of his eventful life, for his deeds of military glory, his ambition that 'o'erselled itself,' the plots in

which he was accused of taking part, and the factions which
rose up against him, at the head of which were the Earl of Warwick, and his own ungrateful brother, Thomas Lord Seymour
of Sudeley, see the Chronicles of the Kings of England.

A majority of the Privy Council, with his deadly foe, Warwick, as leader, was now united against him, and though hitherto
a favourite with the people, they were at last (for the most
part) persuaded that 'the royal person was not safe in the
Duke's hands, whose doings were treacherous, and his proceedings devilish.' Somerset submitted; he resigned the
authority his enemies were bent on wresting from him, and
was committed to the Tower.

The circumstances attending his downfall were most
humiliating. Deprived of all his great offices, save that of
Privy Councillor, he was compelled to own the justice of his
sentence, and that on his bended knees. His first imprisonment did not last long, and his loving nephew contrived to
restore several forfeited estates, and to make up to the ex-Protector, at least for pecuniary losses, as far as in him lay,
—for the Earl of Warwick, though there was no love lost
between them, was yet in no wise averse to the union of his
eldest son, Lord Lisle, with Lady Mary Seymour, Somerset's
daughter.

The Duke was occasionally called upon to take part
in public affairs, and on the reassembling of Parliament, the
Commons, with whom he was still popular, agitated for his
re-election to the Protectorate, but Warwick was bent on his
destruction.

He went so far as to accuse Somerset of a design to
murder him, on which, and many other counts, the Duke
was once more sent to the Tower, together with many other
noblemen, and the next day was followed thither by his
Duchess, Sir John Thynne, and several more.

Wearied, exposed to constant examinations, and arraigned

at Westminster Hall, he demanded a trial of his peers, was acquitted of high treason, but found guilty of felony, and re-conducted to the Tower.

On his road thither there was a demonstration in his favour, for he still stood high with the people; he remained two months in prison, and was then brought out, and, in spite of the poor young King, condemned to die on the scaffold.

On the 22d of January 1552 every householder in London was forbidden to stir abroad, (a rescue being feared,) nevertheless Tower Hill was crowded long before the Duke appeared, surrounded by guards and officials.

On reaching the platform, he kneeled on both knees, and fervently commended his soul to God, then, rising, 'with great alacrity, and cheerfulness,' he addressed the people in quiet, measured terms. He declared his innocence, his loyalty to the King, his love of his country, and of the reformed religion, to which he admonished his hearers to be faithful. Here he was interrupted by a strange kind of tumult, and Sir Anthony Browne appearing on horseback in the crowd, the people cried aloud, 'A pardon! a pardon! God save the King!' But he told them there was no hope, and all the time his arch-enemy, Lord Warwick (or rather Northumberland, as he then was), stood untouched, shaking his cap, and making signs to the people to be quiet.

The Duke of Somerset resumed his discourse, exhorting his hearers to be loyal to the King, and submissive to the laws, concluding with, 'I wish you all to bear witness that I die in the faith of Jesus Christ, desiring you to help me with your prayers.'

We have not space to make more extracts from a dying speech which for manliness, forbearance, and piety could scarcely be surpassed. Unbuckling his sword, he presented it to the Lieutenant of the Tower, gave the executioner money and rings, bade all near him graciously farewell, then, kneeling down, arranged his collar, and covered his face, which showed 'no signs of trouble,' with his handkerchief.

He was required to rise up, once more, to remove his doublet, and again laying his head on the block, and calling thrice, 'Lord Jesu save me!' received the death-stroke.

The head and body were both interred in the north side of St. Peter's Church in the Tower.

There is a story told of a fair enthusiast, who dipped her handkerchief in the ' martyr's ' blood, and afterwards flourished it in the face of the Duke of Northumberland, when he, two years later, was led captive through the City, for his opposition to Queen Mary. Varying as have been the verdicts on the character of the Protector Somerset, surely no one can deny him the attributes of courage, energy, and piety. He had enthusiastic friends, and bitter enemies, among the last his own brother. Edward, first Duke of Somerset, was remarkably handsome, majestic, and naturally of a melancholy aspect, 'every inch a gentleman.' His extravagance, both in public and private matters, was undeniable, and he affected great splendour in dress, not only on State occasions. During his imprisonment he employed himself in works of a religious character. He was twice married—first to Catherine, daughter and co-heir of Sir William Fillol of Woodlands, county Dorset. Respecting this lady there exists a mystery: there were rumours of misconduct, and certain it is her son was disinherited.

There seems little doubt that the Duke's second wife (the daughter of Sir Edward Stanhope of Rampton, county Notts), a proud, ambitious, and violent woman, worked on her husband's mind, to the detriment of her predecessor's children, but in spite of it all, the coveted titles devolved, after some generations, on Catherine Fillol's descendants, ancestors in the direct line to the present Duke of Somerset. Anne Stanhope brought her husband three sons and six daughters.

No. 5.

LUCIUS CAREY, SECOND VISCOUNT FALKLAND.

By Vandyck.

BORN IN 1610, KILLED IN BATTLE 1643.

Half length. Black and white slashed dress.

F the family of Careys of Cockington, county Devon, eldest son of Henry Carey, first Viscount Falkland, by Elizabeth, daughter and heir of Sir Laurence Tanfield, Chief Baron of Exchequer. Lucius was born at Burton, county Oxford, one of the estates his mother brought into the family. Studied at Trinity College, Dublin, and St. John's, Cambridge.

Before attaining his majority he inherited a large fortune from his grandfather, while both parents were still living. With the hope of procuring some command, he went into the Low Countries; but being disappointed, he returned to England, and devoted himself to study. Lord Clarendon says that all the men of note and learning flocked from Oxford to his house, in the neighbourhood, 'where they found a University in a less volume.'

The historian praises the young host for the solidity of his judgment, knowledge, wit, fancy, and extreme humility,—a rare combination of qualities and attainments.

Before Lucius was twenty-three he had read all the Latin and Greek Fathers, and studied diligently all the books he had collected from all parts.

About 1633, the time of his father's death, he became attached to the Court of Charles I.; in 1639 he went with the expedition against the Scots, and afterwards volunteered under the Earl of Essex.

In April 1640 he sat for Newport, Isle of Wight, and after the dissolution was re-elected for the same place, in the same year. He made strenuous opposition in the House to the exorbitancies of the Court, and was a rigid observer of the laws, denouncing those Ministers who, on the plea of expediency, deviated from them. For this reason he withstood Lords Strafford and Finch with a boldness and vehemence at variance with his usual gentleness.

His concurrence in the first Bill, that was passed to deprive the Bishops of their votes, caused him to be suspected of lukewarmness to the Established Church. He maintained his belief in the good faith of Parliament, until he found how far the so-called popular party were carrying their measures, and then he came to a check, voted differently on the second Bishops' Bill, and opposed the Commons on so many occasions as to be accused by them of truckling to the Court.

On this point he was so sensitive of suspicion that he was said to have refused the King's offer of a place about his person, more than once, in a morose and curt manner, although in reality much attached to his royal master. He required persuasion to induce him to accept the office of Privy Councillor, and the positive command of the King, who at length also prevailed on him, to become his secretary. But in these offices Falkland maintained his own strict notions of honour and integrity, and he absolutely refused ever to employ a spy, or open a letter, however important the knowledge he might thus have gained. From this time he was most loyal in his adherence to Charles, and fell in consequence into the displeasure of the Parliament.

The anecdote of his visiting the library at Oxford is well known, and yet we cannot omit alluding to it. Taking down a copy of Virgil, Falkland invited the King to read his destiny therein, by opening the book at random. The passage was, alas! too soon verified :—

> 'Oppressed with numbers, in the unequal field,
> His men discouraged, and himself expelled,
> Let him for succour sue, from place to place,
> Torn from his subjects and his son's embrace,' etc. etc.

It is a part of Dido's curse. The King was very much impressed by the boding passage, and Lord Falkland tried his fortune. This was quite as prophetic as the last, being the lament of Evander over his son, who was killed in battle :—

> 'Well I knew,
> What perils youthful ardour would pursue,
> That boiling blood would carry thee too far,
> Young as thou wert in danger, raw to war.
> O curst essay of arms, disastrous doom,
> Prelude of bloody fields, and fights to come.'

Such predictions were not calculated to cheer the spirits of the inquirers.

As time passed on, and all hope of peace between the Royalists and the Parliamentarians seemed lost, Lord Falkland, to whom his King and countrymen were alike dear, became a prey to profound melancholy.

That worst of all misfortunes, a civil war, affected him deeply; all his efforts at pacification were ineffectual; he would sit often silent when in company, for a long time, and then break forth in shrill accents—'Peace! peace! peace!'

Pale, dejected, negligent of his dress, of which in former days he had been proverbially careful, he passed sleepless nights, and often said his heart was breaking. In battle he exposed himself to so much danger, that a friend expostulated with him, upon which he replied, among other reasons, that it behoved him to be more hazardous than others, lest any one should say that his desire for peace proceeded from pusillanimity.

On the morning of the battle of Newbury 'he appeared more cheerful, put on a clean shirt in case he should be killed, and said he was weary of the times, and did think he would be out of it, before night.'

On the 20th of September 1643, in the front rank of Lord Byron's regiment, Lucius Carey, Viscount Falkland, fell from his horse, pierced by a musket-ball. His body was not found till next morning. Thus, at the early age of thirty-four years, died one of the most remarkable men of his age and country. A true patriot, a loyal and attached subject, learned, witty, wise, honourable, and of so gentle and winning a disposition, that all men could not choose but love him; a soldier, a scholar, deeply attached to the Protestant faith, he withstood all the endeavours of his mother, a strict Roman Catholic, and a woman of great power of mind, to gain him over to her way of thinking.

He was very studious, and used to say he pitied 'unlearned gentlemen on a rainy day.' 'Lord Falkland had dark hair and black eyes, in stature low, and of no great strength.'

No. 6.

THE LORD KEEPER COVENTRY.

In robes of office.

No. 7.

EDWARD SACKVILLE, FOURTH EARL OF DORSET.

By Cornelius Jansen.

BORN 1590, DIED 1652.

White and black slashed dress, gold buttons. Jewel of the Garter.

E was the second surviving son of Robert Earl of Dorset, by Lady Mary Howard, only daughter of Thomas, fourth Duke of Norfolk, of that family; he went to Oxford, and studied there for three years. He seems to have been a great favourite with Lord Clarendon, who paints his portrait in glowing colours: 'His person graceful, beautiful, vigorous, his wit sparkling, his other parts of learning, of that lustre, that he could not miscarry in the world, the vices he had were of the age.'

His grandfather, Buckhurst, the Grand Treasurer, took delight in his education, left him a good fortune, and helped him to a wife, who was heir to another.

In early life, Edward Sackville appears to have yielded to the dissipated examples by which he was surrounded, and a fatal duel with Lord Bruce, a young Scotch nobleman, caused him to incur many a remorseful hour in after days. The quarrel was so inveterate that the two young men went to Flanders and fought under the walls of Antwerp, with only two 'chirurgeons' as witnesses, having bound themselves by the obligation not to stir, till one or other of the antagonists fell. Lord Bruce was the victim, but his adversary narrowly escaped death also, for Bruce's surgeon, seizing his Lord's sword, fell suddenly on Sackville, till stayed by the cry of the dying man, 'Rascal! hold thy hand!' Edward Sackville took refuge in a monastery, there to have his wounds dressed, and to repent his crime at leisure. The cause of the quarrel did not transpire, but from a hint which Lord Clarendon lets drop, it would appear there was 'a lady in the case.'

No notice (to use a familiar expression) was taken, either publicly or privately, of this tragical incident, and Sackville continued high in favour at the Court of James I. He was made Knight of the Bath in 1616, was a leading member of the House of Commons, and spoke very eloquently, more especially in defence of the Lord Chancellor Bacon, when accused of corruption.

His powers of oratory seem indeed to have been of a superior order, and a speech he made on the subject of supplies to the Palatinate, was highly commended. His chivalrous nature was roused in the cause of the Princess Elizabeth, Queen of Bohemia. He spoke of the daughter of their King (in his appeal to Parliament), 'who scarce knew where to lay her head, or, if she did, not in safety.'

He had a command in the forces sent to the aid of Frederic, King of Bohemia, and fought at the battle of Prague, went afterwards to France, as Ambassador, and on his return was made a Privy Councillor.

In 1624 he succeeded to the title of Earl of Dorset, on the death of his brother, who had greatly impoverished the estates by his extravagance. On the accession of Charles I. he received the Order of the Garter, and was named Chamberlain to the Queen's Majesty. Subsequently Lord Dorset was employed in many important offices, such as Joint-Commissioner, with other noblemen, for the management of Irish affairs, likewise for treating with Holland respecting the marriage of Princess Mary and William of Orange.

Dorset was wont to carry matters with a high hand, and at the time of the Bill against the Bishops, finding a mob had been brought down to intimidate the House of Peers, he, as Lord-Lieutenant of Middlesex, in command of the Trained Bands, ordered them to fire, which soon put the affrighted rabble to flight. The House of Commons was very irate, and talked of impeachment, but nothing came of it.

Dorset was a staunch adherent of the King, upholding him by word of mouth, supplying him with money, and fighting by his side in the field, at the battle of Edgehill, where he distinguished himself, and recovered the royal standard from the hands of the enemy. He was, as Clarendon says, 'of most entire fidelity to the Crown,' attending on the royal person constantly, and using every endeavour to bring about peace between Charles and his subjects. It is said, on the authority of Sir Edward Walker, that so deeply did the noble Earl of Dorset take to heart the murder of his royal master, that he never stirred out of his house after the King's execution.

He married Mary, daughter and co-heir of Sir George Curzon of Croxhall, county Dorset, a lady of large fortune, most virtuous and accomplished. Indeed, so highly esteemed and honoured was she, that at her demise in 1645, both Houses of Parliament decreed her a public funeral. By his wife, Lord Dorset had one daughter, and two sons, the eldest of whom succeeded him, and the second, when in arms for the King, was taken prisoner by the Roundheads and barbarously murdered.

No. 8.

HENRY RICH, EARL OF HOLLAND.

By Cornelius Jansen.

EXECUTED 1649.

Breastplate. Order of the Garter. White collar. White and gold sleeves. Flowing hair.

E was the second son of Robert Rich, first Earl of Warwick, by the Lady Penelope Devereux, daughter of Walter Earl of Essex.

Clarendon says of him that 'he was a very handsome man, of a lovely and winning presence and genteel conversation.' He went to France in his youth, was afterwards in arms in Holland; and returning to England, presented himself at Court. Here he attracted the notice and favour of George Duke of Buckingham, then all-powerful with King James I. Young Rich was said to have flattered his patron not a little, and certainly if he did so, it was to some purpose. It seems to have been through Buckingham's intervention that he married the rich heiress of Sir John Cope of Kensington, of which place Rich shortly bore the title of Baron. He also held offices at Court, both about the King's person and that of Henry, Prince of Wales, was made Earl of Holland, Knight of the Garter, Privy Councillor, and sent Ambassador to treat, concerning the marriage of Prince Charles, first in Spain and afterwards in France. On the latter occasion, it was rumoured that his beauty and courtliness made a deep impression on the heart of Henrietta Maria.

He also went to Holland with the Duke of Buckingham on matters regarding the Palatinate, etc.

In 1639, on the first breaking out of an insurrection of

the Scots, he was made General of the Horse in that expedition, and though not in arms at the commencement of the Civil War, when evil days fell on the King, Holland joined him with many other Royalist noblemen, and being appointed General of the King's army, numbers flocked to ask commissions from him. But in July 1648, after several fluctuations of fortune, Lord Holland was pursued, and taken prisoner near St. Neot's, in Huntingdonshire, whence he was conveyed to Warwick House, and finally to the Tower.

A High Court of Justice was appointed to sit for the trial of the Duke of Hamilton, the Earl of Holland, and other Peers; he was in ill-health, and when examined, answered little, 'as a man who would rather receive his life from their favour, than from the strength of his defence.'

But he was condemned with the rest of the Lords, in spite of the influence of his brother, the Earl of Warwick, and the Presbyterian party, who to a man voted for his life. There was a majority against him of three or four votes only; but Cromwell, it appears, had an inveterate dislike to him. Accordingly, on the 9th of March 1649, on the scaffold erected before Westminster Hall, Lord Holland suffered death, immediately after the Duke of Hamilton.

Spent by long sickness, he addressed but few words to the people, recommending them, with his last breath, to uphold the King's government and the established religion.

He left four sons and five daughters. Robert, the eldest, succeeded to his father's honours, and likewise to the earldom of Warwick, on the death of his uncle in 1672.

No. 9.

MALE PORTRAIT—UNKNOWN.

Black gown and cap. Holding a carnation. A scroll with the words 'Supplicatur vos.' The rest is illegible.

No. 10.

HENRY THE EIGHTH, KING OF ENGLAND.

By Holbein.

BORN 1491, DIED 1547.

Inscription in background, 'Anno reg. 36, ætatis 54.' Gold and jewelled dress, slashed. White collar. Chain, alternate columns and H.S. A disk of gold adorned with jewels. He holds a glove. Mantle trimmed with fur. Sleeves of cloth of gold, very full. Hat and feathers.

HE eldest surviving son of Henry VII. by Elizabeth of York. Succeeded his father in 1509. He married six wives, of whom 'the best beloved' was Jane Seymour, with whose family, that of the Thynnes had much intercourse and relationship.

No. 11.

THOMAS LORD SEYMOUR OF SUDELEY.

By Holbein.

EXECUTED 1549-50.

Black gown and cap. Badge of Garter suspended by a ribbon round his neck.

E was the fourth son of Sir John Seymour of Wulfhall, by Margaret Wentworth. He was one of the twelve assistants to the executors of the will of his brother-in-law Henry VIII., and on the accession of Edward VI. he was advanced to great honour. Having already distinguished himself as a sailor, he was made Lord High Admiral and Baron Seymour of Sudeley, also Knight of the

Garter. But these honours did not satisfy the King's ambitious uncle; he turned his thoughts to a royal alliance, and asked the consent of the Council to his marriage with the Princess Elizabeth, then only fifteen.

His suit was refused. He then, having in his pay a gentleman about the King, bade him ask Edward whom he should marry. 'His Majesty,' says Froude, 'graciously offered Anne of Cleves,' and then added he would rather he married Princess Mary, in order that she might change her opinions. But that would neither have suited the Council, nor Mary herself, so Seymour was fain to put up with a Queen-Dowager instead of a future Queen-Regnant, and he proffered his addresses in a quarter where he knew they would be acceptable.

Between him and Queen Catharine Parr there had been love-passages, when she was the widow of Lord Latimer, till a King became his rival. Catharine at first refused to marry until her two years of widowhood should be passed, but Seymour soon prevailed on her to consent to a private union, and letters still extant show that she used to receive him clandestinely, at the palace, Chelsea.

She shared her Lord's hatred, and jealousy of his brother the Protector, and his wife, and said, if they refused their consent, it would be of no consequence. The amiable young King was easily persuaded to do as his uncle wished, and begged Catharine to listen to Seymour's suit. She also desired her lover to ask the Council to intercede with her in his behalf, when she was already his wife.

Princess Mary sensibly refrained from meddling, and while all these schemes were being carried on, the whole truth was discovered. There was a general outcry at the scandal, and it was no wonder that the Protector was much displeased.

Besides, it was a question if it were not high treason to marry a Queen widow, so soon after the Sovereign's death, (at all events it was made into a charge against Seymour later,) as it might possibly have added a fresh difficulty to the vexed question of the succession to the Crown.

On the breaking out of the Scotch war, the Lord High Admiral was ordered to take command of the fleet, but he preferred remaining at home, and superintending the affairs of the Admiralty, and sent a substitute to sea.

Strange as it may appear, after all that had happened, Princess Elizabeth still remained where she had been placed for some time under the guardianship of Catharine Parr. But after a while Seymour's conduct towards the King's sister, his want of respect, and extreme familiarity, scandalised the royal attendants, and roused the tardy jealousy of his easy-going wife. The Princess was, in consequence, removed to safer keeping; but Seymour had other noble wards,—the daughters of the Marquis of Dorset, of whom one was the unfortunate Lady Jane Grey.

The deadly hatred which Seymour bore his brother was shared and fostered by his wife, who writes to him on one occasion, 'This schal be to advertyse you, that my lord your brother has this afternoone made me a lyttell warme. I am glad we were dystant, or I suppose I sholde have bitten him.'

During the time the Duke of Somerset was in Scotland, Thomas Seymour did all he could to injure and supplant him, telling Edward the invasion was madly undertaken, and money wasted—that it was a pity he did not assert himself more—that he was not allowed enough money to be generous to his own servants, etc. Seymour also set about a report that the late King never intended there should be a Protectorate, and he even went so far as to write a letter, which he suggested, the King should copy and sign, to both Houses of Parliament, in his (Seymour's) own favour, but this was refused.

Catharine had two grievances against the Duke and

Duchess: one was the question of precedency between her and her sister-in-law; the other a matter respecting some jewels which Somerset had sequestered as Crown Jewels, but which Catharine affirmed had been left her by the King.

Seymour tried to bring in a Bill to separate the offices of Protector and Guardian, in order to gain possession of the King's person, but he was foiled on all sides. His conduct was so outrageous that he was summoned before the Council to explain it; he defied, and disobeyed the summons.

In spite of this behaviour, and all these machinations against himself, Somerset was lenient to his misguided brother, even to extremes; he palliated his faults, and, 'striving to bridle him with liberality,' gave him fresh grants of land. But Seymour was not of the stuff that can be softened by generosity; he grew desperate, and it was reported, and believed, that he had entered into a treaty with certain privateers then infesting the seas, and that his purchase of the Scilly Islands at this juncture was with the view of acting in connection with them for his own interest.

The Protector, who showed no signs of weakness in public affairs, mildly expostulated with the headstrong man, who was speeding to his ruin, but all his forbearance was thrown away.

Catharine Parr was confined of a daughter, and died a few days after, not without some rumours of her husband having helped her exit from the world; but he was out of favour now with almost all classes, and nothing was too bad to be said of him.

Lady Dorset naturally wished to remove her daughter Jane from the Admiral's roof on the death of his wife, but he, knowing that the Duchess of Somerset was bent on marrying the young lady to her eldest son, so worked on the weakness of Lord Dorset, that Jane Grey remained under Lord Seymour's questionable care. Once more his thoughts reverted to the Princess Elizabeth. He gained over two of her people, who were instructed to praise him to the skies, and keep his name always before her. But Elizabeth, though only sixteen, acted with discretion and dignity, refusing to take any step without the consent of the Council, and positively declining to receive Seymour, in spite of all his tender messages.

The failures in Scotland, religious discontent, and many untoward events, had shaken the Protector's power, and his brother was working strenuously against him. Seymour was warned of his danger; he was told that his designs on the Princess, and his scheme of possessing himself of the person of the King were discovered; but he defied advice, remonstrance, and threats.

Again summoned before the Council, he again disobeyed. He appealed to the Earl of Warwick, on the plea that he was the enemy of the Protector, but Warwick said, if there were to be any change in the Government, it should not be for the advantage of another Seymour, and so he was arrested, and sent to the Tower. All his creatures and accomplices turned upon him, and gave evidence against him, all his intrigues and machinations were discovered; and two months after his committal the Council went to the Tower and caused thirty-three charges against the Lord High Admiral to be read aloud, in his presence. When called upon for an answer, he refused to give any, (though urged to speak on his allegiance,) and demanded an open trial.

The question now arose as to the manner of the trial, and the Chancellor and the rest of the Council gave their opinions for an Act of Attainder, while the Protector, pleading 'what a sorrowful case this was for him, did yet rather regard his bounden duty to the King's Majesty and the Crown of England than his own son or brother, and did weigh more his allegiance than his blood, and therefore he would not resist their Lordships.'

King Edward was present, and although his gentle nature always inclined to clemency, he gave his consent to the decision. Seymour was brought before a committee of both Houses, where he pleaded his own cause; but as the charges grew graver, he stopped short, and refused to say any more.

The next day the Bill was brought before the Lords, and passed without a dissenting voice, the Lord Protector only, 'for natural pity's sake, desiring licence to be away.'

Seymour had a small party of friends in the Commons, but having heard the evidence, the Lower House also passed the Bill. It was sent to the Crown with the request that justice might have place. The sentence was given without reference to the Protector, who would still have interfered to save the ungrateful brother whose inveterate hatred was unconquered, but he was prevented.

The Bishop of Ely visited the prisoner to bid him prepare for death, which he did, by writing to Elizabeth and Mary to incite them to conspire against the Duke.

He concealed the letters in the sole of his shoe, and his last words, as he knelt before the block, were to commission his servant to deliver them.

He died with a courage worthy a better cause. Bishop Latimer said of his death—'Whether he be saved or no, I leave that to God. In the twinkling of an eye He can save a man, and turn his heart. What He did I cannot tell. And when a man hath two strokes with an axe, who can tell but between the two strokes he doth repent? It is hard to judge; but this I will say, if they ask me what I think of his death, I say that he died very irksomely, dangerously, and horribly.'

Latimer says elsewhere that the Admiral was a man furthest from the fear of God that ever he heard of in England. And yet in the picture in which we are treating there are verses that laud him to the skies. Not only his outward form—

> ' Of person rare, stronge limbes, and manly shape ;
> Of nature framed to serve on sea and lande, etc.,
> A subject true to Kinge, frinde to God's truth '—

and so forth, concluding with the lines :—

> ' Yet againste nature, reason, and just lawes,
> His blode was spilte, giltless, without just cause !'

The Bishop and the Poet were at variance in the estimate of Lord Seymour of Sudeley's character.

No. 12.

THOMAS WRIOTHESLEY, LAST EARL OF SOUTHAMPTON.

BY VANDYCK.

DIED 1667.

Order of the Garter.

HE was the second born, but only surviving son of the third Earl, by Elizabeth, daughter of John Vernon of Hodnet, county Salop. He was educated at Eton and Oxford, where he distinguished himself, and then went on foreign travel. He tarried some time in France, where it is probable he espoused his first wife, and afterwards proceeded to the Low Countries.

His father had also gone thither in command of a military expedition, accompanied by his eldest son, but they were both attacked by low fever. The youth died, and the afflicted father, journeying home with the loved remains, ere he was fit to travel, also succumbed, and died at Bergen-op-Zoom.

Thomas, now Earl of Southampton, on his return to England, found public affairs in great confusion, it was soon evident that he did not approve of many of the Government measures, and that he had no sympathy with the Earl of Strafford; in consequence of which, the discontented leaders in Parliament strove hard to gain him over to their side; but neither did he uphold their proceedings, which he considered disloyal, and would take no part therein.

In 1641, he, with Lord Robartes, refused assent to Pym's protestation against 'plots and conspiracies,' which was signed by every other member in each House. This incensed the Parliament, but pleased the King. Southampton was appointed Privy Councillor and Lord of the Bedchamber, and was henceforth, in every sense of the word, attached to the royal person.

He was prudent and zealous in his master's cause, often giving him unpalatable advice, they were now seldom apart, Southampton frequently sleeping in the King's chamber, and trying to soothe his hours of mental anguish. He treated (unsuccessfully indeed, but nobly, and with dignity) between the adverse parties. In 1647, when the unhappy monarch fled from Hampton Court, he took shelter with Southampton at Titchfield in Hampshire, the family estate, and when brought back to the palace, in the hands of his enemies, his first request was for the attendance of his trusty friend.

Southampton was one of the last allowed to remain with the unfortunate Charles, and one of the four to pay the last sad duties to the remains of the master he so dearly loved, in 'privacy and darkness.' He kept up a correspondence with the exiled King, supplied him with large sums, and on Charles's arrival in England, went to meet him, and was rewarded (at the same time as other faithful adherents of the Crown) with the Order of the Garter. He was shortly afterwards made Lord High Treasurer, in which office, says Clarendon, 'he had no dependence on the Court, or purpose to have any, but wholly pursued the public interest.'

Consequently he offended the King by opposing to his utmost the Bill for Liberty of Conscience, as it was called, both in Parliament and Council; yet he was not removed from his office, but held it for a few short years longer, although suffering from a terrible and painful disease, which made business irksome to him. The testimony of Burnet and Clarendon both go to prove that 'he was a man of virtue, and of very good parts, and incorrupt,' and during seven years' management of the Treasury he made but an ordinary fortune, disdaining, unlike many of his predecessors, to sell places.

'He was by nature inclined to melancholy, and being born a younger brother, was much troubled at being called "My Lord." Great quickness of apprehension, and that readiness of expression on any sudden debate, that no man delivered more efficaciously with his hearers, so that no man ever gave them more trouble in his opposition, or drew so many to concurrence in opinion.' The Earl of Southampton was thrice married. His first wife was Rachel, daughter of Daniel de Massey, lord of Ruvigny, in France, by whom he had two sons, who died young, and three daughters, the second of whom was Rachel, the faithful wife and widow of William Lord Russell, who was beheaded, her first husband being Lord Carbery, in Ireland. The second Countess of Southampton was Elizabeth, daughter and co-heir to Francis Booth, Lord Dunsmore, who brought him four girls, one of whom was Elizabeth, Countess of Northumberland. The third wife was the daughter of William, second Duke of Somerset, and widow of Viscount Molyneux.

The Earl died at Southampton House, in Bloomsbury, of a violent attack of the malady from which he had long suffered, and was buried at Titchfield.

No. 13.

GEORGE LORD LANSDOWNE.

By Sir Godfrey Kneller.

Tawny dress. Blue velvet cap.

E was the second son of Sir Bernard Granville, by Anne, sole daughter and heir of Cuthbert Morley, of Normanby in Cleveland, county York, consequently grandson to the gallant Sir Bevil Granville, who was slain at the battle of Lansdowne. He was raised to the peerage as Baron Lansdowne, of Bideford, county Devon, having held the appointments of Secretary at War, Comptroller of the Household, Treasurer, and Privy Councillor. He married, in 1711, Lady Mary, the widow of Thomas Thynne, Esq., daughter of the Earl of Jersey, and mother of the second Lord Weymouth.

No. 14.

SIR HENRY FREDERICK THYNNE.

By Sir Peter Lely.

BORN 1615.

Oval. Dark dress. White cravat. Tawny mantle.

AS the eldest surviving son of Sir Thomas Thynne, by his second wife, Catharine Howard. His royal godmother, Queen Anne, wife to James I., desired he should bear the name of Frederick, after her father, the King of Denmark, Thomas, first Earl of Suffolk, and cousin to Henry's mother, being one of Her Majesty's 'gossips.'

Sir Henry Thynne, who was created a Baronet in 1641, married Mary, daughter of Thomas, first Lord Coventry, by whom he had Sir Thomas Thynne, his heir; James of Buckland, county Gloucester, one of the representatives for Cirencester in Parliament; Henry Frederick; John; Mary, wife to Sir Richard How, Bart., of Wishford, county Wilts; and Catharine, married to Sir John Lowther, afterwards Viscount Lonsdale.

Sir Henry Frederick died at his residence at Kempsford, where he and his wife lie buried.

THIRD LIBRARY.

No. 15.

EDWARD, FIRST LORD THURLOW.
BY SIR JOSHUA REYNOLDS.
BORN 1732, DIED 1806.

Full length. In Chancellor's robes.

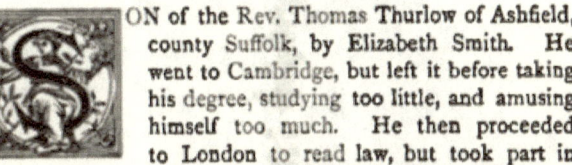

SON of the Rev. Thomas Thurlow of Ashfield, county Suffolk, by Elizabeth Smith. He went to Cambridge, but left it before taking his degree, studying too little, and amusing himself too much. He then proceeded to London to read law, but took part in all the pleasures and dissipations of the town. One time, when opposed to the famous lawyer, Sir Fletcher Norton, he completely worsted his eminent antagonist, which was esteemed a great feat in one so young to the legal profession. But what brought him into prominent notice, and gave him the silk gown, was the able manner in which he conducted the case of Archibald Douglas *versus* the Duke of Hamilton, which made a great noise at the time.

It was by the merest chance that Thurlow was consulted in the matter. Two lawyers belonging to the counsel were conversing together over the matter at a fashionable coffee-house, where Thurlow passed a great deal too much of his time.

They came to the conclusion, that a clear and elaborate statement of the facts of the case in question, must be carefully drawn up, a labour to which they were both averse. They accordingly proposed to young Thurlow, at that moment idling in the bar with the pretty maid, to undertake the task. He did so, and executed the work with so much talent and ability, that he was retained for the defence, and was the chief instrument in gaining his client's cause. This brought him into great notice, and gained him, amongst others, the patronage of Lord Weymouth, then in the Administration, who brought him into Parliament.

Solicitor-General in 1770, and Attorney-General in 1771, he was a firm supporter of Lord North's Administration, and spoke so eloquently on the Ministerial side when the American war broke out, that he was created Lord Thurlow of Ashfield, and next day Lord High Chancellor.

On taking his seat in the House of Lords, the Duke of Grafton made some slighting remark on the obscurity of the Thurlow family, to which the new Peer, although owning the truth of this assertion, retorted in so cutting a manner, with an allusion to the bar sinister in the Ducal coat of arms, as turned the laugh completely against his Grace.

Lord Thurlow retained the Great Seal till turned out by the Cornwallis Ministry, but on Pitt becoming Premier he was reinstated in office. In 1793-4 his opinions were so adverse to those of the Government, that he tendered his resignation, and never returned to office. He still, however, continued to take great interest in public affairs during the remainder of his life, frequenting, and often speaking in the House of Lords. Eloquent, energetic, just, severe, at times morose, he was unpopular (socially speaking) with the members of the legal profession.

Lord Thurlow was a man of pleasure, but a scholar, a patron of literature and the arts, though sometimes accused of bestowing benefits in an ungracious manner. He never married, and his honours devolved on his brother, the Bishop of Durham. He left three natural daughters, to two of whom he bequeathed good fortunes, and to the other only a scanty pittance, in consequence of her having made a marriage which displeased him. On his retirement he gave himself up to literary pursuits, translating the classics, and writing fugitive pieces on various subjects; and in a high-flown dedication of his poem, 'The Doge's Daughter,' to Lord Eldon, he extols the efficacy of 'the light and cheerful airs of poesy' as 'medicine for the mind.' There seems little doubt he derived great amusement from his own poetical effusions, whatever his readers may have done.

BILLIARD ROOM.

BILLIARD ROOM.

No. 16.

FRANCES HOWARD, DUCHESS OF RICHMOND AND LENNOX.

BY VANDYCK.

BORN 1577-8, DIED 1639.

Full length. Black velvet dress. Girdle of pearls. Pearls in her hair. Cap, wimple. In one hand a staff, in the other a handkerchief, marked F. R. Miniature at her bosom. Coronet on the table.

SHE was the daughter of Thomas, first Viscount Howard of Bindon, by his third wife, Mabel, daughter of Nicholas Burton of Carshalton, county Surrey.

A curious contemporaneous account is given of this remarkable woman: 'She was one of the greatest, both for birth and beauty, in the land, but at first she went a step backward.' This alludes to her early fancy for one Prannall, a vintner, and son to a rich alderman. Their union made a great noise in the world of which Frances Howard was a distinguished ornament, the bridegroom having incurred severe censure, wrote a touching and manly appeal, to Lord Burghley on the occasion.

We subjoin some extracts : 'My very good Lorde, hearing to my very grete griefe, how your Honour, by misinformation, shulde be incensed againste me, and daring not presume into your Lordship's presence to pleade pardon for my amisse, I thoughte it my duty to acknowledge my fault, and under your Lordship's favoure, with all humilitie, to allege somewhat for myselfe. Though I have married Mistress Frances Howard, yet I proteste, as I desire your Honour's patronage, I did not begin my suit without the knowledge of her friendes, neither cann they justifie I married her against their willes. The gentlewoman I have a long time dearlie loved, being bounde thereto by her mutuall likinge of me. I expected little or nothing with her, she having little or nothing to maintaine herself, and being destitute of friendes, I thoughte it friendlie to present her myselfe, and thereby to make her partaker of all wherewith God had blessed me,' and so forth. Then he goes on to remark to the great Minister that he did not think 'your Lordship, being busied with serious publick affairs, woulde have time to be troubled with such domestical and private matters,' etc. etc. 'It cannot be justlie suggested that the gentlewoman is cast away, consideringe I will avowe myself a poore gentleman, the son of a deceased alderman of honest fame,—one who is to assure her a large jointure, one whose inward disposition of mynde his outward behaviour can testifie.' Continuing in this quaint style, he encloses a schedule of his estate and property, and concludes with 'all manner of goode wishes for Lord Burghley himself, and his progenie, both in this worlde and that which is to come,' subscribing himself, 'your Honour's poore suppliant, Henry Prannall.'

The true-hearted plebeian did not survive his marriage long, to fret the proud spirit of the Howards ; and, faithful to his promise, he left a large fortune to his young and beautiful widow, unencumbered by children to perpetuate the despised name of Prannall. Under these circumstances, it may well be imagined Mistress Frances did not want for suitors. One Sir George Rodney, we are told, 'a gentleman of the West, well fitted in person and fortune, fixed his hopes upon her, but Edward Earl of Hertford, being entangled by her eyes, she, having "a tang of her grandfather's ambition," left Rodney, and married Hertford. The knight having drunk in too much affection, and not being able to digest it, summoned up his scattered spirits, to a most desperate attempt, and coming to Amesbury in Wilts, where the Earl and Countess then resided, shut himself in a chamber, and wrote a large paper of well-composed verses to the Countess in his own blood.'

A strange sort of composedness, ' wherein he wails his unhappinesse, and when he had sent them to her, he ran himself upon his sword, leaving the Countess to a strict remembrance of her inconstancy, and himself a desperate and sad spectacle of frailty.'

Such trifles made little impression on Lady Hertford, who so wrought upon the good-nature of the Earl, her husband, that he settled above £5000 a year on her, for life. She carried a fair fame during Lord Hertford's time, although she had many admirers, and amongst them the Duke of Richmond, whom she afterwards espoused. She was very fond of boasting of her high descent, and of her two grand, grandfathers, the Dukes of Norfolk and Buckingham, but she would desist when Hertford came into her presence, for, 'when he found her in those exaltations, he would say, "Frank, Frank, how long is it since thou wert married to Prannall?" which woulde damp the wings of her spirit.'

Lodowick Stuart, son of Esme, fifth Duke of Lennox and second Duke of Richmond, as we have already said, paid his addresses to her, while Lord Hertford was still alive; and, says Wilson, (whom we have already quoted,) 'that in very odd disguises.'

She survived the Duke, her third husband, well pleased with the grand title he had bestowed on her. But the proud widow had 'still more transcendent heights in speculation,' for King James, being then a widower, she turned her eyes on him, saying, 'that after so great a Prince as Richmond,' she 'would never condescend to be kissed by, or to eat at the table of a subject. She wished this vow to be spread abroad, that the King might take notice of the bravery of her spirit. But it did not catch the old King, so that she missed her aim.'

'The Duchess was a woman greedy of fame, and loved to keep great state with little cost, for being much visited by the great ones, she had a formality of officers and gentlemen that gave attendance. None ever sat with her, yet all the tables in the hall were spread; but before eating-time, the house being voided, the linen returned into its folds, and all her people grazed on few dishes. Yet when her actions came into fame's fingering, her gifts were suitable to her greatness; for the Queen of Bohemia, to the christening of whose child she was a witness, had some taste of them. The Duchess, either to magnify her merit (or it was done by others in mockery to magnify her vanity) had huge inventories of massy plate writ down that she had given that Queen; yet they were but paper presents. Those inventories had *a non est inventus*. At the Hague, the shell (the inventory) was seen; but the kernel (the plate) was never found.'

The Duchess of Richmond was half-sister to Lady Thynne, second wife to Sir Thomas Thynne. She died at Exeter House in the Strand, and was buried in Henry VII.'s chapel, beside her last husband.

No. 17.
THOMAS THYNNE, SECOND MARQUIS OF BATH.
By Pickersgill.
BORN 1765, DIED 1837.

Full length. Robes of Knight of the Garter.

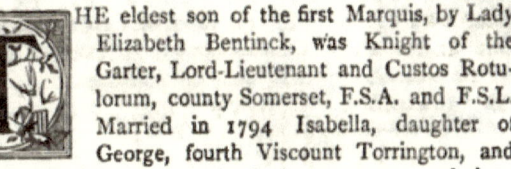

THE eldest son of the first Marquis, by Lady Elizabeth Bentinck, was Knight of the Garter, Lord-Lieutenant and Custos Rotulorum, county Somerset, F.S.A. and F.S.L. Married in 1794 Isabella, daughter of George, fourth Viscount Torrington, and Lady Lucy Boyle, by whom he had seven sons, and three daughters.

Lord Bath, like his predecessors, made considerable alterations in the house, and estate, and died in 1837, deeply and deservedly regretted for his hospitality, and open-handed charity. Not only did he relieve the wants of the poor on his property, but he showed them that personal sympathy which is above all price. He indeed loved to share his good fortune with those around him, and was a benefactor to the neighbourhood where he lived during a long life.

No. 18.

FRANCES ISABELLA CATHERINE, MARCHIONESS OF BATH.

By G. F. Watts, R.A.

Full length.   White dress.

HE is the eldest daughter of Thomas, third Viscount de Vesci, by Lady Emma Herbert, youngest daughter of George Augustus, eleventh Earl of Pembroke. She married John Alexander, fourth and present Marquis of Bath, in 1861.

DINING ROOM.

H

DINING ROOM.

No. 19.

ELIZABETH SACKVILLE, VISCOUNTESS WEYMOUTH.

BORN 1713, DIED 1729.

Plain white dress. Looking at a miniature she holds in her hand.

HE second daughter of Lionel, first Duke of Dorset, by the daughter of General Colyear. She became the bride of the second Lord Weymouth, the respective ages of the pair being sixteen and fourteen. Immediately after the ceremony the bridegroom proceeded on his travels, and the separation was eternal, for the poor child-wife died before the return of her lord to England.

No. 20.

FRANCES FINCH, VISCOUNTESS WEYMOUTH.

BY SIR PETER LELY.

DIED 1712.

Fair hair. Grey gown. Blue mantle. Spaniel in her lap.

LDEST daughter of Heneage Finch, second Earl of Winchilsea, by Mary, daughter of William Seymour, Duke of Somerset. She married the first Lord Weymouth, by whom she had a son, Henry, who died *v.p.*, and a daughter, married to Sir Robert Worsley, Bart.

No. 21.

THOMAS THYNNE, SECOND VISCOUNT WEYMOUTH.

By Dahl.

BORN 1710, DIED 1751.

Tawny coat.   White skirt.   Short hair.

N the death of the first Viscount, the title and estates, by virtue of patent, and entail, descended to the heirs of his youngest brother, Henry Frederick, namely, his grandson Thomas, then only four years old, the posthumous son of Thomas Thynne, by Lady Mary Villiers, daughter of the first Earl of Jersey.

His guardians appear to have been in haste to arrange the young lord's marriage. At the early age of sixteen he espoused Lady Elizabeth Sackville, eldest surviving daughter of Lionel, Duke of Dorset. But the married pair were immediately separated, as before mentioned, and Lord Weymouth sent off to travel, and while absent from his wife she fell sick, and died in 1729. On his return to England in the same year, a second wife was speedily provided for him, in the person of Lady Louisa Carteret, daughter of John Earl Granville, by whom he had three sons; Lord Weymouth, on first coming of age, finding the grounds and gardens round Longleat House, not only in a bad state, but in too antiquated a style to suit his taste, sent for the renowned 'Capability Brown' to improve and modernise them; some of the plans, however, made at that time were not carried out till later. 'The most august house in England' was much neglected during this Lord's lifetime. He did not reside there in his minority, and soon after he came of age he went to live in an old manor-house in the neighbouring village of Horningsham, which had once belonged to the Arundel family. He died and was buried at Horningsham. In 1739 Lord Weymouth was appointed Ranger of Hyde and St. James's Parks.

No. 22.

THOMAS THYNNE, FIRST VISCOUNT WEYMOUTH.

By Sir Peter Lely.

BORN 1640, DIED 1714.

Coronation robes. Holding coronet. Full wig.

THE eldest son of Sir Henry Frederick Thynne, Bart., of Kempsford, by Mary, daughter of the first Lord Coventry. From his schoolmaster, Dr. William Burton, young Thynne imbibed a taste for antiquarian research, which lasted his life. He studied successively under Dr. Triplet and Dr. Henry Drummond, both literary men of mark, and finally at Christ Church College, Oxford, under Dr. John Fell, afterwards Bishop of the diocese.

It was about the year 1657, that Thynne entered the University at the same time as Ken, with whom he then formed a close friendship, which only terminated with the life of that celebrated divine. In 1673 Thomas Thynne was returned M.P. for the University of Oxford, in place of Sir Heneage Finch, appointed Lord Keeper, and later he sat for Tamworth. In 1679 he was chosen Honorary Steward of Sutton Coldfield, county Warwick; and in 1682, in addition to his large paternal estates, he inherited Longleat and other vast possessions on the murder of his cousin and namesake. This was in virtue of an entail made by his uncle, Sir James.

The same year he was raised to the peerage by the titles of Baron Thynne of Warminster, county Wilts, and Viscount

Weymouth, county Dorset, with limitations to his brothers in default of male issue. In 1762 Lord Weymouth was sworn of Queen Anne's Privy Council, and in 1710 Custos Rotulorum, county Wilts, and the ensuing year Keeper of His Majesty's deer, and woods, Forest of Dean. He married the daughter of the second Earl of Winchilsea, by whom he had three children.

Lord Weymouth was much esteemed for many excellent qualities. He died in the seventy-fourth year of his age, and was buried at Longbridge Deverill; his kindness and hospitality towards Bishop Ken is recorded in another page.

He appears to have been worthy of his good fortune, inasmuch as he valued and appreciated the beautiful estate which had fallen to his share. He made considerable improvements in the interior of Longleat House, finished and caused to be consecrated the domestic chapel, and laid out the gardens adjoining the mansion. He was a friend to literature, a patron of literary men, and was deservedly regretted when he passed away.

No. 23.

SIR JOHN COVENTRY.
BY DOBSON.
Grey suit. Blue cloak.

SIR JOHN of Pitminster, county Somerset, and Mere, county Wilts, was the son of John Coventry, by Elizabeth, daughter and co-heir of John Barton, and widow of one Herbert, a gentleman of Hampshire. The Lord Keeper Coventry was his grandfather. He was Knight of the Bath, and sat in the Long Parliament, and others, for Weymouth.

In 1670 an inhuman assault was made on him, which gave rise to the Act since known as 'The Coventry Act,' against wounding, maiming, etc.

Money being asked for in the House of Commons at a time when Sir John, and other members, were advocating economy, the good knight proposed to tax the theatres, the immorality of which was at that time notorious. The courtiers opposed the measure, saying that the players were the King's servants, and part of his pleasure. Whereupon Sir John asked facetiously, 'Whether the King's pleasure lay among the actors, or the actresses?'

This speech was reported to His Majesty by those who were glad to inflame his choler against Coventry, and revenge was projected. Some of the guards were to watch for Sir John in the street, and set a mark upon him.

The Duke of York heard of the plot, and told Bishop Burnet that he had done all in his power to dissuade his brother from so cruel and unjust a proceeding, but in vain. As Coventry came out of his house one evening, he was attacked by three gentlemen, but snatching the flambeau from his servant, with the light in one hand, and his sword in the other, he made a most gallant defence. He wounded one, but was soon overpowered, and the villains cut his nose to the bone,—'to remind him,' they said, 'of the respect he owed the King,' and leaving him in his pain, returned to the Duke of Monmouth's, whence they came. The Duke was much censured for the part he had taken in the affair, and all the more that he and Coventry had been on friendly terms. Fortunately for the sufferer, 'his nose was so well needled up,' that the scar was scarcely perceptible. The members of the House of Commons were furious, and passed a Bill of banishment against the perpetrators of the outrage, with a clause that it should not be in the King's power to pardon them. Sir John died unmarried.

No. 24.

SIR JOHN THYNNE,
CALLED 'THE BUILDER.'

BY HOLBEIN.

BORN 1515, DIED 1580.

White and gold dress, with buttons. Badge. Sword. In the corner an inscription: 'Sir John Thynne, builder of Long Leat. An° Dom¹ 1566. Ætatis suæ, 51.'

HE son of Thomas Thynne of Stretton, Shropshire, by Margaret Eynes.

In 1540 he married Christian, daughter of Sir Richard Gresham, (twice Lord Mayor of London,) who was half-sister and co-heir of Sir Thomas Gresham, builder of the Royal Exchange. In the same year Sir John purchased the old Priory of the Black Canons of St. Augustine, near to Horningsham, county Wilts, with the adjoining lands, and he spent several years in improving and enlarging the estate.

In 1547, being then Secretary to the Duke of Somerset, he was knighted by that nobleman in the camp before Roxburgh, after the battle of Musselburgh and the siege of Leith.

When the Protector Somerset, to whom Sir John was much attached, was sent to the Tower, on being attainted, his Secretary was also imprisoned, and subjected to a heavy fine, but was soon released. In 1555 he obtained a grant of Kempsford, county Gloucester, and was appointed by the Lady Elizabeth (afterwards Queen) Comptroller of her Household, a post he ere long vacated, and went to live on his estate.

He sat in Parliament for county Wilts, for Bedwyn, and

for Heytesbury. Now Sir John's good fortune roused the jealousy of his neighbours, one of whom, an Earl and a Privy Councillor, caused him to be arraigned before the Council, upon the somewhat novel accusation of having amassed a large fortune. Perhaps the worshipful gentlemen were in hopes of discovering Sir John's secret. The knight spake out boldly, and honestly, saying his wife's fortune had laid a good foundation, which he had improved by industry and economy, and he wound up his defence by observing that his Lordship and the other gentlemen had now as good a mistress in the Queen as he had formerly had a master in the Duke of Somerset; and thus terminated the legal (?) inquiry into well-gotten wealth.

It was in 1567 that he began to build that noble structure, the glory, not only of the west, but of all England, respecting the architecture of which, so many pages of controversy have been written.

Both to John of Padua and John Thorpe (unless they be one and the same person) the designs for the house were attributed; but from documents lately discovered, the most probable solution of the mystery is, that Sir John made use of designs prepared many years before by his patron, the Duke of Somerset, for a house on his own estate; this would account for the name of the architect not being mentioned in the records of the building. Be this as it may, the fame of Longleat and its beauty reached the ears of Queen Elizabeth, and she resolved to judge for herself, even before its completion; and so Sir Henry Seymour (the Protector's brother) told poor Sir John roundly, 'that her Grace did not relish his seeming unwillingness to receive her, and making excuses of sicknesses and other letts to divert her from the country.'

Moreover, the said Sir Henry Seymour, and Lord Sussex, a personal friend of Sir John's, were so good as to pacify the Queen, by assuring her, that the master of Longleat hurried

on the building, mainly with the view of receiving his royal
mistress. Thither therefore she repaired in 1574, in her progress
from Bristol. After feasting the royal party in the most
sumptuous manner, the good knight was rewarded for his unbounded
hospitality by a message, through the Earl of Hertford
(son of Protector Somerset), to the effect his illustrious
guest had expressed 'great liking for her entertainment in the
west, especially at your house.' Moreover, the Queen condescended,
in conversation, to praise the charms of Longleat,
an example that has not been lost on succeeding generations.
Sir John finished the south and east fronts, and the interior
from the hall to what was then called the Chapel Court. He
had to his second wife, Dorothy, daughter to Sir William
Wroughton of Broadhinton, county Wilts; he died in 1580,
and by his own desire was buried by his first wife at Longbridge
Deverill. Amidst all the persecutions of Mary's reign,
he was a staunch supporter of the Reformed Church.

No. 25.

SIR EGREMONT THYNNE.

Red robe. Ruff. Holding a scroll.

E was the eldest son of Sir John Thynne of
Longleat, by his second wife. He was
Serjeant-at-Law, and married Barbara,
daughter of Henry Calthorpe, whose brother
was Lord Mayor of London. Aubrey has
a strange story connected with him, in his
Miscellanies, which is interesting to those who love the marvellous.
One of Sir Egremont's sisters married (as his second
wife) Sir Walter Long of Draycot, county Wilts, and had

several children; it would appear that this lady used every means in her power to induce her husband to disinherit his son by the first marriage, sowing dissension between the father and his first-born in a most unpardonable manner. She persuaded her brother, Sir Egremont Thynne, to draw up a paper, by which Sir Walter, if prevailed on to sign the same, cut off his eldest son from the inheritance. This was at Bath, during the Assizes, where the learned serjeant-at-law was engaged in his legal duties; Sir Egremont accordingly drew up the document, and gave it to his clerk one night, bidding him sit up and engross it.

The man set to work, but no sooner had he commenced, than he was startled by a shadow falling on the parchment; he looked up hastily, and perceived a hand between him and the candle; he rubbed his eyes, and roused himself to his work, in the belief that he was falling asleep. Once more came the dark blot on the deed, and this time he saw quite clearly a small, white, lady's hand, that vanished each time, as he gazed on it. He flung down his pen in terror, and, hastening from the room, went and told his master he would have no more to do with so unpleasant a transaction. But Lady Long found some one else to do her bidding, and the obedient husband signed and sealed.

No good came, as may well be imagined, of such dealings. The rightful heir's maternal relations rose in his defence, seized the body of Sir Walter (who died shortly afterwards) in the church porch, and began a law-suit against the second son, by which they compelled him to accept of a moiety of the property, and to relinquish the principal estate to his half, and elder, brother.

No. 26.

LOUISA VISCOUNTESS WEYMOUTH.

BY VAN DER BANK.

In a fancy dress of pink and black. Pearl ornaments. Aigrette in her hair.

ADY Louisa Carteret was the daughter of John Carteret, Earl Granville, by Lady Grace, daughter of John Granville, Earl of Bath.

She married the second Lord Weymouth (as his second wife) in 1733, and had by him two sons—Thomas, who succeeded his father; and Henry, who became Lord Carteret.

The dress in which Lady Weymouth is painted, was worn by her at a fancy ball at the Spanish Ambassador's, and was so much admired, that she sat for her portrait in the same.

No. 27.

THOMAS THYNNE, THIRD VISCOUNT WEYMOUTH, FIRST MARQUIS OF BATH.

BY SIR THOMAS LAWRENCE.

BORN 1734, DIED 1796.

In Parliamentary robes.

ON of the second Viscount, by Lady Louisa Carteret. In 1753 he set out on a foreign tour to complete his education; in 1760 he was appointed Lord of the Bedchamber to the King; in 1763, Master of the Horse to the Queen; in 1765, Lord-Lieutenant of Ireland, which post he did not occupy more than a few months, and in 1768, Secretary of State. He was also a Privy

Councillor, High Steward of the Corporation of Tamworth, and an Elder Brother of the Trinity House. In 1759 he married Lady Elizabeth Cavendish Bentinck, eldest daughter of William, second Duke of Portland, by whom he had three sons and six daughters.

In 1789 he was created Marquis of Bath, and in the autumn of that year their Majesties and the Princesses, with a numerous suite, were sumptuously entertained at Longleat. By the way, it is mentioned, in an elaborate account of this visit, that 30,000 people pressed into the park, and 125 guests, independent of servants, slept in the house. The King, George III., who had just recovered from a serious illness, and was on his road from Weymouth, was delighted with his reception. He went out on the roof of the house, and there observed, what many have said before, and since, that Longleat far exceeded its reputation for beauty.

Lord Bath continued the alterations begun by his father, and died in 1796.

No. 28.

SIR THOMAS THYNNE.

Black dress. Pointed beard.

E was the eldest son of Sir Thomas Thynne, by his first wife, the daughter of Lord Audley. He was seated at Richmond, in Surrey, and married the daughter of Walter Balquanhill, Dean of Durham, by whom he had Thomas, called of 'Ten Thousand,' who was murdered. He died *v.p.*

No. 29.

THE HONOURABLE HENRY COVENTRY.

By Sir Peter Lely.

BORN 1620, DIED 1686.

Scarlet and gold dress. Tawny mantle. Wig.

E was the third son of Lord Keeper Coventry, by the daughter of John Aldersley; educated at All Souls College, Oxford. A firm Royalist, on the Restoration he was appointed a groom of the Bedchamber, and in 1664 was sent Ambassador-Extraordinary to Sweden, where he remained till 1666. The following year he and Denzil, Lord Holles, went as Joint-Plenipotentiaries to Breda, where they concluded a peace with France, Denmark, and the States-General. In 1668 he went again on an embassy to Sweden, and on his return was made one of the Principal Secretaries of State, and Privy Councillor. He gave so much satisfaction in office that when compelled to retire from bad health, the *Gazette* had a notice respecting him: 'His Majesty has accepted the resignation with some unwillingness, because of the great satisfaction he always had in his services.' Lord Clarendon commends his diplomatic duties, and says he was beloved of every one.

He retired into private life, and died at his house in the Haymarket, unmarried, leaving his estates to his namesake Henry Coventry, and his nephew James Thynne, with several charitable bequests.

No. 30.

SIR JAMES THYNNE.

DIED 1670.

In armour. Flowing hair.

THE eldest surviving son of the first Sir Thomas Thynne of Longleat, whom he succeeded.

No. 31.

THOMAS THYNNE, Esq.

By Sir Peter Lely.

MURDERED 1682.

Tawny-coloured dress. Wig and ruffles. Holding a cane.

THE son of Sir Thomas Thynne of Richmond, Surrey, by Stuart, daughter and co-heir of Dr. Walter Balquanhill, Dean of Durham and Master of the Savoy. On the death of his uncle Sir James, Thomas Thynne inherited Longleat and other large estates, and was thenceforward known by the nickname of 'Tom o' Ten Thousand.' He enlarged and improved the house of his inheritance, built stabling, made good roads, which were a benefit to the country round, and was proverbial for generosity and hospitality.

Indeed, his hospitable treats are immortalised in Dryden's poem of 'Absalom and Achitophel,' for Absalom (the Duke of Monmouth) and the Master of Longleat were sincerely attached to each other. And on the Duke's return from banishment to Holland, in 1680, his staunch friend Thynne gave him so enthusiastic a welcome at his house, that he was in consequence deprived of the command of a regiment of militia in the county.

Thomas Thynne now turned his thoughts to matrimony, and resolved to take a wife whose birth and fortune qualified her to reign as mistress of his lordly mansion. He therefore selected the first match in the United Kingdom, and engaged himself to a widow lady of the mature age of thirteen years, Lady Elizabeth Percy, daughter and heir of the eleventh Earl of Northumberland. She had been removed from her mother's guardianship on that lady's second marriage, and committed to the care of her grandmother, the Dowager Lady Northumberland, by whom she was betrothed to Lord Ogle, son of the Duke of Newcastle, 1679. But the bridegroom dying the next year, the heiress was once more free to bestow her hand, and the Duke of Monmouth interested himself to further the suit of his friend, 'Tom o' Ten Thousand,' but it was whispered that the grandmother favoured the idea more than the granddaughter. However, in June 1681 they were contracted, and in July Mr. Thynne gained the young lady's consent that the marriage should be solemnised, on condition that it was kept secret until her year of mourning should be over. In the Marriage Service, when they came to the passage 'with all my worldly goods I thee endow,' the husband placed on the open Prayer-Book one hundred pieces of golden guineas, mixed with silver, 'which the lady put into her handkerchief, and then pocketed.' No sooner was the ceremony concluded than the bride announced her intention of going abroad to spend a year with Lady Temple, the wife of the celebrated

Sir William Temple, in Holland, a proceeding which was the cause of much gossip, some saying that she disliked her husband, and preferred another, and hoped to procure a dissolution of the marriage, etc. Be this as it may, there is no doubt that Count Königsmark, a handsome and distinguished officer, the head of one of Sweden's noblest families, then residing in London, was Thynne's rival. It is said he followed the young bride to the Continent, at all events he laid a deep scheme to rid himself of the obnoxious husband, by whom, he affirmed, he had been insulted. He accordingly secured the services of a German officer, who on his part hired two men, to one of whom (a Pole) was intrusted the actual murder. Königsmark kept out of the way, while his three creatures watched Thynne's proceedings, and lay in wait for him.

On the night of February the 12th, 1682, as the unfortunate gentleman was returning from a visit to the Countess of Northumberland, his coach was stopped, one villain riding up to the horses' heads, another alongside pointing to the occupant of the carriage, when the Pole fired, lodging several shots in the body of Thomas Thynne. On hearing the sad news, his faithful friend, the Duke of Monmouth, from whom he had just parted, hastened to the sufferer's bedside, tending him through the night with the utmost care, and taking the most energetic measures for the detection of the murderers. Indeed, it was at first supposed that the shot was intended for the Duke himself, but this Königsmark strenuously denied. Thomas Thynne lingered till the next morning.

The instigator of this foul deed was acquitted; the three men in his employ suffered death, the Duke of Monmouth witnessing the execution. The German officer behaved with gallantry worthy a better cause, his accomplice protested against the hardness of his fate, seeing he was about to die for two men, and a woman, on not one of whom he had ever set his eyes; and the Pole pleaded that he had only obeyed orders, as a soldier should do.

The Count, so unjustly acquitted, found, however, that his reputation had suffered by the dastardly and cruel deed, and confessing that it was a stain on his name, he entered the Venetian service, went to the wars, was sent to Greece as second in command, and fell at the siege of Argos, August 1686. The well-known marble monument erected by Thomas Thynne's family to his memory, in Westminster Abbey, has an elaborate bas-relief representing the murder.

Dying without children, he was **succeeded by his second** cousin and namesake, afterwards first **Viscount Weymouth**.

No. 32.

ELIZABETH, FIRST MARCHIONESS OF BATH.

PASTEL.

BORN 1734, DIED 1825.

White déshabille. Blue scarf.

LADY Elizabeth Cavendish Bentinck was the eldest daughter of William, second Duke of Portland, by Lady Margaret Harley, only daughter and heir of Edward, second Earl of Oxford.

She married, in 1759, Viscount Weymouth, who became Marquis of Bath in 1789. Their children were Viscount Weymouth, who succeeded to the Marquisate, and George, second Lord Carteret, married to Harriet, daughter to the second Viscount Courtenay. Lord Carteret died 1838, *s.p.*, and was succeeded in the title by his brother John, married to Mary Anne, daughter of Thomas, Master of the

Abbey, Cirencester. This Lord Carteret also died childless, when the title became extinct. Lord and Lady Bath had four daughters,—Louisa Countess of Aylesford, Henrietta Countess of Chesterfield, Sophia Countess of Ashburnham, and Mary, wife to Osborn Markham, son of the Archbishop of York. Two died unmarried, Isabella and Caroline, of whom the former was Lady of the Bedchamber to the Princess Mary, Duchess of Gloucester.

No. 33.

SIR HENRY FREDERICK THYNNE.

Plum and fawn-coloured dress. Long and flowing hair.

No. 34.

GEORGE, FOURTH VISCOUNT TORRINGTON.

BY HOPPNER.

DIED 1812.

Dark coat. Full wig.

THE **eldest son** of the third Viscount **by Miss** Daniel; he married, in 1765, the Lady Lucy Boyle, only daughter of John Earl of Cork and Orrery, by whom he had four daughters, —Lady John Russell, the Countess of Bradford, the Marchioness of Bath, and Emily, married to Henry, eldest son of Lord Robert Seymour.

No. 35.

VISCOUNTESS LANSDOWNE.

In a white deshabille. Flowers on the table beside her.

HE daughter of the Earl of Jersey, the wife of Thomas Thynne, (by whom she had the second Lord Weymouth,) and afterwards of Lord Lansdowne.

No. 36.

LADY ISABELLA THYNNE.

Buff gown. Pearls. Ringlets. Oval.

DAUGHTER of the Earl of Holland, and wife to Sir James Thynne of Longleat.

No. 37.

JAMES THYNNE.

BY CLOSTERMANN.

DIED 1708-9.

Grey coat. Red mantle. Cravat and ruffles.

ECOND son of Sir Henry Frederick Thynne by the daughter of Lord Keeper Coventry; seated at Buckland, county Gloucester; LL.D. at Oxford; was M.P. for borough of Cirencester, 1700-1. He died unmarried.

No. 38.

JOHN ALEXANDER, FOURTH MARQUIS OF BATH.

By George Richmond, R.A.

BORN 1831.

Shooting dress.

ARQUIS of Bath, Viscount Weymouth, Baron Thynne of Warminster, county Wilts, and a Baronet, succeeded his father in 1837. Was educated at Eton, and Christ Church, Oxford; married the daughter of Viscount de Vesci in 1861. Has six children, three sons, and three daughters.

No. 39.

THE LORD KEEPER COVENTRY.

By Cornelius Jansen.

BORN 1578, DIED 1640.

In robes of office.

HE founder of the family's fortunes was one John, who, assuming the name of his native town, went to London, where he became a mercer, and, doing well in business, was elected Lord Mayor in 1425.

Thomas, a descendant of the worshipful aforesaid (a lawyer, and eventually a Judge of Common Pleas), married Margaret, daughter and heir of —— Jefferies of Croome d'Abitot, county Worcester, still the residence of the Earls of Coventry. The subject of this notice was his son and heir, educated under the eye of his father, till he was fourteen, afterwards at Baliol College, Oxford, where he remained three years, then passed to the Inner Temple, London, to study law, which he did zealously. 'By an indefatigable diligence he attained the bar, and appeared in the lustre of his profession above the common expectations,' according to the magniloquent phrases of the time. In 1616 he was elected Recorder of London, and in the following year Solicitor-General, and shortly afterwards he was knighted at Theobalds.

1620 saw him Attorney-General, and in 1625 Buckingham recommended him to the King, as Lord Keeper, the Duke being most anxious to oust his old enemy Bishop Williams, who then held the Seals. A letter is extant from Coventry to the Duke, in which, with many circumlocuting paragraphs, he accepts the responsible post, which it would appear he had at first declined from diffidence. 'But after a great conflict in himself against those disabilities,' he laid himself 'in all humility and submission at the feet of his Sovereign, hoping that God and His Majestie would accept his true hart and willing endevor,' etc. etc.

But although he wrote in a style that may seem to us timeserving, it should be rather attributed to the fashion of the day, since not long after he had the independence to resist the grasping ambition of the Duke, his original patron.

Buckingham was moving heaven and earth to induce the King to revive in his favour the dormant post of Lord High Constable. The Lord Keeper was well aware what a dangerous power would thus devolve on a dangerous man, and he strongly advised the King to refuse.

Buckingham, furious, insolently demanded, 'Who made you, Coventry, Lord Keeper?' 'The King,' was the reply. '"Tis false, 'twas I, and you shall see that I who made, can and will unmake you.' 'Did I conceive,' answered the Lord Keeper, with dignity, 'that I held my place by your favour, I would presently unmake myself by resigning the Seals to His Majesty.'

The arrogant Buckingham dashed off, breathing revenge, and there is little doubt that he would have done his worst against the man who presumed to oppose him, had not his career been so soon ended by the knife of the assassin.

But Coventry had other enemies, and he offended the Marquis of Hamilton and the Earl of Manchester by the rigid discharge of his duties; the Earl of Portland, Lord High Admiral, was also much opposed to him, nevertheless he stood high at Court. In 1628 he was created Baron Coventry of Aylesborough, and Lord Clarendon says that 'he discharged all his offices with great ability and singular reputation of integrity. He enjoyed his place of Lord Keeper for sixteen years, and sure justice was never better administered, even until his death; no man had held the post so long, for the lapse of forty years.' The whole character of the man by Lord Clarendon is most admirable, and shows what a true friend he was to the King he loved, by opposing him in any unwise or unjust proceeding, even on his deathbed sending him good and wholesome counsel. Another witness says of him, 'He had a noble fame—not that he passed unaccused, for envy is a constant follower of greatness, and detraction an utter enemy of desert.' 'Amongst all and the many felicities of his life,' we again quote Clarendon, 'that of his short sickness and willing embracement of deathe with open armes, were of the most remarkable observacion, for it is our *finis qui coronat opus.*'

The venial charges brought against this great and good man are so slight as to demand no place in these pages. 'He was of a venerable aspect, wise, grave, and severe almost to moroseness, yet tempered with courtesy, discreet and reticent, speaking to the point without much eloquence—few enemies and some well-wishers—a man rather exceedingly than passionately loved.' He died at Durham House, Strand. His first wife was the daughter of Edward Sebright of Besford, county Worcester, by whom he had a daughter, and a son, his successor, the mother dying in childbirth.

His second wife was the daughter of John Aldersey of Spurston, county Chester, and widow of William Pitchford of London, citizen—'lovely, young, rich, and of good fame.' She brought him four sons, of whom two at least, and four daughters, were all celebrated for some high quality—Anne, married to Sir William Saville; Mary, wife to Sir Henry Frederick Thynne of Kempsford; Margaret, to the first Earl of Shaftesbury; and Dorothy, to Sir John Pakington, Bart., of Westwood, county Worcester. 'This lady,' says Lodge, 'stood at one time first candidate for the honour of having written *The Whole Duty of Man*, a possibility which at least speaks well for the consideration in which her talents and piety were held at the time.'

Lord Coventry published some legal works.

No. 40.

SIR WILLIAM COVENTRY.

BY SIR PETER LELY.

BORN 1626, DIED 1686.

Tawny coloured coat. Wig. Hand resting on book.

E was the youngest brother of Sir John Coventry. Went to Queen's College, Oxford, as gentleman-commoner, when sixteen; then travelled in foreign parts: on his return, declaring himself a loyal subject of King Charles, he was appointed secretary to the Duke of York, and also to the Admiralty. Other honours succeeded—Privy Councillor, Commissioner of the Treasury, etc.

Evelyn calls him a 'wise and witty gentleman.' Burnet says of him: 'A man of great notions and eminent virtues, the best speaker in the House of Commons, and capable of leading the best Ministry, as it was once thought he was very near it, and deserved it more than all the rest did.'

Having quarrelled with the Duke of Buckingham, and a duel being in contemplation, he was forbid the Court, and retired to Minster-Lovell, near Witney, in Oxfordshire, where he led a quiet country life, refusing all offers of public appointments. He was never married, and died at Somerhill, near Tunbridge Wells, where he had gone for the benefit of the waters. He was buried at Penshurst, in the same county.

He left in his will £2000 for the relief of the French Protestants lately banished on account of their religion, who had taken refuge in England; also £3000 for the redemption of captives from Algeria.

No. 41.

THOMAS THYNNE, Esq.

By Sir Godfrey Kneller.

DIED 1710.

Tawny suit. Full wig.

THE only son of Henry Frederick Thynne, by the daughter and co-heir of Francis Philips of Sunbury, county Middlesex; born at Little Holland House, Kensington; educated at Eton and Oxford. He afterwards travelled on the Continent for two years, and on his return, Lord Weymouth, who was his uncle, godfather, and guardian, arranged a marriage for him with Lady

Mary Villiers, daughter of the first Earl of Jersey. By his father's will he was not to come into possession of his estates till he was twenty-four, which age he never attained, but his guardians purchased property for him in Dorset, Wilts, etc. etc. He died of the small-pox in London, leaving his wife near her confinement, and accordingly, the month ensuing, she gave birth to a son, afterwards the second Viscount Weymouth.

LOWER CORRIDOR.

LOWER CORRIDOR.

No. 42.

MARIA AUDLEY, THE HONOURABLE LADY THYNNE.

By Mytens.

Full length. Richly embroidered crimson skirt, laced and fringed, over gown of white. White shoes. Holding fan.

THE first wife of Sir Thomas Thynne, daughter and co-heir of Lord Audley, by Lucia, daughter and heir of Sir James Mervin of Fonthill. Strange enough, there had been a negotiation of marriage between Miss Mervin and Sir John Thynne, father of Sir Thomas. We are not told why the owner of Longleat disapproved of the match for his son, but the families were destined to be united.

Maria, Lady Thynne, had five children,—John, who died unmarried; Thomas, seated at Richmond in Surrey, died *v.p.*; James, who succeeded his father; and two daughters,—Stuart, married to Sir Edward Bayntun of Bromham Bayntun, county Wilts, and Elizabeth, married to John Hall of Bradford, in the same county.

The reason assigned for Lady Thynne having sat for her portrait in an interesting, rather than a becoming condition, is as follows: she had a dream that she should not survive her confinement, and told her husband, if he wished to possess a picture of her no time must be lost. It is possible that her fears may have hastened the event, for the story goes that the foreboding was fulfilled at the appointed time, but we have only family tradition as our authority.

Biographical Catalogue.

No. 43.

CATHARINE HOWARD, THE HONOURABLE LADY THYNNE.

By Mytens.

DIED 1650.

Full length. White gown, richly embroidered in coloured flowers. Blue and gold band on left arm.

HE was the daughter of Charles Viscount Howard of Bindon, and second wife to Sir Thomas Thynne of Longleat, by whom she had (beside two sons who died unmarried) Sir Henry Frederick Thynne of Kempsford.

Lady Thynne was buried in Henry VII.'s Chapel, Westminster Abbey, near the steps of the Duke of Richmond's monument.

No. 44.

LADY ISABELLA THYNNE.

By Dobson.

Full length. White gown. Coloured scarf. Ringlets. Holding a handkerchief.

HE daughter of Henry Rich, Earl of Holland, by the heiress of Sir William Cope of Kensington. There is a most tragical story connected with this lady's youth. King James I., with the shameful injustice that characterised him, had wrested the estates and revenues of the noble family of Butler from their rightful owner, the Earl of Ormonde, and bestowed them on a favourite of his own, Preston by name, who was, moreover, created Baron Dingwall, and eventually Earl of Desmond.

Lord Dingwall married Lady Elizabeth Butler, whose brother, Lord Ormonde, had been despoiled in his favour. Their only child Elizabeth became the Earl of Holland's ward, and was brought up chiefly under his roof; she was a beautiful and engaging girl, when her cousin, Lord Thurles, (Lord Ormonde's son,) fell in love with her. It was a most suitable match, and so thought Lord Holland and his wife, and, indeed, the whole household. The cousins pledged their troth, Lord Thurles's visits were encouraged, and all went well for a time, but so great a prize as Lady Elizabeth Preston was sure to be coveted. The Duke of Buckingham desired her hand for his nephew, and induced the King to forbid the marriage with young Lord Thurles.

Elizabeth's affections were irrevocably fixed, and she had many friends and confidants; her guardian durst not assist her openly, having received the King's commands on the subject; but there was one who was in a position to do so, and that was his daughter Isabella, Elizabeth's chosen friend, and sister, (in all but blood,) a beautiful sharp-witted girl of her own age, who admitted Lord Thurles every day, at all hours, in a clandestine manner, (as was necessary,) nor did her parents object, or interfere with her proceedings, but allowed her to make a feint of receiving Lord Thurles's addresses, and implicit trust was placed by all parties in Isabella's rectitude.

Alas! for the compact which we must believe was begun in good faith: Lord Thurles was young, handsome, agreeable, captivating in fact, and the *rôle* of confidante is proverbially dangerous. In an evil moment he forgot his loyalty to his betrothed, and Isabella forgot her friend, herself, her duty, and all but her infatuation for the man, who was playing a double part by the two girls.

Surely no romance can outdo this real history in sensational incident. Lord Desmond was drowned about the same time his wife died, leaving as her last injunction that Elizabeth should marry no one but her cousin, and by that means restore him the property, the acquisition of which had weighed heavily on poor Lady Desmond's mind. Buckingham was assassinated, the King died, and Charles I., on his accession, gave the royal consent to the union of the cousins. 'And so,' says the biographer of the great Duke of Ormonde (who, by the way, makes very light of this episode with his bride's friend), 'the marriage was joyously consummated, and every one content.' We are not informed how the unfortunate Lady Isabella fared on the occasion, but the *dénouement* remains to be told. Several years afterwards, when Ormonde was in Paris, he went to the Academy there to visit a handsome and intelligent youth, whom he had sent thither for his education, whereupon he sat down and wrote a long description of the boy to Lady Isabella (then the wife of Sir James Thynne), being a subject in which they had a common interest. As ill-luck would have it, he at the same time indited a letter to his wife, and misdirected the covers; while Lady Ormonde was occupied in making the discovery that she had been cruelly betrayed, and deceived by the two people she loved best, and trusted most, in the world, Isabella came in, and found her reading the fatal letter.

An agitating scene ensued, Isabella humbled herself before the woman she had so grievously injured, and sought by every means of fascination which she possessed to soften her just resentment.

Tears, sobs, caresses, remorse. Elizabeth, generous and high-minded, almost beyond belief, raised the suppliant who was kneeling at her feet, with the promise not only of pardon, but of unchanging friendship; a promise nobly kept, as we shall see later. Still more marvellous is the fact, (for we can scarcely doubt the evidence,) that Lady Ormonde not only never upbraided her husband, but maintained a profound silence on the subject. As to Lady Isabella's marriage to Sir James Thynne, we have been unable to ascertain the date, or any circumstances attending it. But it would appear she lived apart from her husband for some time before the legal separation, which took place (according to Longleat documents) in 1653. She led a most independent life during the time the Court was at Oxford: we are told a great deal about Lady Isabella Thynne, who lodged at Baliol College; strange stories of her doings; of 'how she and Mistress Fanshawe went to morning chapel dressed as angels,' *i.e.* in scanty drapery; of 'how our grove is converted into a Daphne, for the ladies and their gallants; how Lady Isabella used to make her entry there, in a jaunty manner, with a lute before her, dressed in a fantastical costume;' also how she and her friend Fanshawe paid a visit for a frolic to a great Don, and behaved in so extravagant a manner, that the learned man rebuked the two ladies sharply.

Lady Isabella seems to have carried her eccentricities a little too far, according to some contemporary evidence: 'They say there is a lady banisht from Court lately—the Lady Thinne. It is a bad sign when such stars fall.' Again: 'It was reported that Her Majesty should strike the good Lady Thynne; methinks it should not be true. Yet they say Her Majesty gave her a box on the ear, which Lady Thynne gave Mr. Gorman to keep.'

In 1647 the paper entitled *Parliament of Ladies* for that year said, 'The rattle-headed ladies having assembled at Kate's in the Covent Garden, and choosing a speaker, at last resolved on Lady Isabella Thynne.' But we have dwelt perhaps too long on the vagaries of one whom we are assured 'was most beautiful, most accomplished, most humble, most charitable.' The destinies of the two women who had been early friends, but whose characters were so opposed, seem to have been strangely entangled. Lady Isabella was fated to cross Lady Ormonde's path once more ; the occurrence is a curious one, and is related in the life of Lord Broghill (afterwards better known as the Earl of Orrery), who was at the time in high favour with Cromwell, and had pleaded Lady Ormonde's cause to some purpose, with the autocrat, being deeply attached to that most noble lady and her husband. He had just returned from Ireland, where he had distinguished himself, when he was summoned to the Protector's presence.

'If you are still interested in my Lord Ormonde's safety,' said Oliver, 'you had better advise him to leave London. We know all about him, where he is, what he is doing, and he had best absent himself.' The hint was given and taken, and Lord Ormonde left England in haste. A short time elapsed, when one day Lady Ormonde was much distressed by receiving a domiciliary visit from one of Cromwell's functionaries, who ransacked the house, and carried away every paper he could find.

She immediately sent for her faithful friend, and besought him to intercede once more in her behalf.

Broghill lost no time, but hastened off to Whitehall, where he found the great man in a towering passion.

'You have undertaken, indeed, for the quietness of a fine person,' he said. 'I have allowed my Lady Ormonde £2000 a year, out of her husband's estates, because they were sufferers in Ireland. But I find she is a wicked woman, and I promise you she shall pay for it.' It was some time before Lord Broghill could gain a hearing, but when he was permitted to speak, he asked what proof could be adduced of Lady Ormonde's treachery, upon which Cromwell threw him a letter, that certainly left no doubt of the writer's Royalist tendencies and disaffection to the existing Government.

'This had been found,' he said, 'in searching the escritoire at Ormonde House.' Lord Broghill could not help laughing. 'But this,' he said, 'is not the writing of my Lady Ormonde.'

'Indeed,' exclaimed Cromwell angrily, 'and pray who wrote these lines?'

Bent on saving Lady Ormonde's credit, Lord Broghill not only told him the letter was from Lady Isabella Thynne, (between whom and Lord Ormonde there had been undoubted love-passages,) but he produced some other letters of the same lady, to identify the handwriting, and further proceeded to relate several anecdotes of a most lively nature, respecting her, which turned all Cromwell's anger into mirth, and he laughed immoderately.

Broghill's judicious conduct had gained Lady Ormonde's cause. But some time afterwards she went to reside at Caen, her husband being on the Continent, and Lady Isabella having got herself into hot water once more, recalled and claimed her friend's promise. Nor did she do so in vain: Lady Ormonde welcomed her to her house, where Isabella remained two years, during which time Lord Ormonde was a frequent visitor. We do not give the dates, as they are not clearly set down by our authorities; but to the best of our belief she was in England in 1653. Lord Clarendon tells us 'that Hyde's heart ached for poor Lady Isabella Thynne.'

No less a poet than Waller wrote verses to her, on her playing the lute, on her exquisite cutting of trees in paper, etc.

In 1665 one Flecknoe's Muse was also inspired by her charms.

Of her death we know nothing; but there was a story current that both she and her sister, the Lady Diana, had warnings of their approaching dissolution by meeting their own 'fetches,' the latter lady in Kensington Gardens.

No. 45.

MARY COVENTRY, THE HONOURABLE LADY THYNNE.

By Sir Peter Lely.

Full length. White gown. Blue scarf over her shoulders. Pearl ornaments. Ringlets.

HE was the daughter of Lord Keeper Coventry, and the wife of Sir Henry Frederick Thynne, by whom she had three sons and two daughters,—Thomas, who succeeded his father, James, who died unmarried, and Henry Frederick; Mary, wife of Sir Richard How, Wishford, county Wilts; and Catherine, wife of Sir John Lowther, afterwards Viscount Lonsdale.

No. 46.

SIR WALTER COVERT.

By Mytens.

Full length. Black dress and sword belt. Lace collar and cuffs.

HE Coverts were an ancient and knightly race, supposed to be of Norman origin; settled in Sussex about the middle of the twelfth century. A marriage with an heiress of the Norman family of the D'Aiguillon brought them good estates, Broadbridge and Sullington in the same county, and at the latter place they remained for several generations; in the church there is the tomb of a mailed knight—*temp.* Henry III.—supposed to be that of Sir William de Covert. They formed

alliances with some of the oldest families in Sussex, and were reckoned the richest untitled gentry in that part of the country, where they were held in good repute.

In the reigns of Henry VIII., Elizabeth, and James, there is so much confusion in the printed pedigrees and county histories respecting the Coverts that we are unable to mention names and circumstances relating to Sir Walter, with any degree of certainty. In a Sussex archæological journal, we find that in 1587 a survey of the county was made by Thomas Parker and Sir Walter Covert (two deputy-lieutenants) in order to ascertain how far the shores were prepared for defence. Sir Walter was twice married. By his first wife, Anne Covert, he had a son, the first and only Baronet. It is difficult to decide if he obtained the estate of Slaughane by this marriage, or by inheritance, but he is reputed to have been the builder of the noble mansion there. His second wife was Jane Shurley. Sir Walter died before the year 1632.

No. 47.

JANE SHURLEY, LADY COVERT.

By Cornelius Jansen.

Full length. White dress. Red under-skirt. Red and white ribbons. In a garden.

AUGHTER of Sir John Shurley of Ifield, county Sussex, who died in 1631. She married Sir Walter Covert as his second wife, and after his death became the second wife of Denzil Lord Holles. The dates which are given of this lady's birth, marriage, and death are so different, according to different authorities, that we think it best not to adopt any.

No. 48.
GASPARD DE CHÂTILLON, SIRE DE COLIGNY, GRAND AMIRAL DE FRANCE.

BORN 1517, MURDERED 1572.

Black dress. Black hat.

E was the son of Jean de Châtillon, Sire de Coligny, and was born at the ancestral estate of Châtillon-sur-Loing. His mother was Louise de Montmorency; his father dying when he was quite a child, the guardianship devolved on Gaspard's maternal uncle, the celebrated Connétable de Montmorency. The boy was educated in the Roman Catholic religion, and he showed much talent and intelligence, but rather drew back from distinguishing himself, lest his family should insist on his entering the Church, a step to which he was much averse.

He showed, on the contrary, an early predilection for a military career, and the King (Henry II.), whose favour he had gained, appointed him, while still young, to a high post in the army. Coligny, when at Court, had formed a close intimacy with François Duc de Guise, and joining the army together, they were for some time inseparable brothers-in-arms. In De Coligny's first campaign he was twice severely wounded, and also made prisoner of war; he served in Flanders, in Italy, in Picardy, etc. etc. His courage and endurance were proverbial, and when intrusted with diplomatic negotiations he showed great ability. In 1552-3 he was appointed Lord High Admiral of France, and about two years afterwards he, with the royal consent, vacated his military command in favour of his well-loved brother and brave comrade, François de Coligny (better known as

D'Andelot), and returned to his home and family at Châtillon, where he gave himself up for some time to theological studies, more particularly to the investigation of the doctrines of the Reformed Church. This was done at the earnest request of his brother, who had become a Huguenot. His conversion was owing to the perusal of several religious books on the subject, procured for him while a prisoner of war at Milan. The Admiral was not slow in following D'Andelot's example, and he became an ardent proselyte, although the fear lest the step should prove disadvantageous to his family prevented him from making an open profession at first. But Gaspard de Coligny was not a man for half-measures, and ere long he stood forth as a staunch champion of the Huguenot party, only second in importance to the Prince de Condé. He spent large sums of money in establishing reformed colonies in Florida and Brazil (neither of which were long-lived), and he memorialised the King to allow the Huguenots freedom of worship, and to grant them exemption from many persecutions. An edict was passed which seemed favourable to this oppressed people, but it was not of long duration. The murder of a Huguenot by one of the Guise faction again lit the flame, and the war was resumed. At the first call to arms, Coligny hastened to join the Prince de Condé, then Generalissimo of the Huguenot army, and the two friends took the field together, against the Duke of Guise.

For some time fortune smiled first on one, and then on the other side of the opponents, until the battle of Dreux, where the Duke of Guise was victorious and marched off in triumph to Orleans. But his days were numbered. At the moment of giving orders for storming the town, a shot fired by Poltrot de Mery, a Huguenot enthusiast, struck him down in his tent, mortally wounded. There were not found wanting some who dared accuse the noble Coligny of being the instigator of this deed; but few of either party gave credence to so foul a calumny, although the Guise faction made it a plea for hunting their enemy even to the death.

Another religious truce, and Coligny once more disbanded his soldiers, and returned to his beloved Châtillon. Another outbreak, when the Huguenots, confirmed in the opinion that the Queen-Mother, Catherine of Medicis, was their deadly enemy, formed a project to possess themselves of the person of the young King, which failed. In the meantime the wily Catherine 'babbled of peace,' and strove by every means in her power to allure Condé and Coligny to Paris—an invitation they wisely refused. The Huguenots had acquired a valuable ally in the person of Jeanne d'Albret, Queen of Navarre, sole daughter and heir of the late King, and widow of Antoine de Bourbon, Duc de Vendôme. This Princess, called when a child 'La Mignonne des Rois,' from the tender love which her father and her uncle (Francis I.) both bore her, was remarkable for her courage, her judgment, and her devotion to the tenets of the Reformed Church. She had arrived from the Pyrenees with a large escort and a considerable sum, (realised by the sale of her jewels,) to join the Huguenot camp, and swell its treasure. She was accompanied by her son Henry, Prince de Béarn, (afterwards Henry IV.,) about fourteen years of age, who pleaded earnestly, though vainly, to be allowed then and there to flesh his maiden sword. A terrible blow awaited the Huguenots in the death of their leader, the great Condé, who was slain at the battle of Jarnac, in 1655. Jeanne d'Albret did all in her power to raise their drooping spirits, and entering the camp in person, with her son on one side, and the young Prince de Condé on the other,— 'My friends,' she said, 'here are two new chiefs with whom God has provided you, two orphans I intrust to your care.'

Coligny, indeed, acted the part of a second father to the young Prince de Béarn, who studied the art of war under this great master, and did him early honour, for at a time when

Coligny was invalided, the young warrior took the command of the army and greatly distinguished himself. Time passed on; the Queen, Catherine, having matured a terrible plan for the ruin of the Huguenots, set about bringing it to bear. She negotiated a marriage between Henry, then heir to the **throne of** Navarre, **and** the Princess Margaret, sister to the **King of France.** The hitherto prudent Jeanne d'Albret fell **into the snare, and repaired to** Paris with her betrothed son, **in** order **to consummate a union** that promised so many advantages for **all parties concerned.** Her example was followed by Coligny, whose reception **at Court was as** flattering as the wily Italian thought prudent. The young King, well tutored, assured the Admiral by his **mother it was the** happiest day of his life, and offered him **as a bait a high** command in Flanders. The Huguenots flocked to the capital in numbers, and there were only a comparative few, who still harboured any suspicion. To the friendly warnings he received, Coligny replied, 'I am resigned, it shall all be **as** God pleases.'

One of his own household, after striving in vain to persuade his master to seek safety at Châtillon, or at least to be allowed, himself, to leave Paris, was asked what he feared. ' Ils vous font trop de caresses,' was the wise reply.

The preparations for the marriage were not concluded ere **the** sudden death of his beloved mother overwhelmed the *fiancé* with **deep** sorrow. But he was allowed no time to indulge **his** natural grief, for the nuptials were hastened.

There were rumours of poison, but the matter was hushed; the **next** incident that was calculated to alarm the Huguenots was the attempted assassination of the Admiral. A miscreant, supposed to be a creature of the Duchess of Nemours, (widow of the Duke of Guise, who died at Orleans,) fired a shot from an arquebuse, as Coligny was passing a window, and wounded him in the right hand and left arm.

But the time had not yet arrived. The King hastened to the Admiral's house, Rue de Béthisy, now Rue des Fossés, to inquire, to sympathise, and to condole, promising that the assassin should be brought to justice. Whether De Coligny's eyes were opened at last or not, it was now too late.

On the night of the Feast of St. Bartholomew, the Duke of Guise, at the head of a body of men, forced the door of Coligny's house, and killed the guard, while a Bohemian, by name Behme, rushed up to the Admiral's bedchamber. Awaked by the noise, the man who had braved danger in almost every form, opened the door, and stood face to face with the intruder. Being asked if he were the Sire de Coligny, he replied in the affirmative, and then added, 'Jeune homme, respectez mes cheveux blancs.' The miscreant's only answer was by a sword-thrust on the head, then seizing his victim by the heels, he dragged him to the window, and flung him headlong into the court below, at the feet of the Duke of Guise. This brutal man kicked his expiring enemy several times, and then delivered him up to the mob, who tore him to pieces. The body was gibbeted at Montfaucon, and the King went to look at it, saying, with the Emperor Vitellius, 'that a dead enemy is not a horrible sight, and does not smell bad.' The Admiral's faithful servants carried off the corpse at great personal risk, and buried it at Châtillon, but it was afterwards transported to Maupertuis, whose proprietor caused a grand monument to be erected. Thus died this brave and noble man, after a life full of vicissitude, leaving behind him a name dear to all lovers of human greatness and goodness, whatever their creed or nation.

As a general he was not reckoned successful, yet so energetic and skilful at 'reparation,' that De Coligny was considered more dangerous after defeat 'than his enemies after victory.'

Although a staunch disciplinarian, he was much beloved

by his soldiery on account of his benevolence and consideration. He spoke and wrote well, and was the author of several works, some of which are still extant.

Gaspard de Coligny was twice married—first to Charlotte de Laval, daughter of Guy, fifteenth of that name, Comte de Laval, by Antoinette de Daillon, by whom he had several sons and daughters. The circumstances attending his second marriage are of so remarkable and romantic a nature that we cannot pass them over in silence. Jacqueline de Montbel was the daughter and sole heir of a noble and wealthy Savoyard, the Comte d'Entremonts, and widow of Claude de Bastarnai, Comte de Bonchage. She was moreover a zealous Huguenot, and the reputation of Coligny, as the champion of that persecuted party, and the fame of his valour and piety, had so inflamed the fancy of the beautiful Savoyarde, that even before they had ever met, she conceived an unconquerable passion for the far-famed hero. The Duke of Savoy was very much averse to the marriage, probably wishing to retain the lady and her wealth within the precincts of his own dominions. He therefore caused her to be watched, but woman's wit eluded his vigilance; the Comtesse Jacqueline escaped to La Rochelle, and bestowed her hand on the man she had chosen from the world beside. The Duke of Savoy, enraged at her disobedience, seized on the lady's estates.

About the same time Louise, Coligny's daughter by his first wife, was united to M. de Téligny, 'un simple gentilhomme, de la compagnie de l'Amiral de Châtillon.' He was much beloved by his father-in-law, whose fate he shared, being also murdered on the day of St. Bartholomew; Louise survived, to become the wife of William of Nassau, Prince of Orange.

There is a curious historical parallel between more than one circumstance in the lives of these two heroes, both heads of the Huguenot party, both beloved, from their reputation alone, by noble and beautiful women, and both victims of a cruel murder. By De Coligny, Jacqueline had a posthumous daughter named Beatrice; we cannot close this brief notice without inserting a translation of the characteristic epitaph which was written in Latin :—

'Ci gissent les os de Gaspard de Coligny, Grand Amiral de France, Seigneur de Châtillon, son ame est dans le sein de Celui pour lequel il combattit avec tant de constance.'

No. 49.

ROBERT DEVEREUX, EARL OF ESSEX.

BORN 1567, EXECUTED 1601.

Full length. White dress. Embroidered vest. George, Ribbon, **and** *Garter. Left hand resting on the pommel of his sword; right hand holding a cane.*

HE eldest son of Walter, first Earl of Essex of the Devereux family, by Lettice, daughter of Sir Francis Knollys, Knight. He succeeded to the title and estates before he had reached his ninth year. But his father's solicitude had provided him with worthy guardians; Lords Burghley and Sussex, and Dr. Waterhouse, of whom, in his last moments, Walter, Lord Essex, took leave in these terms—'Farewell, Ned; thou art the friendliest and faithfullest gentleman that ever I knew;' and well did Waterhouse fulfil the trust imposed on him by his dying friend, he took the direction of the minor's affairs, which he managed with great ability, and watched over the boy himself, with paternal care.

In 1577 young Essex went to Cambridge, where he bore an excellent character, and gained the reputation of 'an elegant scholar,' while his refined and genial manners made him generally popular. He remained at the University till 1581, when he retired to his country house in Pembrokeshire, and seemed to have 'become enamoured of a rural life.' In 1584, on his first presentation at Court, he found his stepfather, the Earl of Leicester, reigning supreme, with whom he was in no way inclined to stand on friendly relations. The sudden death of Essex's father, and the indecent haste of his mother's marriage with Robert Dudley, were too vivid in his remembrance. But the royal ægis had been thrown over the pair, and the matter had been hushed up. Lord Leicester strove by every means in his power to propitiate his wife's son, and the young man was not proof against the professions of affection, or the prospects of advancement. At least so it would seem, for in the following year the two Earls went together to the Low Countries, Leicester as Captain-General, and Essex (though not more than eighteen at the time) as General of the Horse. Here the latter was greatly commended for his valour, more especially at the battle of Zutphen.

On his return to England he was made Master of the Horse, and not only intrusted with a high command in the army, at the time of the threatened Spanish invasion, but invested with the Order of the Garter—a proceeding which excited no little jealousy. Lord Leicester dying in the same year, the post of first favourite became vacant, and to that dangerous elevation was the new knight elected without loss of time; and now began afresh the disgraceful farce which Elizabeth Tudor had already enacted with Leicester, and in a minor degree with Sir Philip Sidney, and others. Alas! this time the curtain was to fall on a tragedy. The Queen's coquetries, her advances and retreats, her attacks on the citadel of the handsome and accomplished courtier's heart, are part of history, and need not be detailed here. Notwithstanding the honours she heaped upon him, his eager spirit was often 'vexed past patience,' even in these early days.

In 1589 he absented himself without leave from Court, even as Sir Philip Sidney had done before him, and sailed with Sir Francis Drake on his expedition to Portugal. Elizabeth ordered him to return in a most peremptory letter written with her own hand; but when he did so, she received him with open arms, keeping up for some time a skirmish of lover's quarrels. At length her indignation was seriously aroused on learning the old story, that her favourite had married without her permission.

She called it a *mésalliance*, a word that could scarcely apply in the case of the daughter of Sir Francis Walsingham, and the widow of Sir Philip Sidney.

In 1591 he commanded troops sent to the assistance of Henry IV. of France, and on his return was made a Privy Councillor; but jealousy was rife, plots were hatching against him, and the train was laid which was to be fired some years later.

He was appointed to the joint command of the fleet in the expedition against Spain, with Admiral Howard, and on their return, the marked difference between the manner in which the Ministers received Essex and his coadjutor was most distasteful to the former. Howard was treated with honour and consideration, while Essex was exposed to blame and mortification. He now retired to the country in disgust, and would not even attend Parliament till the question arose of a proposed treaty with Spain, when he hastened up to London to be present at a Council, and to advocate war, which he did in such vehement and passionate terms that his quondam guardian, Lord Burghley, rose from the table, and drawing a prayer-book from his pocket, pointed to a passage in the Psalms which proved too prophetic—

'The bloodthirsty and deceitful man shall not live out half his days.'

Burghley, who died soon after, was indeed a tried and trusty friend, ever ready to defend him against all his enemies, even the worst of all, Essex's own self. Peace was concluded, however, and Robert Devereux added to his general unpopularity, while he angered the Queen, by rushing into print on the occasion, and that in most unmeasured terms. Not long afterwards, occurred the well-known scene at the Council, where was a hot discussion relative to the choice of a Governor for Ireland, and Lord Essex's language was so intemperate that Elizabeth in a rage rose from her seat and struck him on the cheek. Stung to the quick, he half drew his sword, and swearing he would not endure such treatment, left the royal presence in a fury, and once more hurried off to his country house, whence it required much persuasion to induce him to return to his allegiance. The ill-fated man did not realise (after he had made a species of proud apology) how far he was playing into his enemies' hand, by accepting the command now given him, to put down a rebellious outbreak in Ireland. The complete failure of this expedition is well known. Essex incurred the unmitigated censure of the Government, and of the Queen herself.

His mind was at this time in a very wretched and unsettled state, and on the receipt of a letter from Elizabeth full of reproaches, he left Ireland, and drew no breath till he stood suddenly in her presence at Nonsuch Place, coming, he said, to throw himself on her mercy, and implore her to listen to his vindication. After a conference of some duration, she dismissed him with the desire that he should remain in the custody of the Lord Keeper. In this species of honourable imprisonment he continued for some time in suspense, probably relying on Her Majesty's constancy to pardon him. But there were those who whispered distrust and slander in the royal ear.

Alas for the proud spirit of Robert Devereux! he was examined for eleven hours before the Privy Council, during most of the time compelled 'to remain on his knees.'

When released, he once more retired to the country, and then came up to London, where he made his house the centre of the disaffected; and although still professing unshaken loyalty, yet his actions and the companions he drew around him were well calculated to excite the suspicions both of the Queen and of her Ministers. Again summoned before the Council, he refused to appear; and when the Lord Keeper and the Lord Chancellor went to his house to expostulate, he detained them prisoners. A climax to his rashness was the step he took in sallying forth into the city to enlist volunteers, at the head of a large body of armed adherents, and on his return to his house he fortified himself therein. He was proclaimed a traitor, besieged, and taken prisoner on the 8th of February 1601, and on the 19th brought to trial, and condemned to die.

The struggle between anger, tenderness, and compassion in the breast of Elizabeth has been recorded in history, drama, and fiction; and the story of the ring, which will be found in another page, is one of the widest circulated of historical romances. There is little doubt that Elizabeth never recovered the shock of Essex's death, although her own hand dealt the blow to both.

On the night preceding his execution, the noble prisoner opened his window, and addressing the guards and pages, regretted he had nothing to give them; 'for I have nothing save what I am going to pay the Queen on the morrow.' He rose soon after midnight, and prayed with the chaplain, saying, 'God bless you, as you shall comfort me.' He dressed himself with care in a black suit, velvet gown, felt hat, and starched ruff. On his road to the scaffold he continued instant in prayer. 'God grant me true penitence, true patience, true humility, and put all worldly thoughts from my mind.' No one can deny that Robert Devereux made a noble end.

He spoke earnestly to the crowd, asking them to join in prayer with him, repeated the Lord's Prayer with great fervour, desired forgiveness of God and of the Queen, 'whom he had never intended to harm,' and answered the executioner with gentle courtesy, who kneeling, asked his forgiveness. 'Thou art but the minister of justice,' said Essex; then taking off his velvet gown and doublet, he continued to pray till the cruel blow silenced that noble voice for ever. He was deeply mourned by many. 'My Lady of Essex,' says a contemporary writer (she had made strenuous efforts to save him), 'is a most sorrowful creature, she wears black of the meanest price, and will receive no comfort.'

She loved him dearly, and was his chosen companion in the quieter moments of his life, sharing and lightening his literary studies and labour. They had an only son, Robert, the last Devereux who bore the title of Essex, and two daughters—Frances, married to William, Marquis of Hertford, afterwards Duke of Somerset; and Dorothy, married, first, to Sir Henry Shirley of Stanton Harold, county Leicester, and secondly, to William Stafford of Blatherwyck, county North Hants.

No. 50.

GUSTAVUS ADOLPHUS, KING OF SWEDEN.

BORN 1594, KILLED IN ACTION 1632.

Full length. Drab leather coat, grey and gold embroidered sleeves, and trunk hose. High drab boots. Helmet with grey and drab feathers on the table beside him.

HE son of Charles IX., King of Sweden, by Christina of Holstein, and grandson of the great Gustavus Vasa. He ascended the throne when only fifteen, and at that early age showed great capacity for government, and discrimination in the choice of his ministers. But his education and tastes led him to a military career; he engaged in wars with Denmark, Muscovy, and Poland with wonderful success, and he then entered into an alliance with the Protestant powers of Germany against the Emperor of Austria, and was the hero of the Thirty Years' War, the friend and comrade-in-arms of all those brave spirits whose names live for ever in the pages of Schiller, and the memory of all lovers of religion and valour.

After a series of brilliant campaigns, where he appeared to bear a charmed life, Gustavus Adolphus fell at the battle of Lützen. It was said of him, 'He died with the sword in his hand, the word of command on his tongue, and the victory in his anticipation.'

When surrounded by enemies, his page tried to hide the rank of his royal master, but the hero exclaimed, 'I am the King of Sweden, and I seal with my blood the Protestant faith and the liberties of Germany.' Then he called on the God he had served so well, and with the name of his beloved

Queen on his lips he expired. The body was instantly stripped, for every one was anxious to possess some relic of Gustavus Adolphus; but his noble and commanding form, though divested of all the trappings of royalty, caused it to be recognised amid the heaps of less eminent slain.

In appearance the King of Sweden was fair, his eyes were light blue, but most expressive, his features aquiline, his complexion florid. All his portraits resemble each other so nearly that we cannot but feel familiar with the personal aspect of this great and good man. He was idolised by his friends, subjects, and comrades. His death seems to have stricken down the unfortunate King of Bohemia, who loved him dearly, and on all the Protestant princes it fell like a thunderbolt. He cultivated the arts and sciences, and improved the social position of Sweden, although so often absent on foreign campaigns. By his beloved and beautiful wife, Maria Elenora, Princess of Brandenburgh, Gustavus left an only daughter, the famous Christina, who succeeded her father on the throne of Sweden; but after reigning about twenty years she abdicated.

No. 51.

VISCOUNTESS TORRINGTON.

Blue mantle trimmed with fur.

ADY LUCY BOYLE, only daughter of John Earl of Cork and Orrery, by Margaret, daughter and sole heir of John Hamilton of Caledon, county Tyrone, Ireland, and wife of George, fourth Viscount Torrington.

No. 52.
LOUISA CARTERET, VISCOUNTESS WEYMOUTH.
THE SECOND WIFE OF THE SECOND VISCOUNT WEYMOUTH.
In the Coronation robes of a Peeress.

No. 53.
THOMAS, SECOND VISCOUNT WEYMOUTH.
By Sir GODFREY KNELLER.
Full length. In a Peer's Parliamentary robes.

No. 54.
VISCOUNTESS LANSDOWNE.
By Sir GODFREY KNELLER.
In the Coronation robes of a Peeress.

SHE was the daughter of the Earl of Jersey, by Barbara, daughter of Chiffinch, the closet-keeper and close confidant of Charles II., who has gained no enviable fame from the sketch which Sir Walter Scott has drawn of him in *Peveril of the Peak.* She married first, Thomas Thynne, Esq., of Old Windsor, who died, leaving her with child. Her son succeeded to the title of Weymouth. Lady Mary Thynne afterwards married Lord Lansdowne, by whom she had four daughters.

No. 55.

WILLIAM, EARL, AFTERWARDS MARQUIS, OF HERTFORD AND DUKE OF SOMERSET.

OLD STONE. AFTER VANDYCK.

DIED 1660.

In armour. Holding a truncheon.

E was the eldest surviving son of Lord Beauchamp (consequently great-grandson to Protector Somerset), by Honora, daughter of Sir Richard Rogers of Bryanston, county Dorset.

He was educated at Magdalen College, Oxford, at the time that James I. and his Queen were keeping Court at Woodstock. Amongst the fairest and noblest of Her Majesty's ladies, was the King's own cousin, the Lady Arabella Stuart. As soon as she and William Seymour met, they loved, and the young lady, suspecting that her royal kinsman would be averse to their union, impressed on her lover the importance of secrecy.

Their attachment was discovered, and Arabella Stuart and William Seymour were summoned before the Privy Council, and reprimanded in no moderate terms, but the affection had taken so deep a root, that even the tyrannical decrees of James could not prevent the consummation of the marriage. As we have told at length in the notice of Arabella Stuart's life, they were privately united, for which crime they were both imprisoned, and both in the course of time made their escape. Seymour was far more fortunate than his wife, and it was supposed that the authorities were not unwilling that he should regain his liberty. Disguised, in a black peruke, and tawny suit, he followed a cart out of the courtyard of the Tower, which had brought in firewood, and found a faithful friend at the iron gate, in whose company he travelled with all speed to the sea-coast, where it had been arranged he should meet Arabella.

Foiled in this hope, he made his way to Ostend, and resided some time in Flanders, after the death of his wife, until that of his grandfather, when he succeeded to the titles of Lord Beauchamp and Earl of Hertford. He then returned to England, and went to reside on his estates, and in the society of a few chosen friends, passed his time in study, and the improvement of the fortune, which had been sadly diminished, at the time of the attainder of Protector Somerset.

For some time after the accession of Charles I., Lord Hertford voted on the popular side, but he became disgusted with their ultra views, and with the injustice of the proceedings at the trial of Lord Strafford, although that nobleman was no personal friend of his. As was the case with many leading men of the time, Hertford now seceded from the party he had hitherto upheld, and devoted his services, his fortune, and his influence to the Royal cause.

In his new career he displayed an energy and activity of which he had hitherto appeared incapable. He proved his zeal, moreover, by accepting the post of Governor to the Prince of Wales, for which Clarendon tells us he was not fitted, neither did he incline to the duties. But so conscientious was he in their discharge, that he boldly withstood Parliament in a matter where the Prince of Wales's interests were involved.

About this time he succeeded to the Marquisate of Hertford. In 1643 he was named Lieutenant-General Commandant of the western counties, with power to raise troops at his discretion for the King's service. He was not very successful at first, but was afterwards joined by the Princes Maurice and Rupert, who served under him, and was present at the victories of Lansdowne and Roundway. At the taking of Weymouth a dispute arose between him and Rupert as to the nomination of a Governor to that town. Hertford waived his claim in submission to the King's wish, but, throwing up his military command, went to reside with Charles at Oxford, who gave him a place in the household, and he was elected Chancellor of the University. He now served the King in a civil capacity, taking part in the negotiations between his Majesty and the Parliament, and that with so much rectitude and moderation as to procure him the respect of both parties. His generosity kept pace with his loyalty; his coffers were open to his King; and during the time of Charles II.'s exile, Hertford allowed him an annual income, and he was one of the few mourners permitted to pay their last tribute to their martyred King by attending his funeral. At the Restoration he met Charles at Dover, who invested him with the Garter to which he had been named some years before; Cromwell had deprived him of the Chancellorship of Oxford, which he now resumed, and the King, in the most flattering manner, restored to him the Dukedom of Somerset, forfeited by the Protector, and after expressing his gratitude for the loyalty which Lord Hertford had evinced to his father and himself, hoped 'no man would envy the honours thus bestowed,' observing 'that it was no more than a good master should do for such a servant.'

The Duke did not survive this mark of royal favour very long. He died in 1660, and was buried at St. Bedwin in Wales.

His second wife was the Lady Frances Devereux, daughter of Robert, the second Earl of Essex, and sister and co-heir of Robert, the third Earl, and Parliamentary General.

Of his five sons, three died unmarried, and his four daughters all married Peers of the realm.

Lord Clarendon said of him, 'He was a man of good parts and conversant with books, both Greek and Latin; he loved study better than exercise, and a country better than a public life. By nature he was indolent, and though brave and faithful, he was by no means a good soldier.'

He was succeeded by his grandson and namesake, William Duke of Somerset, who died young.

No. 56.

JOAN HAYWARD, LADY THYNNE.

By Zucchero.

Full length. Black and white embroidered dress. Ruff. Holding a feather fan.

YOUNGEST daughter of Sir Rowland Hayward, Knight, who was twice Lord Mayor of London. She was co-heir to her mother, Joan Tylsworth, and brought into the Thynne family Cawse Castle, the Manor of Tretton, county Salop, and other lands. She married Sir John Thynne, (the second of that name,) by whom she had Sir Thomas and other children.

Lower Corridor.

No. 57.

THE LADIES DEVEREUX.

By Zucchero (?).

(*According to one Catalogue of an earlier date, ' Two Ladies, by Honthorst,' or as it is spelled, Hunthurst.*)

Two sisters dressed alike, in one picture. Half length. Light hair. Red and gold velvet bodices. White sleeves. Pearl necklaces.

IN all probability, the Lady Frances and the Lady Dorothy Devereux, daughters of Robert, the second Earl of Essex (Queen Elizabeth's favourite)—the eldest married to the Earl of Hertford, widower of Arabella Stuart, afterwards Duke of Somerset; and the younger to Sir Henry Shirley of Stanton Harold, county Leicester, and secondly, to William Stafford, Esq. of Blatherwyck, county North Hants.

No. 58.

SIR JOHN THYNNE, THE SECOND.

DIED 1604.

Black dress. White collar and sleeves. Right hand resting on hip, left on pommel of sword.

ELDEST son of Sir John, the builder of Longleat, by Christian, daughter of Sir Richard Gresham. He married Joan, daughter of Sir Rowland Hayward, who brought many estates into the family.

No. 59.

LADY ARABELLA STUART.

A head. Dress as in large picture on staircase.

No. 60.

GRACE, COUNTESS GRANVILLE.

By Sir Godfrey Kneller.

Full length. In the Coronation robes of a Peeress.

HE was the daughter of John Granville, first Earl of Bath, by Jane, daughter of Sir Peter Wyche. The Granvilles, or Grenvilles, as they were originally called, were a noble and heroic race; witness the exploits by sea of Sir Richard, immortalised in history and poetry, who lived in the time of Queen Elizabeth, and of the brave Sir Bevil, who perished in arms for King Charles 1. at the battle of Lansdowne, he on whose death it was written—

'Where shall the next famed Grenvil's ashes stand?
Thy grandsire fills the sea, and thou the land,'

a couplet most characteristic of the high-flown language of the period. Lady Grace was destined to be allied with heroes, for she married Sir George Carteret, afterwards raised to the Peerage as Baron Carteret, in consideration of the services of his father, and his grandfather, the gallant Earl of Sandwich. These two brave men died at Solebay fight in 1682, in an engagement with the Dutch, when Lord Sandwich's ship held out singly for five hours, at fearful odds with the enemy. After Sir George's death, his widow was created

Countess Granville and Baroness Carteret, in her own right, with limitation of her first title to her eldest son; she also succeeded to vast wealth and estates on the death of her nephew, the Earl of Bath.

But both these titles soon became extinct, that of Carteret being renewed in the person of Henry Thynne, son of the second Lord Weymouth by Lady Louisa Carteret, Lady Granville's grand-daughter. The Peerage of Carteret was destined to be short-lived, as it is now again extinct.

No. 61.

EDWARD VILLIERS, FIRST EARL OF JERSEY.

DIED 1711.

Full length. In Peer's Coronation robes, holding a wand.

THE eldest son of Sir Edward Villiers, by Frances, daughter to the Earl of Suffolk. He accompanied Princess Mary to Holland on her marriage with the Prince of Orange; returned to England with them in 1688, and was appointed Master of the Horse to the Queen, with other marks of royal favour.

In the third year of King William's reign he was created Viscount Villiers of Dartford and Baron Villiers of the Hoo, both in county Kent. On the Queen's death he went to the Hague as Plenipotentiary; in 1697 was employed in the same capacity for the Treaty of Ryswick, and shortly afterwards Ambassador to the States-General, on which occasion he was created Earl of Jersey. In 1698 he went to Paris as Ambassador-Extraordinary, where he kept up great state. On his return Lord Jersey was made one of the Principal Secretaries of State and one of the Lords Justices for the administration of the government, during the King's absence in Holland. He joined William at the Loo, and held other diplomatic posts, besides being chosen Lord Chamberlain of the Household, an office he continued to hold under Queen Anne until 1704, when he retired from public life. He died in 1711, the day before his intended nomination as Privy Seal, and was buried in St. Michael's Chapel, Westminster. He married Barbara, daughter to William Chiffinch, by whom he left three sons and a daughter—Mary, wife of Thomas Thynne of Old Windsor, (and mother of the second Viscount Weymouth,) who was afterwards Lady Lansdowne.

No. 62.

THE HONOURABLE LADY SAVILE.

DIED 1662.

Oval. Black dress. Jewels. Ringlets.

ANNE, eldest daughter of the Lord Keeper Coventry, married Sir William Savile of Thornhill, county York, a distinguished officer, enthusiastically devoted to the cause of Charles I.

He had served under his relative the Earl of Arundel against the Scots in 1639, and in 1643 he was appointed by his kinsman William Cavendish, Earl (afterwards Duke) of Shrewsbury (at that time in command of the Royal Forces in the northern counties), Governor of Sheffield. But his services were soon required elsewhere, and Thomas Beaumont was named Governor-Deputy in his absence. Sir William was anxious that his wife should accompany him, but she was too near her confinement to be able to follow him in his frequent marches and countermarches.

The separation was for ever. Sir William died early in 1643-44, and in the August of that year the town of Sheffield was besieged by the Roundheads under Major-General Crawford, who sent a summons to Beaumont to surrender. But the garrison, the Governor, and the brave widow of their late commander, were all of one mind. The reply, accompanied with a volley of shot, was to the effect that they refused to parley. Batteries were raised, and artillery kept playing for twenty-four hours without effect.

Crawford then sent for the 'Queen's Pocket Pistol,' a celebrated piece of ordnance, and a culverin, which did sad damage to the walls, already full of cracks.

At length the garrison showed signs of wishing to capitulate, but Lady Savile, whose time of trouble was drawing very near, assured the soldiers she would rather perish than give up the fortress intrusted to them by her gallant husband; even though her state was all the more distressing in consequence of the besiegers refusing admittance into the town of a female attendant, whose services the noble lady so much required. Such is the testimony of a zealous Royalist, Dr. Barwick, Dean of St. Paul's. But there was no help for it, and the garrison surrendered, having made honourable terms for the lady whose courage had so endeared her to them all:—

'Lady Savile, with her family, with her own proper goods, shall pass with horses, coaches, and wagons to Thornhill, or elsewhere, with guard befitting her quality, and without any injury to their persons, or plundering of their goods, or otherwise; she, they, or any of them to go, or stay, at their own pleasure, until she or they be in a condition to remove themselves.'

Terms so honourable to both parties seem at variance

with the spirit of cruelty which could forbid help, but a few hours before; but then the fortress was still unconquered. The day after the surrender Lady Savile gave birth to a son, who became Earl of Halifax.

She married, as her second husband, Sir Thomas Chicheley of Wimpole, Cambridgeshire. Finding herself very ill, 'this illustrious example of piety towards God and love to her country sent for her constant friend, Dr. Barwick (whose counsel in doubtful, and whose advice in difficult affairs she had often experienced), to make use of his pious ministrations. She resigned her breath easily, dying at Wimpole one year and a half after the Restoration.'

No. 63.

OLD PRINCE OF CONDÉ.

O called in the Catalogue, but no evidence to say which Prince of Condé, as they none of them lived to be old.

No. 64.

AN ECCLESIASTIC.

No. 65.

SIR JAMES THYNNE.

By Dobson.

DIED 1670.

Full length. Buff jerkin. Slashed sleeves. Red scarf. Red ribbons at knees and on shoes.

E was the eldest surviving son of Sir Thomas Thynne, by his first wife, the daughter of Lord Audley. He married the Lady Isabella Rich, daughter of the Earl of Holland. An ill-starred union; for even before her marriage the lady bore a sorry reputation, and her subsequent conduct was such, that in 1653 she was legally separated from her husband, having doubtless tried his forbearance too far.

Sir James was a staunch Royalist, and we are told his house of Longleat was plundered by a party of Roundheads in 1643, under the command of Sir Edward Hungerford and Colonel Slade.

The marauders seemed to have turned their attention especially to the contents of the stables and harness-room. Handsome saddles, caparisons, plumes, bits, pleased the fancy of the two officers, while their men made free with the contents of the wardrobes, cellars, larders, and what not. In 1663 Charles II. and his Queen visited Sir James at Longleat.

Dying without children at Richmond, in Surrey, in 1670, he was succeeded by his nephew.

No. 66.

SIR THOMAS THYNNE.
By Mytens.
DIED 1639.

Full length. Black and gold dress. Close-fitting vest. Lace collar. Scarlet stockings. Shoes with rosette.

E was the eldest son of Sir John (and the grandson of Sir John the builder) of Longleat, by Joan Hayward. He was twice married—first to a daughter of Lord Audley, and secondly to a daughter of Lord Howard of Bindon. He had children by both wives, and was succeeded by his eldest surviving son, James.

No. 67.

VIDÂME DE CHARTRES.
By Zucchero.

White close-fitting vest. Trimmed beard and moustaches. Inscription, ' Ætatis suæ 33, año 15 .' An escutcheon in the corner.

ESSIRE PREJAMN de la Fin, Vidâme de Chartres, Prince de Chabanois, Baron de Confolant et Pousaujes, Seigneur de la Ferté, et Sire de Gravlie; Capitaine de cinquante hommes d'armes, des ordonnances du Roi très Chretien.

We read in Strype that when peace was concluded between France and England in 1550, and Boulogne ceded to France, a large sum was to be paid to King Edward vi., and several of the highest French nobles came over to this country as hostages.

Among many distinguished names, we find that of the Vidâme de Chartres, but we cannot be quite sure whether allusion be made to the subject of this notice or the kinsman, François de Vendôme, from whom he inherited his title and estates. There is mention of him in 1560 as an agent of the Bourbons, sent on a mission to the Connétable de Montmorency, where he is described as a Huguenot of high birth, and akin to the Connétable himself. There was some rumour of a scandal between this nobleman and Queen Catherine de Medicis, for which probably there was no foundation.

In 1567 the Condé party had taken possession of St. Denis, demanding the diminution of taxes and the summoning of the States-General, in consequence of which a royal herald was sent to call upon the chiefs (Condé, the Vidâme de Chartres, and others) to lay down their arms, on pain of being proclaimed rebels.

The King, after much discussion, came to a compromise with Condé, for a time at least, but a decree was passed against Coligny, the Vidâme, and others, of confiscation of property, execution, etc., the latter sentence being carried into effect, but fortunately at that time only in effigy.

In 1569 we hear of him again, for Lord Leicester writes to the Ambassador of the Emperor of Muscovy: 'The Vidâme de Chartres is come to England, with his wife and familie, on a "snuffe," having in the last action (a battle near Coignac) proved himselfe neither fishe nor fowle.'

We also find in the Life of Archbishop Grindal, speaking of the same: 'A great nobleman of France, and of chief account among the Protestants, was here on some business relating to religion, and was favoured much by the friends of religion, but not so much by all at Court. The Bishop of

London obtained for him the Bishop of Ely's house in Holborn, where he remained some time.'

He was one of those who, just before the Massacre of St. Bartholomew, strove to persuade Coligny and his son-in-law to leave Paris, but in vain, though the life of the brave Admiral had already been attempted. At this time a colony of Huguenots lived outside the walls of Paris, the Vidâme included, and it had been arranged that on the day of St. Bartholomew the Provost-Marshal should let loose a thousand men to attack that quarter. But by good fortune the murderers stopped by the way to plunder, and never reached their destination. The Huguenot population was aroused by a tumult, and believing it to be a rising of the Guises, they were about to fly to the assistance of the King; so little did they suspect the truth. But the frightful reality was soon forced upon them, the massacre had already begun, and turning away, the chief part fled into the country.

The Vidâme's escape was almost miraculous, the Duke of Guise had actually followed him into his own house with the intention of murdering him, but the fugitive contrived to elude his pursuer, and to conceal himself until he procured a safeguard from the King. Charles was suspected of having promised it while the Vidâme was still in hiding, with the conviction that he, being thrown off his guard, would return home, and thus fall into the hands of his enemies. But the hunted man was too wary: he stole away, and got safely on shipboard for England.

Immediately on his arrival, he wrote to the Treasurer to admonish him 'to arouse Queen Elizabeth to a sense of her own danger, to excite her warmly to resent what had passed, and not to be too lenient to the Papists, believing they would become more gentle by a few light words, for he was assured they would become more insolent if too easily dealt with.'

In several letters from Secretary Smith to Lord Burghley,

both in 1572 and the ensuing year, he mentions frequent interviews which the Vidâme and other noble refugees had with the Queen relating to the interests of the Huguenot party in France.

England, who has never been found wanting in sympathy or hospitality towards the oppressed or exiled of other nations, welcomed the fugitives from the Massacre of St. Bartholomew with more than usual warmth, and the Queen showed some of them great consideration, and especially the Vidâme de Chartres. We once more quote Secretary Smith, who, writing to the English Ambassador, then in France, observes that it did him 'good to see the princely compassion that was in Her Majestie towards the poor Vidâme, who was escaped by good fortune into England, for whom the Queen had, at his humble and lamentable suit, written to the King of France in his favour, which she bade her Ambassador deliver with as good words as he might, and to require an answer.' To which the King gives this answer: 'That as he was glad to gratifie Her Majestie, so he could not grant this earnest request without touch of his honour, to suffer any of his subjects to live in a foreign countrie without a kind of defiance of his sincerity. Yet he could for gratifying Her Majestie be content that the Vidâme should return home and enjoy his livings there, as he could not have occasion to doubt his safety.' But the exile dared not trust himself to these protestations of a hypocrite.

Queen Elizabeth answered the King, that in the present state of France, his subjects in England did not think it safe to return there. These particulars, though somewhat disjointed, are all we have been able to gather of a man, whose life was most eventful. Neither can we tell if he died in England.

CHAPEL CORRIDOR.

CHAPEL CORRIDOR.

No. 68.

MARY, QUEEN OF ENGLAND.
By Sir Godfrey Kneller.
BORN 1661, ASCENDED THE THRONE 1689, DIED 1694.

Red and white brocade dress. Blue mantle. Flowers in her hand.

HE was the eldest daughter of King James II., by Anne Hyde, daughter of the Earl of Clarendon. Married in 1677 her first cousin, William, Prince of Orange, by whom she had no children. They reigned jointly as King and Queen on the abdication of her father.

No. 69.

FAIR ROSAMOND.

Black and scarlet dress. Scarlet mantle. Holding a golden cup in one hand, and the cover in the other.

HE second daughter of Walter Fitz-Pons or Poyntz, who took the name of Clifford, having married Margaret de Toeni, the heiress of the Clifford family. The pitiful story of 'the Rose of the World,' her amours with Henry II. of England, the beauteous labyrinth in which he concealed the sweet flower, and her murder by Queen Eleanor, are amongst the best known of the romances of early English history; and few even endeavour to disentangle truth from fiction. All is doubtful, even dates; but it is said Rosamond was buried at Godston, near Oxford, by her royal lover. She had two sons—William Longespée, Earl of Salisbury in right of his wife; and Geoffrey, Archbishop of York.

No. 70.

THE EARL AND COUNTESS OF CARNARVON.

AFTER VANDYCK.

THE EARL WAS KILLED IN ACTION, 1643.

Full length. Drab coat and boots. Brown trunks. Lace collar. Sword-hand on hip. Countess holding her husband's hand. Blue dress trimmed with pearls. Ringlets. Black page in scarlet dress, trunks, and hose. Badge on breast.

THE eldest son of William Dormer, by Alice, daughter of Richard Molyneux, of Sefton, county Lancaster. He succeeded his grandfather, who had been created first a Baronet and then Baron Dormer of Wenge, county Bucks (by James I.), in these titles, but was himself raised to the dignity of Viscount Ascot, and Earl of Carnarvon by Charles I. In early life he travelled further than most young nobles of the time, not only visiting France and Italy, but also Spain, Turkey, etc. etc. Clarendon seems to regret that 'he brought home some foreign tastes.' But another biographer (David Lloyd) says that 'if he had contracted a taste for gambling he hated drunkenness most perfectly.'

He took his degree of Deacon of Civil Law at Oxford, but did not come forward publicly till the impeachment of

Strafford, whom he strove to befriend. On the rising of the Buckinghamshire men, under Hampden, when they came to London in 1642 to present 'seditious petitions' to both Houses of Parliament, Lord Carnarvon went down into the county, where he owned a large property, to raise troops in conjunction with other Royalists, and used all his influence to advance the King's cause. He was with Charles at York, and was one of the Peers who signed 'the Declaration.' He afterwards joined His Majesty at Nottingham, with a force of a thousand men levied and equipped at his own cost; so zealous was he in the Royal service that his name was excepted from the list of those to whom the Parliament offered a pardon, in its instructions to the General Lord Essex.

Carnarvon was present at almost every action of importance about this time, and his courage, which often amounted to rashness, made him much beloved by the soldiery. At the battle of Edgehill (when in command of a squadron of horse under Prince Rupert) he pursued a body of the rebel cavalry so fast and so far, as to endanger the safety of his own men. He was appointed General of the Horse in the army of Lord Hertford, whom he joined in the west of England.

He maintained his reputation for valour at the battle of Stratton, and at Chewton, in the vicinity of Wells, he charged, Lord Clarendon says, 'with incomparable gallantry, for Lord Carnarvon always charges home.' But once more his hot pursuit brought him into imminent danger, when venturing too near the enemy's quarters he encountered a superior force of Sir William Waller's dragoons; Prince Maurice hastened to the rescue, but was himself wounded, unhorsed, and in his turn saved by Carnarvon, who rallied his men, and again sent the rebels flying. At the battle of Roundway Down he served as volunteer in Sir John Byron's regiment, and greatly contributed towards gaining the victory; he then marched on Dorchester, at that time fortified by the rebels, which soon surrendered. But on the arrival of Prince Maurice there arose a difference of opinion between them.

Lord Carnarvon, being 'full of honour and justice,' was desirous of restraining the licence of the soldiery, a point on which the Prince was somewhat lax. The result was, that Carnarvon threw up his command, and marched on Gloucester, which the King was besieging. He had scarcely arrived when Lord Essex compelled the Royalists to raise the siege, and they accordingly took their way towards London. But they had not proceeded far when they were obliged to give battle, and on the 20th of September was fought the memorable battle of Newbury, when so many of England's proudest chivalry were laid low. Lord Carnarvon, as usual, had been rash in pursuit, and was returning carelessly, when a stray trooper recognised his person, and closing on him suddenly, ran him through the body. He did not survive above an hour, but was most anxious in his inquiries as to the safety of his beloved master. A friend who was attending on him inquired if there were any last request he would wish conveyed to the King. 'Nay,' he replied, 'I will not die with a suit in my mouth to any king, save the King of Heaven.'

Lord Clarendon, after paying a fine tribute to his memory, sums up by saying, 'If he had lived he would have been a great ornament to his profession, and by his death the King found a sensible weakness in the army.'

Lord Carnarvon married Anne Sophia, eldest daughter of Philip Herbert, fourth Earl of Pembroke and first Earl of Montgomery. They had no children, and the title became extinct, although afterwards revived in the Herbert family.

No. 71.

GIACOMO ROBUSTI, DETTO IL TINTORETTO.

By Himself.

DIED 1594.

A VENETIAN, son of a dyer; hence his sobriquet. Studied under Titian, but was desirous of forming a new school combining the colouring of his great master with the drawing of Michael Angelo. On the door of his studio was inscribed, 'Disegno di Michelangelo, colorito di Tiziano.' His best works are in his native Venice, but there are many at the Louvre (where is his own portrait) and elsewhere. He was celebrated for his quickness in finishing his pictures on occasions; which may account for the inequality of their excellence. His son Domenico, and his daughter Marietta, were also painters.

No. 72.

JOHN ALEXANDER, FOURTH MARQUIS OF BATH.

By James Swinton.

BORN 1831, SUCCEEDED 1837.

Full length. Brown coat. White waistcoat. Cane and hat. A large dog beside him.

No. 73.
ELIZABETH BYNG, SECOND MARCHIONESS OF BATH, WITH THREE CHILDREN.
By Sir Thomas Lawrence.
DIED 1830.

Unfinished. Red gown. Gold-coloured scarf. Girls in white frocks and blue sashes. Boy in jacket and trousers.

DAUGHTER of George, fourth Viscount Torrington, by Lady Lucy Boyle. Married in 1794 Thomas, second Marquis of Bath, by whom she had ten children. The three portraits in this group are Elizabeth, afterwards the Countess of Cawdor, Lord John Thynne, afterwards in Holy Orders, and Lady Louisa, afterwards Countess of Harewood. The other children were Viscount Weymouth, who died *v.p.*, Henry, who succeeded to the Marquisate, but only survived his father three months, William, Francis, Edward, George, Charlotte Duchess of Buccleuch, and Charles.

No. 74.
GEORGE I., KING OF ENGLAND.
BORN 1680, SUCCEEDED TO THE ENGLISH THRONE 1714, DIED 1727.

In royal robes.

SON of the Elector of Hanover, by Sophia, daughter of Elizabeth, Queen of Bohemia. Succeeded his father in the Electorate in 1698, and Queen Anne on the Throne of England in 1714. Married Sophia of Zell, his cousin, whom he divorced and imprisoned. By her he had an only son, who succeeded as George II.

HOUSEKEEPER'S ROOM.

HOUSEKEEPER'S ROOM.

No. 75.

ELIZABETH, DUCHESS OF ALBEMARLE.

By Sir Peter Lely.

DIED CIRCA 1734.

Seated. Brocaded dress, short sleeves, deep lace. Blue mantle. Jewels. Ringlets.

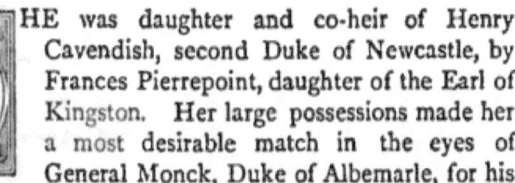

SHE was daughter and co-heir of Henry Cavendish, second Duke of Newcastle, by Frances Pierrepoint, daughter of the Earl of Kingston. Her large possessions made her a most desirable match in the eyes of General Monck, Duke of Albemarle, for his son Christopher. Feeling his end approaching, the anxious father hurried on the negotiations for the marriage, which were pending with Elizabeth's family, and went so far as to insist that the nuptials should be celebrated in his own bedchamber, a few days previous to his death in 1670.

We have at this time no means of gaining much information respecting the married life of Christopher, second Duke of Albemarle, and his wife; but in 1687 he went out as Governor-General to Jamaica, and died there the following year. Neither are we in a position to ascertain the circumstances attending the insanity of his widow, as we have no trace of her life until the mention of her second marriage with Ralph, **Lord** (afterwards Duke of) Montagu. This eccentric man, after losing his beautiful and accomplished wife (Elizabeth Wriothesley, widow of Josceline Percy, Earl of Northumberland) in 1690, thought to console himself with the wealth of the Duchess of Albemarle, whose madness was then well known. This trifling impediment was not considered by any means insurmountable, and the unfortunate woman, or rather her large fortune, had many suitors.

One of the disappointed band, Lord Ross, gave vent to his spite, on hearing of Lord Montagu's success, in the following lines :—

> 'Insulting rival, never boast
>   Thy conquest lately won,
> No wonder if her heart was lost,
>   Her senses first were gone.
>
> From one that's under Bedlam's laws
>   What glory can be had?
> For love, indeed, was not the cause,—
>   It proves that she was mad.'

Finding that the poor maniac had announced her determination of marrying no one but a Sovereign, Montagu caused himself to be presented to her as the Emperor of China, and doubtless the mumming and masquerading which ensued suited his volatile and eccentric humour. But if he looked forward to enjoying his wife's wealth without her society, he was disappointed, as she survived him twenty-six years. Happy in her royal illusions, served to her dying day on bended knee, addressed always as Majesty, while even after death, her wishes were obeyed by the sumptuous funeral which was given to her remains in the lofty pile of Westminster Abbey compatible with her imperial dignity.

No. 76.
POPE INNOCENT XI.

AFTER RUBENS.

BORN 1611, ELECTED 1676, DIED 1689.

ENEDETTO, of the noble House of Odescalchi, of Como, went to Rome, and on to Naples, when about twenty-five years of age, with no possessions save the weapons which he required for the military profession he had chosen. But a Cardinal, with whom he became acquainted, dissuaded him from becoming a soldier, and on his return to Rome Odescalchi entered on the career of the 'Curia,' where he was soon distinguished for zeal and ability, and gradually rose to elevation in several public offices. In 1645 he obtained the Cardinal's Hat, and the Bishopric of Novara, a step which his enemies unjustly attributed to the influence of the celebrated Donna Olympia, for Odescalchi was ever remarkable for the morality, and even austerity, of his life.

He became so popular in Rome, that when the Conclave was sitting, a large concourse assembled under the portico of St. Peter's, and shouted out his name; and the election of Innocent XI. to the Papal Chair gave very general satisfaction.

The new Pontiff, upright and conscientious by nature, first turned his thoughts to financial reform. He reduced the annual expenditure, inquired into all the abuses of Government sinecures, and though he had a worthy kinsman to whom he was much attached, he eschewed nepotism; he also watched over the state of the money market, and after the lapse of a a few years, his efforts were rewarded by a great increase of the public revenue. Innocent showed himself a firm opponent of Louis XIV., when that King encroached, as His Holiness deemed, on spiritual privileges. He embraced the cause of the Jansenist priests who had fallen under the displeasure of the 'Grand Monarque' for withstanding some of the decrees they considered arbitrary, more especially on the long-vexed question of the 'Regale.' They appealed to the Pope, who wrote once, and yet twice, to the King on the subject, admonishing him not to listen to flatterers, and not to lay hands on the immunities of the Church, lest by so doing, he should 'dry up the fountains of divine grace from his kingdom.'

Finding his homilies of no avail, Innocent spoke out more boldly still, assuring Louis that he 'would suffer no storm nor danger to appal him, but would use every resource of that power he held at the hands of God' to resist his injustice. But so completely were the mass of the French clergy enslaved by His Majesty that the Prince de Condé was used to say that if Louis chose to go over to the Protestant faith, the priests would be the first to follow him. Therefore they feared to stand by the Pope, who had defended their rights so zealously, and the 'Declarations' that were published from year to year increased and strengthened the royal authority in spiritual concerns.

This was especially manifest in the Articles of the Convocation of 1682; but the Pope was not easily disheartened. To those members of the Declaration whom Louis had preferred before all other candidates for Episcopal offices, Innocent denied spiritual institution. They might indeed receive the revenues of the sees, but ordination was refused them, neither could they exercise one spiritual act of their office.

About this time, the King, it was said, thought to ingratiate himself with the Holy See by his cruel persecutions of the Huguenots, but such measures were not calculated to please a man of Odescalchi's character, and fresh disputes arose. One of the abuses which the Pope had endeavoured to abolish in Rome was the 'right of asylum,' as it was called, hitherto claimed by foreign Ambassadors. Not only on their arrival in the imperial city had they a palace assigned them, but quarters for innumerable hangers-on, in several adjacent streets. The Emperor, the King of Spain, and others, had listened to the remonstrances of His Holiness, and waived their claim to these unreasonable privileges; but Louis was glad of a fresh opportunity to oppose the Pope, boasting that he was not in the habit of following the example of others.

Accordingly, he sent his Ambassador, with a considerable armed force, to demand the rights of 'asylum' in the name of his royal master. The formidable array brought no fear to the brave heart of Benedetto Odescalchi. 'They come with horses and chariots,' he said, 'but we will walk in the name of the Lord.' The French emissary was excommunicated, and the Church of St. Louis (the patron saint of France), where he attended mass, was placed under interdict.

Reprisals were now the order of the day. The Papal Nuncio was detained a prisoner in Paris, many French bishops deprived of their canonical institutions, a territory of the Holy See occupied by France; in fact, daggers drawn! But other Powers besides Rome were jealous of the encroachments and arrogance of the French monarch, and Innocent allied himself with them from political motives. He made a friend of Austria, by assisting her with subsidies in the war with Turkey, and he incurred blame from some of the Catholic bystanders by an alliance with the Protestant Prince William of Orange. The plea was, that William had undertaken the command of the Rhine, and would defend not only the rights of the Empire, but also those of the Church, against Louis XIV. Be this as it may, it seems strange that the Pope should perhaps unwittingly have assisted in the elevation of the enemy of James II., to whose son he had stood godfather. But if the head of the Roman Catholic Church proved indirectly instrumental in furthering the Protestant cause in England, the Protestants, on their side, by maintaining the balance of power in Europe, did His Holiness a good turn. Innocent died soon after these events, leaving behind him a character for courage and steadfastness, combined with great humility and gentleness of manners. As we have already said, he was remarkable for the purity of his morals, and made himself very unpopular with the women of all classes by denouncing, in no measured terms, the indecency of dress and laxity of manners, which were (he considered) unusually prevalent in his reign. He was much opposed to the sect of the Quietists, and confirmed the sentence of the Inquisition against their unfortunate founder Molinos, who was imprisoned, and eventually died in the cells of that dread institution. He was but a poor scholar, and his secretaries were obliged to translate or turn into Italian, all Latin documents with which he had to deal.

Innocent XI. was charitable to the poor, and much beloved, especially by his dependants, of whose wellbeing he was most careful. He died in the month of August 1689, and the Roman people flocked round his tomb, invoking him as a saint, and disputing with each other any available relic of their favourite Pontiff.

GREAT STAIRCASE.

GREAT STAIRCASE.

No. 77.

GEORGE VILLIERS, SECOND DUKE OF BUCKINGHAM.

By Sir Peter Lely.

BORN 1627, DIED 1688.

Steel cuirass. Buff leather coat. Black and white sleeves. One hand resting on a helmet. Red plume.

HE was the second son of the first Duke of Buckingham, (of the Villiers family,) by Catherine, daughter and sole heir of Francis Manners, sixth Earl of Rutland. No sooner did Charles I. learn the news of the murder of his friend (the first Duke) than he hastened to the residence of the sorrowing widow, to pay her a visit of condolence; the little Duke being then but an infant, and his mother expecting her confinement. The King, much touched by her sad position, said all he could to comfort her, and promised to be a father to her children; nor did he forget to fulfil the self-imposed trust. At the proper age, George Villiers was sent to Cambridge, and afterwards to travel abroad, accompanied by his brother Francis, under the care of a tutor provided for them by their royal guardian. On the breaking out of the civil war the two youths returned to England, and hastened to proffer their services to their Sovereign, a proceeding which brought down upon them the vengeance of the Parliament. Their property was confiscated, but in consideration of their youth the estates and revenues were soon restored to them. Poverty was ill suited to the splendid tastes, and profuse style of living, which characterised the Duke, on his second trip abroad, or indeed wherever he went, and in later life he was in constant pecuniary difficulties.

The war broke out afresh between Charles and his subjects; he was a prisoner in the Isle of Wight, when the loyal brothers returned home, and joined the Royalist army, under the Earl of Holland, who had unfurled his standard in the county of Surrey. Lord Holland was quartered at Kingston-on-Thames, and it was on the 11th of July 1648 that Lord Francis Villiers, 'after performing prodigies of valour,' was killed in a skirmish with the Parliamentarians near Nonsuch, to the sincere regret of his comrades and the inexpressible grief of his brother. 'He was a youth,' says Clarendon, 'of rare beauty and comeliness of person.'

The expedition proved most disastrous; Lord Holland himself was taken prisoner shortly after, near St. Neots, and beheaded, the Duke of Buckingham narrowly escaping the same fate. He contrived to conceal himself, but one morning, finding the house in which he lay, surrounded by a troop of the enemy's cavalry (with the dashing bravery which always characterised him), he leaped on his horse, and followed by one faithful servant, cut his way through the troopers, killing the officer in command, and gained the sea-shore, where he joined the Prince of Wales, who was on board a vessel lying in the Downs. A proclamation was issued by the Parliament, to the effect that if the Duke did not return in forty days, his property would a second time be forfeited.

Buckingham stood the test, and remained faithful to his

allegiance. He lived for some time on the proceeds of a sale of magnificent pictures bequeathed to him by the Duke, his father (the chief part once the property of Rubens), which he disposed of at Antwerp. He remained abroad for some time, but accompanied his King on the expedition to Scotland, and after the battle of Worcester had another of his 'hair-breadth 'scapes,' almost as miraculous as that of his royal master.

After leaving the King concealed in Boscobel House, the Duke, with other Royalist nobles, rode northward, and were intercepted by a body of Roundheads (who took many of them prisoners). Buckingham, according to his wont, escaped, by the aid of some friendly labourers and workmen, with one of whom he changed habits, and was concealed in a wood. He afterwards went from one house in the neighbourhood to another, and again made his way to the Continent in safety, first to Holland, and then to France, where he gained fresh laurels by his conduct at the sieges of Arras and Valenciennes.

Buckingham now resolved on a bold and daring step. The Parliament had awarded the chief part of his estates and revenues to General Lord Fairfax, but this noble-minded man had already set apart a considerable portion for the service of the widowed Duchess; and the Duke (although an outlaw) deemed it politic to return to England and appeal to the further generosity of 'my Lord Fairfax.' He repaired, then, forthwith to the home of his ancestors, ingratiated himself not only into the favourable feelings of the father, but still more into those of the daughter.

The handsome and irresistible George Villiers was not likely to sue long in vain; he proposed, was accepted, and became the son-in-law of the man who was in possession of his rent-roll. Cromwell, on hearing of the marriage, was exasperated beyond measure, and the Duke was again forced to go into hiding. Most likely this was not difficult, surrounded by his own tenantry, with the assistance of a loving bride; but he was rash, and doubtless trusted to his own talent for evading danger; and so one day, riding to visit his sister in the neighbourhood, he was waylaid, taken prisoner, and carried off to the Tower.

Fairfax, already disgusted with many of Cromwell's proceedings, was furious, and expressed himself boldly. But the Protector was not one to listen patiently to any strictures on his own conduct, and laughed the General to scorn. Fortunately for the captive, Cromwell did not survive much longer, and on the abdication of Richard Cromwell the Duke regained his liberty. At the Restoration he was marked out for favour by the King, to whose fortunes he had been so faithful; he was made Lord-in-Waiting, Lord-Lieutenant of York, Master of the Horse, etc. etc. But his restless and intriguing spirit led him into many dangerous plots, so much so that in 1666 he was deprived of all his offices, and summoned to take his trial. The King came to the rescue, and caused him to be reinstated in many of his posts. Buckingham joined Lord Shaftesbury against Clarendon, became President of the Council, and his initial, as is well known, stood for the third letter of 'Cabal.'

In 1670 he was sent Ambassador to the King of France, ostensibly to condole with him on the death of the Duchess of Orleans, but in reality with the project of breaking 'The Triple Alliance.' About this time there was an attempt on the life of the Duke of Ormonde by one Blood, and Lord Ossory (Ormonde's son) accused the Duke of Buckingham of being an accomplice of the villain. His plea was that his father was a friend of Lord Clarendon's, to whom Buckingham had vowed deadly enmity, but the charge soon fell to the ground.

Buckingham was one of the Plenipotentiaries (with the Earl of Arlington and others) to Holland, but the negotiations with which they were intrusted, failed. The Cabal breaking up, the Duke once more found himself accused of many heavy charges,—of treasonable correspondence with the King's enemies, and the like.

He also made himself obnoxious to his royal master by the part he took respecting the Test Bill, and above all, by maintaining that the King had exceeded his royal prerogative in proroguing the Parliament for a longer time than was legal. He was sent to the Tower, and when once more liberated, mixed himself up (with a restlessness he doubtless called patriotism) in fresh plots and cabals. On the death of Charles II., the Duke of Buckingham, well aware that he could not expect the same indulgence from King James as from his predecessor, retired to the country (being in failing health at the time), and gave himself up to literary occupations and the sports of the field. One day, while intent on unearthing a fox, he was imprudent enough to sit for some time on the damp ground, in consequence of which he caught a chill that proved fatal in three days. His wife, who long survived him, was a most exemplary woman, who loved him in spite of his numerous and flagrant infidelities. They had no children, and the title became extinct.

The witty, handsome, profligate Duke of Buckingham is a well-known acquaintance to all readers, both of history and fiction. His manners were genial, even captivating; his anger or revenge generally vented itself in pointed satires or pungent *bon-mots*. Dryden immortalised him as Zimri in 'Absalom and Achitophel.' Pope drew his portrait in the *Moral Essays* (Epist. iii.); his love for astrology and alchemy helped him to squander his living, but all his tastes were extravagant. His comedy of 'The Rehearsal' (in which, however, he is supposed to have been much assisted by friends) made a great noise, and his delineation of Dryden under the character of Bayes was much admired.

No. 78.

CATHERINE CAREY, COUNTESS OF NOTTINGHAM.

DIED IN 1603.

Black dress. White lace cap. Ruff and cuffs. Black veil. Holding a glove.

HE daughter of Henry Carey, Lord Hunsdon, who was first cousin to Queen Elizabeth his mother being Mary Boleyn. Nor did 'her Grace disdain to call him cousin,' and her visit to Hunsdon House is immortalised in a painting (engraved) by Mark Gerrard, where she is carried in procession. The picture contains many portraits, including Lord and Lady Hunsdon, and Catherine, their daughter, the subject of this notice.

Grainger, speaking of Lord Hunsdon in his usually quaint manner, tells us 'he was of a soldierly disposition, and a great seller of bargains to the maids of honour,' and the Queen esteemed him much, and offered to create him an Earl on his deathbed, which somewhat tardy dignity he refused.

Catherine married the gallant Charles Howard, Lord High Admiral of England, whose name is invariably connected with the glorious defeat of the Spanish Armada. He was first created Baron of Effingham, and afterwards Earl of Nottingham; and it was to his wife that the unfortunate Essex intrusted the ring which Elizabeth had given him in the height of his favour, with the promise that whatever crime he should commit, she would pardon, provided he returned the pledge.

The story connected with this ring has been so often and so variously told, so many times asserted and disbelieved, that we might be tempted to let the subject pass in silence were it not for the fact that the actual relic is in the possession of Lord John Thynne, uncle of the present Marquis of Bath, (1879,) and therefore claims a comment in these pages. We subjoin what appears to us the most authentic account:—

Not very long before the death of Queen Elizabeth, she being then in failing health, and much depressed in mind, after the execution of her favourite, Her Majesty received a message from the Countess of Nottingham (one of the ladies of her household, and a connection of her own), to say that she lay a-dying, but that she had something on her mind which she would fain impart to the Queen before her death. Elizabeth lost no time in repairing to the house of the Earl of Nottingham, and taking her place by the sufferer's bedside, listened to the following confession. When Lord Essex lay under sentence of death, he bethought himself of the Queen's present, and the promise which accompanied it, and he began to devise means how to send it to his royal mistress. He dared not trust any one near him, but watching from the window, he perceived a boy, whose appearance inspired him with confidence. He contrived to get speech of him, and induced him, by means of money and promises, to be the bearer of the ring, which he drew from his finger and intrusted to him. The Earl's injunctions were that it should be carried to his friend Lady Scrope, (one of the royal household, and sister to the Lady Nottingham,) with the earnest request that she would present it to the Queen.

The boy, by some unfortunate mistake, carried the ring to the Countess of Nottingham, who immediately consulted her husband on the subject. It is further said (although it may appear inconsistent with the character of the gallant sailor for generosity) that he peremptorily forbade his wife to undertake the mission, or to interfere in the matter. Yet we are also told that on the downfall of Essex, Lord Nottingham evinced the greatest friendship for the man with whom he had once been at enmity, visiting him in prison, and the like. Certain it is that the lady whose conscience was so ill at rest, screened herself under the prohibition of her husband, who, she added, insisted on her keeping the ring, and returning no answer to the unfortunate captive. The secret being divulged, the dying woman entreated the Queen to pardon her. The answer she gave is well known: 'God may forgive you, but I never can;' and she left the room in a fury.

Strange, if she believed that Lord Nottingham was in fault, that Her Majesty should not only forgive him, but keep him constantly in her presence, in her last days, (for she did not survive this scene above a fortnight,) talking with him on matters of the greatest importance, and sometimes accepting nourishment and medicine from his hand, which she would refuse from that of others.

Lady Nottingham died soon after the stormy interview with the Queen, having borne two sons and three daughters to her husband. It would appear that the cause of the doubt and perplexity which have been thrown over the romantic story of the Essex ring, can be accounted for in this manner: The fact is there were two historical rings, and the Carey family were connected with both, as also, to make the confusion more complete, the name of Lady Scrope, born Carey, is mixed up with both.

When Queen Elizabeth was dying, Robert Carey, Earl of Monmouth, was stationed on horseback under the window, and no sooner was the Queen's last breath expended, than a lady (said to be Lady Scrope) threw a ring from the window, with which Monmouth rode post-haste to Scotland, it being a pledge agreed upon between King James and a member of Elizabeth's Court, to inform him, betimes, of the death of the English Queen. This ring is a sapphire, and in the possession of the Earl of Cork and Orrery, to whom it descended by inheritance.

Two rings, both secret pledges, and with both of which the names of Queen Elizabeth and Lady Scope are connected, it no longer appears strange that confusion and perplexity should have arisen on the subject. The ring in the possession of Lord John Thynne has a gold hoop of delicate workmanship engraved, and relieved with blue enamel. The centre is an onyx, with a cameo head of Queen Elizabeth, a perfect likeness, in relief, and is surmised to have been the work of Valerio Vincentino, an Italian artist of great merit, who executed several works of the kind, for the Queen, Lord Burghley, and others. There is no record to inform us how this ring returned into the possession of the Devereux family. But it seems more than likely that Lady Nottingham, or her husband, may have bequeathed or restored it to the rightful owners. It descended to the present possessor in unbroken succession from the Duchess of Somerset, Frances Devereux, Essex's daughter, who was grandmother to the first Lady Weymouth.

No. 79.

SIR HENRY SIDNEY.

Full length. Black dress. White ruff. High hat on table.

HE was the son of Sir William Sidney, Chamberlain to Henry VIII., and was born at Penshurst, a royal grant from Edward VI. to the family.

Henry became the bosom friend of the young King, who knighted him, and sent him as Ambassador to France when only twenty-one. Sir Henry was much admired and esteemed at the Courts of France and

England. His friend, King Edward, expired in his arms. He also found favour in the eyes of Queen Mary, after whose husband he named his son Philip. She made him Vice-Treasurer and general governor of the royal revenues in Ireland, also Lord Deputy of that country, where his administration was more than commonly popular, considering the state of the times. In the reign of Elizabeth he was appointed Lord President of Wales, and he placed his son Philip at school at Shrewsbury, so as to be near him. The boy was delicate in health, and extant letters prove his father's tender solicitude for the bodily and mental education of his first-born. Sir Henry Sidney married Lady Mary Dudley, the daughter of the Duke of Northumberland—a woman of 'rare merit.' Later on in years, when leading 'a quiet and contented life at home,' a proposal was made to him to resume the government of Ireland, on which subject he consulted his son Philip: would he accompany him with the hope of succeeding to the post when he should vacate it? etc. etc., but he made so many stipulations and conditions to the Queen, dependent on his acceptance, that the matter fell through, probably from the fact of Elizabeth declining to be dictated to, though here we speak without book. Sir Henry Sidney shone in domestic as in public life, and his wife was worthy of her husband. They both died in 1586, within a few months of each other, Sir Henry being buried at Penshurst, though his heart was lodged at Ludlow.

SIR WALTER RALEIGH.

BY ZUCCHERO.

BORN 1552, EXECUTED 1618.

Full length. White and scarlet dress. Scarlet garters and rosettes. Brown trunk hose. White hat. Ruff and sash.

HE was the younger son of Walter Raleigh, Esq. of Cornwood, near Plymouth, by his third wife, daughter of Sir Philip Champernon, and widow of Otho Gilbert.

At sixteen Walter went to Oriel College for a year, and left it with a good character for study. In 1569 he became a volunteer in a troop raised by a relative, Henry Champernon, attached to the expedition which Elizabeth was sending out to the relief of the Huguenots in France. He was engaged in this campaign five years, and in 1577 he served in the Low Countries; in the following year he embarked with his half-brother, Sir Humphrey Gilbert, who had obtained a patent from the Queen, to colonise North America. This expedition failed. The English were attacked, and defeated on the high seas by a superior force of Spaniards.

On Raleigh's return to England he found that an insurrection had just broken out in Ireland; thither he proceeded, and soon gave token not only of his courage, but of his capacity for military command.

He was shortly afterwards appointed to the joint government of Munster, and to that of Cork. In 1581, there being a lull in Ireland, he returned to England. It would appear that he was bent on making his way at Court, and we all know, and most of us believe, the story of his flinging down his velvet cloak before his royal mistress, that she might step across the mire, likewise his writing with a diamond on a window-pane, which would necessarily attract Elizabeth's attention:—

'Fain would I climb, but fear to fall.'

The tale goes on to say that the Queen wrote underneath,

'If thy heart fail thee, climb not at all.'

We hope to be excused for alluding to stories which, if 'fables,' are at least characteristic of the times.

In 1583 he appeared before the Privy Council to plead his cause in the matter of a difference that had occurred between him and Lord (Deputy) Grey de Wilton, when they were together in Ireland.

On this occasion, says Sir Robert Naunton, 'what advantage Raleigh had in the controversy I know not; but he had much the better in the telling of his tale, inasmuch as the Queen and the Lords took no slight mark of the man, for from thenceforth he came to be known, and have access to the Lords,' etc. etc. Naunton goes on to say, 'that he does not know if Lord Leicester had recommended him to her Majesty, but true it is, Raleigh had gotten the Queen's ear at a trice, and she began to be taken with his eloquence, and loved to hear his reasons to her demands, and in truth, she took him for a kind of oracle, which nettled them all.'

Raleigh, whose whole soul was bent on enterprise, made use of his favour at Court to enable him to prosecute his maritime discoveries. In 1583—in a ship he had, however, manned and victualled at his own expense, and named after himself—in company with his brother, he sailed for Newfoundland. But they were again unfortunate; as Gilbert was returning to England he was lost, with two of his ships.

Yet Raleigh's heart never 'did fail him,' and the following

year he obtained a grant from Queen and Council, 'free liberty to discover remote and barbarous lands.'

He proceeded to Florida, discovered and colonised Virginia, and for several years prosecuted his voyages, discoveries, and colonisations, all of which belong to the record of naval history.

In 1584 he was knighted, and honours and dignities of all kinds bestowed on him, together with good estates from the Queen.

At Sherborne, county Dorset, he built 'a fine house, with gardens and groves of much variety and delight.' Notwithstanding all the favours he received at her hands, Raleigh never truckled to Elizabeth, and although she often fell out with him, she invariably in the end listened to her loyal but independent subject.

He was always ready to intercede for others, and one day, when asking a service for a friend, the Queen said, 'When, Sir Walter, will you cease to be a beggar?'

'When your Majesty ceases to be beneficent,' was the reply. But he fell into disgrace at Court when Elizabeth found out that he was too high in the good graces of one of her own maids of honour, and although he married the lady, (Mistress Elizabeth Throckmorton, daughter of Sir Nicholas of Beddington, county Surrey,) yet the lovers were imprisoned for some months in the Tower.

Voyages innumerable, fresh projects of colonisation followed, but unfortunately in two expeditions the Earl of Essex had the chief command, and he and Raleigh had a deadly quarrel. On their return it was continued, and there can be little doubt Raleigh hated and worked against Essex, at a time when there were many intrigues going on, to get rid of the Queen's unfortunate favourite. More honours, more places of trust, were bestowed on Raleigh. In 1600 he went Ambassador to France, and soon after was named Governor of Jersey; in fact, while Elizabeth lived, she never swerved in her friendship, but on her death, Cecil, who was Raleigh's enemy, undermined his favour with James, who received him ungraciously, and dismissed him from the offices he held.

Sir Walter, on discovering his secret foe, tried to impress on the King's mind that Cecil had been instrumental in the execution of his mother, but this made no difference in his Majesty's demeanour, and only insured the minister's bitter hatred. So commenced Raleigh's downfall. He was accused, with several other noblemen, of a plot to place Arabella Stuart on the throne; tried for high treason, and in spite of deficiency of evidence, in spite of his gallant defence, he was found guilty by a shameful jury, for even Coke, the Attorney-General, who, we are told, made 'brutal speeches,' on the trial, exclaimed, when informed of the verdict, (not being in Court at the time,) 'Surely thou art mistaken, for I only accused him of misprision of treason.'

Sir Walter remained at Winchester under sentence of death for a month, during which time he appealed to the justice and mercy, of a King who was devoid of both. He was reprieved, and sent to the Tower, where they held that noble spirit captive for twelve years. He occupied his melancholy hours with works which would have sufficed to make his name immortal, had it not already become so by ' his hairbreadth 'scapes, and moving accidents by flood and field.'

It having been made worth his while, Villiers Duke of Buckingham interceded for Raleigh's release, and he was accordingly liberated in 1616.

Stripped of all his possessions, and cast entirely on his own resources, the gallant knight once more embarked for Guiana, James, in the hope of wealth accruing to himself, granted him a commission, as Admiral.

But on his arrival he found he had been betrayed to the

Spaniards, who were drawn up against him in great numbers. 'Never,' he says himself, 'was poor man more exposed to the slaughter as I was.' Information was sent to the King of Spain; the cowardly and cruel James, terrified at the prospect of a rupture with that monarch, issued a proclamation setting forth that he had forbid Raleigh to enter on any hostilities, and threatening severe punishment.

The brave, enterprising, noble-minded sailor returned to England, his heart bowed down with sorrow, for the loss of his first-born, who had died on the field of battle.

He was arrested on his road to London, made two ineffectual attempts to escape, and was once more closely imprisoned in the Tower; he was brought to the bar of the King's Bench, and demanded why the former sentence should not be held good against him. His defence was a model of manly eloquence, but it did not avail him, and he was beheaded in Old Palace Yard, Westminster, the 29th of October 1618.

By Elizabeth his wife he had two sons—one killed in South America, and the other, Carew, who bought an estate called West Horsley, in Surrey, where, as tradition goes, he kept his father's head, and in consequence gained for the quaint old house the reputation of being haunted.

Sir Walter Raleigh, according to his portraits, merits Sir Robert Naunton's description of him: 'He was of a good presence and well-compacted person. He had a strong natural wit, and was an indefatigable reader both when at sea and on land.'

He was also remarkable for great magnificence in dress, he tilted in silver armour, with a belt of diamonds, pearls, and rubies, and his retinue was most costly. In the portrait before us his costume is certainly elaborate.

No. 81.

CATHERINE OF BRAGANZA, QUEEN OF ENGLAND, WIFE OF CHARLES II.

By Sir Peter Lely.

BORN 1638, DIED 1705.

Full length. Seated. Black dress. Jewels. Mantle lined with ermine. Crown on the table beside her.

HE was the only daughter of the Duke of Braganza, afterwards Juan IV., King of Portugal, by Luisa de Guzman, daughter of the Duke of Medina Sidonia. Catherine died childless.

No. 82.

CHARLES II., KING OF ENGLAND.

By Sir Peter Lely.

BORN 1630, RESTORED 1660, DIED 1685.

Full length. Seated. Crimson robes. Mantle. Collar of the Garter. Long flowing wig.

HE was the eldest son of Charles I., by Henrietta Maria of France. Married Catherine of Braganza, by whom he had no children.

No. 83.

PETER PAUL RUBENS, WIFE, AND CHILD.

By Himself.

BORN 1577, DIED 1640.

Both seated. He is in a black dress, reading; his wife in a red gown, blue mantle. The child standing on her lap.

HE family of Rubens was of noble Styrian origin. The father of the illustrious painter settled in Antwerp about the time of the coronation of Charles v., Emperor of Germany. He became a magistrate, and married Maria de Pipelingue of that city; but the religious differences, which were then very fierce, determined him (being a Roman Catholic) to quit Antwerp, and take up his abode at Cologne, where many children were born to him, the youngest of whom was Peter Paul, of world-wide fame.

On the death of Rubens the elder, the widow returned with her family to her native city. She placed her youngest son as page in the house of the Countess de Lalain, a noble lady, destining him at a later period for the magistrature; but neither of these vocations pleased the youth's fancy, whose decided bias for art soon declared itself. He had some difficulty in overcoming his mother's repugnance to the profession he had chosen, but she loved him too well to be obdurate. He began his studies as a painter in the school of Adam van Oort, a man of brutal manners, who soon disgusted the fine taste and good feeling of young Rubens. His next instructor was Otho Venius, but the pupil soon threw both masters into the shade.

Rubens now commenced his travels, to Venice first, and

to Mantua, where the reigning Duke showed him the greatest favour, gave him a place at Court, appointed him Painter-in-Ordinary, and intrusted him with a diplomatic mission to Philip III. of Spain.

Our painter afterwards visited Rome, and all the principal cities of Italy, working as he went on all subjects, religious, historical, mythological, and making splendid portraits, gaining in fact golden opinions from Popes, Princes, and Potentates.

When at Genoa he heard of the dangerous illness of his mother, to whom he was tenderly attached; he started immediately for Antwerp, but the news of her death arrested him on the road, and he went into retreat near Brussels, to nurse his grief, design a monument to her memory, and write her epitaph.

The Governor of the Low Countries, the Archduke Albert, and his wife Isabella, who admired the painter, and esteemed the man, did all they could to fix him at their Court in Brussels. They gave him a pension and the key of Chamberlain, and showed him marked proofs of a friendship which proved lasting, but Rubens preferred returning to Antwerp, where he could pursue his art with less interruption. Here he built a splendid house, and formed a noble collection of pictures, which he sold afterwards to the Duke of Buckingham, with whom he became intimate at Paris. He was summoned to the French capital by Marie de Medicis, and executed for her the well-known decorations of the Luxembourg. His superb talent, his handsome person, his acquaintance with dead and living languages, and his noble and genial disposition, made Rubens welcome in every country, and with every class. He proceeded to England, ostensibly to paint portraits, but in reality to negotiate a peace between the Courts of Madrid and London, and we are told how discreetly and warily he entered on his mission, while Charles I. was sitting for his picture. The King took the greatest delight in the society of Rubens, loaded him with princely gifts, knighted him in Parliament, (an especial honour,) presenting him on the occasion with a sword set in diamonds; and when the new Knight took leave, Charles hung his own miniature round the painter's neck, which Rubens wore till his death. He was now constantly employed in diplomatic missions of all kinds, and appears almost always to have been successful; he made Antwerp his headquarters, usually giving the preference during a pressure of work to the orders of his own countrymen, particularly as regarded religious fraternities.

His zeal was unwearied; there is scarcely a town in Flanders that is not enriched by his glorious talent. He loved literature, and while busy at his easel, would employ a secretary to read aloud to him, generally selecting some portion of the classics. He lived well, without excess of any kind, but had always a love for beautiful surroundings. He was an excellent horseman, and took great interest in the breeding of horses; but he had a taste for more serious avocations also, and delighted in presiding over the education of his children. He was twice married, first to Isabella Brant, whose charming portrait, sitting on the ground by her husband's side, holding his hand, is in the Pinakothek at Munich. His second wife was the beautiful Helena Forman, whose lovely smiling face, and full rounded form greet us in every gallery in Europe, sometimes alone, sometimes with a blooming little child beside her. Rubens made her his model, and painted her in every shape, and in every costume, and frequently without any costume at all.

By his first marriage he had two sons, to the eldest of whom the Archduke Albert stood sponsor, and gave his own name; by the second he had several children.

Marie de Medicis, in her last exile from France, went to Cologne, bought Rubens's house, and died there. For some

x

time before his death he was a martyr to the gout, which at length proved fatal; he lies buried in the church of St. James, at Antwerp, where his widow caused one of his most beautiful pictures to be placed.

He painted himself as St. George presenting his two wives to the Madonna, who carries the Holy Child in her arms.

No. 84.

JOHN FISHER, BISHOP OF ROCHESTER.

BORN 1455, EXECUTED 1535.

Ecclesiastical robes.

BORN at Beverley, in Yorkshire, but little is known of his early years; having taken his degree at Cambridge, he was appointed confessor to Margaret, Countess of Richmond, (mother of King Henry VII.), by whom he was much esteemed, and over whose mind he gained a powerful influence, which he exerted for no selfish ends.

By his advice and co-operation this Princess, after founding the Colleges of St. John's and Christ's at Cambridge, collected famous Professors from all parts, to be members of the same. The University was not ungrateful to Fisher for the part he had taken in the aggrandisement of Cambridge, and elected him Chancellor in 1504. The King (Henry VII.) preferred him to the See of Rochester, and it is said by some that he was made preceptor to Prince Henry (afterwards the Eighth). Certain it is that that Prince after his accession was very partial to the Bishop, and showed him much favour.

Until the question arose of the divorce of Catherine of Arragon, to which step Fisher was strenuously opposed on every account, he was personally much attached to the Queen, and his creed as a Roman Catholic caused him to deny the validity of such a proceeding. He was also loud in his disapprobation of the King's assumption of spiritual supremacy. It cannot be wondered at, under these circumstances, that Fisher should fall into thorough disgrace at Court, or that Henry (who could not bear to be thwarted) should catch at any pretext to persecute him. Added to all this, Fisher became mixed up in the affair of the 'Holy Maid of Kent,' as she was called, which plunged him into further trouble. His goods having been confiscated, he was imprisoned during the King's good pleasure in the Tower of London, whence he was only released on the payment of a heavy fine.

It will be remembered that the 'Holy Maid of Kent' (an impostor) pretended to be possessed of the gift of prophecy, and was made an instrument by some Roman Catholic priests to denounce the doctrines of the Reformed religion, and to predict a violent death within one month for Henry, should he proceed with the divorce suit against the Queen. The unfortunate woman suffered death with some of her upholders, and most assuredly her predictions were not verified. Henry, exasperated by Fisher's determined refusal to acknowledge him as head of the Church, once more sent the venerable ecclesiastic to the Tower as a rebel, and when there, in spite of his age and position, Fisher was treated with shameful indignity. They stripped him of his priestly garments, and dressed him in scanty rags. But the old man had a dauntless spirit. He had already been captive for a year, when the Pope, Paul III., hearing of his sufferings, chiefly on account of his creed, intimated to him that he should be raised to the grade of a Cardinal, a fatal step as far as Fisher was concerned. The King, in a fury, forbade the Hat to be brought into his dominions, and he sent Thomas Cromwell to the Tower to inquire whether Fisher intended to accept it.

The brave old man replied it was his duty to accept the honour done him by His Holiness, but he had neither solicited nor desired it, and such was his indifference to all human grandeur, that if the Hat were lying on the floor, he would not even stoop to pick it up.

The King was transported with rage when he learned the details of the interview, and cried out, 'Let the Pope send it then, and it shall be placed on John Fisher's shoulders, for by the mother of God, I will not leave him a head to carry it.' This cruel word was kept; the captive was tried by corrupt judges, creatures of the tyrant, condemned, and beheaded immediately after his trial. Fisher was remarkable for his erudition, his knowledge of Holy Writ, and the writings of the Fathers.

He was likewise an eminent controversialist, and his argumentative writings against Luther and the doctrines of the Reformation made a great noise on the Continent. Yet he was honoured even by his opponents, and Erasmus spoke in the highest terms of his integrity and the purity of his life. The cruelty to which he was subjected roused the indignation of many writers, and there is more than one foreign as well as English biography of this learned and good man. He was deeply attached to his See of Rochester, and although, when in favour in high places, he had the offer more than once of translation to other dignities of a more lucrative nature, he refused to leave his beloved cathedral. 'Is she not my dear wife?' he was wont to say, 'and how then can I separate myself from my spouse?'

No. 85.

HENRY FITZALAN, EARL OF ARUNDEL.

By Holbein.

BORN 1512, DIED 1579-80.

Black dress. Gold buttons. Gold chain. Ermine cape.

E was the only son of William the seventeenth Earl of Arundel, by Anne, daughter of Henry Percy, fourth Earl of Northumberland, and succeeded to the title and estates when about thirty years of age, until which time he had lived apart from public life.

In 1544 he accompanied Henry VIII. to Boulogne, which Brandon, Duke of Suffolk, was then besieging. With the wonderful precipitancy which characterised the period, Arundel suddenly found himself raised to the grade of Field-Marshal in the English army. Nor was the choice misplaced, for a manœuvre on his part carried the town, which he was the first to enter by a breach, at the head of his troops.

The King, delighted with the success of the undertaking, granted Lord Arundel the government of Calais, and subsequently the Comptrollership of the royal household.

Not long after, Arundel was appointed one of the Commissioners to negotiate a treaty with the Scots, when it so happened that the terms proposed were distasteful to the King, although unanimously approved by his Ministers. Henry sent no less a person than William Cecil (afterwards Secretary) to tell Arundel that whatever he (the King) might write by letter, his royal pleasure was that the treaty should be broken.

Cecil demurred, but was ordered off to Scotland.

Whatever impartial opinions may decide as to the honesty of the proceeding, Arundel gained the King's approbation, insomuch as he followed his master's injunctions, and that with so much discretion as to take the *onus* upon himself. Henry defended him when censured by the Government, ordered his pardon to be drawn up, and not only made him Lord Chamberlain, but named him one of the guardians to his successor, the youthful Edward.

After some attempts to remain or appear neutral during the struggle for power between the Protector Somerset and the Earl of Warwick, Arundel at length joined the party of the latter nobleman, and was chosen one of the six Lords intrusted with the custody of the King's person. We are told that he was 'circumspect and slow,' and 'a man of integrity.' Such a character was not likely to be acceptable to Warwick; Lord Arundel was deprived of his Chamberlain's staff and his seat at the Privy Council, and some frivolous accusations were brought against him, on the strength of which he was sent to the Tower. He was, moreover, subjected to a heavy fine, and banished into the country.

'Doubtless,' says Sir John Hayward, 'the Earl of Warwick had good reason to suspect that they who had the honesty to disapprove his purpose, would not want the heart to oppose it.'

Arundel remained on his own estates till the King's death, when he came forward as a zealous supporter of Mary's claim to the Crown. At a meeting of the friends of that Princess he made a most stirring and impressive speech, nor did he lose the opportunity thus offered him of attacking the Duke of Northumberland (the Earl of Warwick) for his conduct, past and present, namely, his disloyalty in the reign of Edward, and his actual treason in setting up his daughter-in-law, Jane Grey, as Queen.

Arundel took upon himself to make promises to the Protestants in Mary's name which she unfortunately did not fulfil. But his speech was received with such enthusiasm that at its conclusion the whole assembly escorted the speaker to the city, and summoning the Lord Mayor and Aldermen, proceeded then and there to proclaim Mary Tudor Queen of these realms. Lord Arundel immediately took horse and rode down into Suffolk to announce in person to Mary herself the success of the exertions made in her behalf, and at Cambridge he arrested his old enemy, the Duke of Northumberland, and led him a prisoner to the Tower of London.

These proceedings only occupied three days, and were completed by the 21st of July 1553. The Queen was becomingly grateful; she made Arundel, Steward of her household and President of her Council.

In 1558 he was elected Chancellor of the University of Oxford, but in 1560 was obliged to resign that dignity on account of his creed, when the Protestant faith was re-established. In spite, however, of the difference of their religious views, Queen Elizabeth treated Lord Arundel with marked distinction, continued him in his office of Lord Steward, and named him, in addition, High Constable and High Steward of England at her coronation.

He appears to have thought himself higher in the good graces of the royal coquette, than was actually the case, and finding himself somewhat slighted by her and by other friends at Court, we are told he grew 'troubled in mind, and to wear off his grief, asked leave to travel.'

Accordingly, he went abroad, returned for a short time, and then repaired to Italy, where he resided for some years. He contracted 'a great fondness for foreign fashions,' and on coming home introduced many, and in particular the use of coaches, the first known in England being the property of the Earl of Arundel.

He remained unemployed until the year 1569, when he was named one of the Commissioners to inquire into the murder of Henry Darnley, King of Scots. He pleaded Mary's cause, (believing firmly in her innocence,) and spoke out boldly in her behalf to Elizabeth herself, at the Council table when he considered the proceedings unjust. He never failed in his loyalty to the English Queen, although the intercourse he held with 'Mary's friends,' as they were called, rendered him an object of distrust.

In 1572 he suffered a brief imprisonment in the Tower, and on his release found he had forfeited the royal favour, which he did not go the right way to regain, by his resolute opposition to the proposed marriage with the Duke of Anjou.

He continued in retirement until the beginning of the year 1580, when, says Camden, 'Henry Fitzalan, Earl of Arundel, rendered his soul to God—in whom was extinct the surname of this most noble family, which had flourished with great honour for three hundred years and more'—from the time, indeed, of Richard Fitzalan, who, in the reign of Edward I., received the title of Earl of Arundel without any creation, from being possessed of the castle and lordship of Arundel, in Sussex. Henry married, first, Catherine Grey, daughter of Thomas, second Marquis of Dorset, (and aunt to Jane Grey,) by whom he had three children, who all died before their father, viz. :—

Henry, died unmarried at Brussels; Joan, married to John Lord Lumley; and Mary, the wife of Thomas Duke of Norfolk, in right of whose descent the present Duke of Norfolk enjoys the title of Earl of Arundel. Henry Fitzalan's second wife was Mary, daughter of Sir John Arundel of Lanherne, county Cornwall, by whom he had no children.

No. 86.

SIR RICHARD GRESHAM.

Dark coat. Yellow sleeves. Black cap. Chain.

HE Greshams took their name from a town so called in the county of Norfolk. Richard was the second son of John Gresham of Holt, in the same county, by Alice Blyth of Stratton, who brought her husband a large fortune. He was bred a mercer in London, where he was most successful in trade, and was appointed royal agent, or 'King's merchant,' as it was called, a trust of great importance and profit, which consisted in transacting the trading interests of the Crown in foreign countries. This Richard Gresham conducted for Henry VIII. and Edward VI. He amassed great riches, bought estates in several counties, was knighted in 1531, and elected Lord Mayor of London in 1537. He enjoyed much esteem and consideration in the city, and first conceived the idea of building the Royal Exchange, (which his son carried out,) beside many reformations and improvements for the benefit of the commercial community.

The merchants had suffered much inconvenience from being exposed to the weather in Lombard Street, when they met for the transaction of business.

Richard Gresham married, first, Audrey, daughter of William Linn of Southwick, county North Hants, by whom he had two sons—the second was Sir Thomas, usually called the founder, and at all events the builder, of the Royal Exchange,—and two daughters, Christian, or, as some call her, Margaret, who married Sir John Thynne, the builder of Longleat, to whom she brought a large dower as co-heir with her brothers, and Elizabeth, who died unmarried. Audrey died in 1522, and Sir Richard married again a widow named Taverson.

Y

No. 87.
ARABELLA STUART.
By Van Somers.
BORN 1575, DIED 1615.

Full length. Dark gown, richly embroidered in flowers of gold. *Ruff. Jewel. Cord of pearl* across the shoulder and round the waist. *One hand resting on a table.*

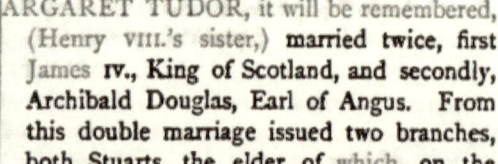

MARGARET TUDOR, it will be remembered, (Henry VIII.'s sister,) **married twice, first James IV., King of Scotland, and secondly, Archibald Douglas, Earl of Angus.** From this double marriage issued two branches, both Stuarts, the elder of which, on the death of Elizabeth, succeeded to the Throne, in the person of James I., the younger remaining heirs-expectant in case James had no children. To this branch belonged the Lady Arabella, and the jealousy shown by the elder to the younger is the key to her melancholy history. By her second husband, Margaret Tudor had a daughter, who bore her name; Lady Margaret Douglas was remarkable even in early life for her ambitious and intriguing spirit; according to modern parlance, she was always in hot water, and in the constant habit of paying compulsory visits to the Tower of London. Having secretly betrothed herself to Lord Thomas Howard, son of the first Duke of Norfolk of that name, they were both imprisoned on that account, and both fell ill of fever. Howard died, but his betrothed was set at liberty. A short time elapsed when she espoused Matthew Stuart, Earl of Lennox, this time with the concurrence of the Court, and by him she had several children, of whom only two sons grew up to manhood, the unfortunate Darnley, and Charles, who succeeded his father in the earldom of Lennox. On the marriage of her eldest son with Mary Queen of Scots Margaret was again imprisoned. Her husband's estates had already been confiscated on a charge of treason; by the time she was released Lord **Lennox was** dead, and she went to reside with her son Charles, **to whom** King James had granted his father's titles (as also **to his heirs** without restriction), at her dwelling-house in Hackney. Here **they** remained till Charles was about nineteen, when his mother thought it **high** time to provide him with a wife. So **in October 1574 the** mother and son mounted their horses, and took their way towards Scotland, but they were waylaid and intercepted, by **a sumptuous welcome.** Bess of Hardwicke, (there are few who do not **know** how to apply that nickname,) then Countess of Shrewsbury, heard of the travellers being in the neighbourhood, **and it suited her to receive** them as her guests.

A word to **enlighten, or remind, respecting this remarkable** woman:—

Elizabeth, daughter of **John Hardwicke of Hardwicke** Hall, in Derbyshire, was beautiful, vivacious, practical, and headstrong. At fourteen she married Mr. Barlow, a rich country gentleman, who soon left her a widow. She espoused secondly, Sir William Cavendish; thirdly, Sir William Saintlow, and fourthly, George Talbot, Earl of Shrewsbury.

Each husband brought her money, and most of them children and step-children. Bess was **as** fond of marrying (herself) **and** giving in marriage as she was of building; and so, **as we said before,** she waylaid the equestrians, and invited them to one of her numerous homes—Rufford House, county Notts. Her husband, Lord Shrewsbury, **gives an amusing** account of what took place during the visit:—

'The Lady Lennox being sickly, rested her at Rufford five days, and kept most her bedchamber, and in that time **the** young man, her son, fell into liking with my wife's daughter, Elizabeth Cavendish, and such liking was between them that my wife says she makes no doubt of a match. The young man is so far in love, that belike he is sick without her. This taking effect, I shall be well at quiet, for there is no nobleman's son in England that she hath not prayed me to deal for, at one time or another.'

The poor man reckoned without his host when he spoke of quiet. There was another Bess in the field, and one not easily hoodwinked. A few days' courtship, and a secret marriage! But the news soon reached the Queen's ear. The whole party (with the exception of Lord Shrewsbury, in whose custody Mary Queen of Scots then was, and who exonerated himself in the transaction) was summoned in a body to London.

So the first days of the honeymoon were spent in a dreary ride through wintry weather, by the two poor young lovers, attended by their respective mothers, to meet a welcome on their arrival which matched but too well with the severity of the atmosphere. The match-making mothers were lodged in the Tower, and left there for some time to reflect on the imprudence of giving so near a kinsman of the Queen's away in marriage, without her consent, one (more especially) who had pretensions to the succession.

It was some time before the ladies were released, and by then little Arabella had appeared on the scene, having been born at Chatsworth, the beautiful estate which Bess had induced or commanded her second husband, Sir William Cavendish, to purchase. No sooner did Lord and Lady Lennox hear that the Dowager was at liberty than they joined her with the new-born infant at the old house at Hackney. The Queen of Scotland having written graciously on the occasion of the birth, both mother and grandmother wrote to thank her for the remembrance 'of our little daughter, who some day may serve your Highness.'

The death of Charles Lennox, which happened shortly afterwards, plunged his family into poverty as well as sorrow. In spite of all her relations could say in her behalf, Arabella's English possessions were pounced on by *good* Queen Bess, while both James and the Regent Murray ignored the orphan's pretensions to titles, and land in Scotland, heedless of Queen Mary's exertions and expostulations. James, indeed, was so kind as to propose that Arabella should marry the man on whom he had bestowed the Earldom of Lennox—a favourite scheme of his. The child was about two years old when her grandmother died, in whom she lost a zealous, though not always judicious champion. Illustrious as was her birth, Margaret Dowager Countess of Lennox's finances were so low as not to be sufficient to defray her funeral expenses; and the Queen, doubtless glad to be rid of her importunities, gave orders for a sumptuous interment in Westminster Abbey to the woman she had not scrupled to defraud in her lifetime.

In 1582 Elizabeth Lady Lennox followed her mother-in-law to the grave after a short illness, and her death brought deep grief to the heart of the otherwise worldly-minded Lady Shrewsbury, who took the little orphan to reside with her.

In spite of her proud spirit, Bess of Hardwicke did not disdain to write to Lord Burghley that her love for the child was more than that of a natural mother, on account of her near relationship to the Queen, to whom both Lord and Lady Shrewsbury made periodical and ineffectual appeals in behalf of their charge.

The early days of Arabella Stuart's childhood were passed at Chatsworth and Hardwicke, and when she was about seven, proposals of marriage commenced, which went on without intermission for years. Lord Leicester, it seems, was minded to betroth her to his son (by Lettice Knollys, widow of the Earl of Essex). The bridegroom-elect's age was two, yet we are gravely informed that the children were told of their engagement, and portraits exchanged.

The Queen did not approve of the idea, but a sterner mandate forbade the banns. 'The noble imp, Baron of Denbigh,' as he is called on his monument at Warwick, died, to the inexpressible grief of his father. At 'Hardwicke Hall, more glass than wall,' (one of the most interesting of England's 'proud ancestral homes,' and a glory to Bess the builder, beside the older house, now a ruin, where her father lived,) amongst a treasury of portraits, there is one of little Arabella, which is doubtless the identical picture alluded to as painted at this time.

A sweet little face peeps out of a formal dress of the period—richly embroidered gown, high head and cap, numerous ornaments, with a jewel bearing this ambiguous and no way prophetic motto, '*Pour parvenir j'endure.*'

In her hand she carries a doll dressed in the same quaint and stiff manner as the young mistress. The picture is full of pathos to those who remember the subsequent history of the then loved and petted child. Arabella's bedroom is shown at Hardwicke, and her memory blends well with the picturesque background of those time-honoured walls.

Lord Burghley, who was very friendly to Arabella's interests, (and the feeling proved hereditary,) writes to Bess to warn her 'there are plots to carry off the child.' She thanks him; says she is 'careful Arabella takes the air near the house; goes not to any one else; lieth in my own bedchamber. Is most loving and affectionate.'

The grandam appeared really to have a very soft place in her heart for the pretty intelligent, amiable, amenable child; but Arabella's early life was passed in the midst of domestic strife, as Bess was always at variance with her husband, and his, her, or their children. But with these squabbles the present narrative has nothing to do.

Sir Walter Mildmay, on a visit to Lord Shrewsbury, was captivated by the little lady, then about eleven, and bade her write a letter to the Queen; but he reckoned without his host when he thought so innocent and simple an appeal could touch so tough a heart. Surely never was one young maiden made the centre of so many matrimonial speculations as the Lady Arabella. All kinds of husbands, of all countries, grades, religions, and ages, were selected for her; plots and schemes for the aggrandisement of the plotters, laid, while the unconscious object was still playing with the doll we saw at Hardwicke Hall.

In the course of time, James King of Scotland, (we do not pretend to place them in chronological order,) Henry d'Albret, (Henry IV. of France,) Philip of Spain, the Duke of Parma, or his brother, whom the Pope would have released from his ecclesiastical vows for such a prize, the King of Portugal, the Duc d'Anjou, as many pretenders as there are sands on the sea-shore; but the poor girl chose (and that unfortunately) for herself. Soon after the death of Mary Queen of Scots, Elizabeth sent for Arabella (then twelve years old) to Court, showed her great favour, invited her to dine at the royal table, and gave her precedence over all the nobility. She won all hearts, pretty, witty, amiable, unsuspicious, and gentle-hearted. The Queen treated her with characteristic inconsistency, now with indulgence, now with severity.

One day at Court, calling Arabella to her side, and presenting her to Madame Chateauneuf (the French Ambassadress), she bade the lady look well at that child. 'She is not so unimportant as you may think. One day she will be even as I am, and be lady mistress.' This speech was doubtless intended to spite the King of Scotland, rather than to be believed by those who heard it. M. and Madame Chateauneuf were delighted with the child, observing that 'she spoke Latin, French, and Italian well, sufficiently handsome in the face, and without doubt the lawful heritress of the kingdom, if James of Scotland be excluded.'

The grave old Lord Burghley loved the child, and made much of her at supper, on the first night of her presentation at Court.

Years passed on, and Arabella was made the centre of intrigues of all kinds, both abroad and at home; and she became the object of jealousy and suspicion. The Queen's fury was roused by hearing her young kinswoman had betrothed herself to William Seymour, grandson to the Earl of Hertford, and the unfortunate Katherine Grey.

The alliance was most distasteful to Elizabeth, who was inimical to the whole house of Hertford. Arabella was arrested, and Her Majesty, much perturbed, fell sick; it was even reported that the illness was of the Lady Arabella's contriving! Alluding to this, she writes most pathetically:—
'While we wash our hands in innocency let the grand accuser, and all his Ministers do their worst. God will be on our side, and reveal the truth to our most gracious Sovereign.'

Elizabeth died. James succeeded, and Cecil spoke to him in behalf of his cousin, then a kind of honoured prisoner at Wrest House, the seat of the Earl of Kent, who had married a Talbot. Cecil besought and advised the King to deal gently with her, and she was set at liberty, but went by her friend's advice to dwell at Sheen, with my Lady Northampton, whence she wrote many letters petitioning for some allowance suitable to her birth. James at first showed her much favour, and appointed her nominally governess to his daughter, Princess Elizabeth. She accordingly set out for Welbeck to meet the Queen (Anne of Denmark) and her retinue on her way from Scotland. Sir Charles Cavendish (Arabella's uncle) gave the royal travellers a royal welcome at his house of Welbeck with revellings and maskings, and beautiful girls dressed as nymphs, and the goddess Diana, who came to bid the Queen welcome, 'and proved to be no other than the Lady Arabella.'

Bess of Hardwicke had deputed her granddaughter to invite Queen Anne to Chatsworth, but to the old lady's disgust her invitation was not only rejected but waived in favour of her deadly enemy, her step-son and son-in-law, Lord Shrewsbury.

Princess Elizabeth was charmed with her governess, and was never so happy as in her company. At Queen Anne's first drawing-room, we are told that Arabella was present with her aunt, Lady Shrewsbury, and that 'both were sumptuous in apparell, and exceeding curious in jewellery.' From letters preserved at Longleat we find that Lord Shrewsbury was in constant correspondence with his niece, urging her to prudence, warning her of pitfalls around her, in consequence of her being made the unwilling and unconscious nucleus of political plots, and her answers invariably testify to her sense and her affection for her counsellor. She was at Woodstock with the Court during the Plague, and writes delightful letters thence, which we regret not having the space to insert. Her own views were in no ways dazzled by Court life; her playful description of a Dutch lady who came over from the Duchess of Holstein to learn the English fashions, must perforce be inserted:—'She hath been here twice from Oxford, and thinketh every day long till she be at home, so well she liketh her entertainment, or loveth her own country. In truth, she is civil, and therefore cannot but look for the like which she brings out of a ruder country. But if ever there were such a virtue as courtesy at the Court, I marvel what is become of it, for I protest I see little or none of it but in the Queen, who speaketh to the people as she passeth, and receiveth their prayers with thankful countenance.'

Another letter bemoans the loss of time which the royal pair lost in their immoderate passion for hunting, to the great disgust of many courtiers, who were not equally enamoured of the noble science. She says: 'I could believe I had become a child again; we are seeing the ladies-in-waiting take delight in the most frivolous games, such as "Arise up, pig," and the like.'

She was also much disgusted at the manner in which the dead lioness, the late Queen, was kicked at. Small as was the pittance allowed her, she was expected to offer Christmas and other seasonable gifts to Her Majesty Queen Anne, and others.

Poor Arabella, considerate and wise, whose leisure was spent, 'scant as it was, in reading of service and preaching.'

In 1603 the celebrated trial of Sir Walter Raleigh took place, in which, among numerous counts, he was accused of plotting to place Arabella Stuart on the throne. But when her name was mentioned in Court, Robert Cecil, her friend, rose and said, 'Let us not scandal the innocent by confusion of speech; the Lady Arabella is as innocent of these things as I, or any man here,' and then followed an able defence.

Arabella, who was much attached to her uncle, Lord Shrewsbury, was always striving, at least by letter, to make peace between him and her grandmother, which was perhaps the reason that she lost favour with that irascible old lady.

We hear of 'the Lady Arabell riding in a procession through the city, next to the Queen, on a crimson velvet caparisoned horse, acting in masques and pageants, sumptuously arrayed; but the poor lady was deep in debt, and her uncle of Shrewsbury in the like plight, unable to help her.' She was, however, much liked at Court, and chosen sponsor to little Princess Mary, (who died young,) and, says Birch, 'she was very dear to Prince Henry, not less for her near relation to him, than for her accomplishments of mind, both natural and acquired.' The Duke of Holstein was a zealous suitor, 'but the Lady Arabella will not hear of marriage.'

The King of Denmark, when on a visit to the Queen, his sister, was captivated by her, and they corresponded in Latin.

In 1608 died Bess of Hardwicke, Countess of Shrewsbury, 'feared by many, flattered by some, beloved by none,' having disinherited the grandchild whom she professed to love. Arabella's favour at Court lasted up to 1609, at the close of which year she was placed in restraint, and her servants arrested, and early in the ensuing year she was accused of having entered into a secret treaty of marriage with her old love, William Seymour. A fitter husband could scarcely be found, but what availed that fitness, if the match did not please the tyrant who ruled his unfortunate kinswoman's destinies?

Seymour was 'a quiet, steady young man,' loving his book above all other exercise. They are supposed to have met frequently when the youth was at College, and the lady at Woodstock with the Court; be this as it may, the lovers met, and solemnly plighted their troth. Twice they saw each other, at the houses of confidential friends, and ere a third interview could be effected, they were both summoned before the Privy Council, admonished, forgiven, and betrayed into promises impossible to keep. They were separated for a time, and Arabella, with a heavy heart, was called upon to parade her comeliness and her talent in a Court masque, where she enacted a nymph of Trent, her costume, most elaborate and minutely described, of gold, silver, seaweeds, sedges, and cloth of both metals, all embroidered, and shells and coral on the crest of a helm. That was the end of her grandeur and her prosperity, and now came tribulation of all kinds. At Whitsuntide, Seymour, accompanied by a friend and confidant, by name Rodney, went down to Greenwich, where they arrived at midnight. They waited till morning, and then found access to Lady Arabella's apartment, where the lovers were united; Rodney and two servants serving as witnesses. The secret soon transpired, and the luckless bride was placed in the custody of Sir Thomas Parry at a house in Lambeth, 'opposite a capital mansion called Fauxhall,' to remain there with one or two of her women, without access of any other person till His Majesty's further pleasure should be known.

Hence she addressed letters which seemed indeed to soften the King's hard heart; the Queen, it appears, frequently interceded, as did many other influential persons, but without effect. The bridegroom was lodged in the Tower; Arabella continued to write letters to her uncle, to her husband, and innumerable petitions to the Council in most pathetic terms, 'that had not God for some high purpose steeled the hearts of men, they must perforce have pitied her.'

James now ordered her off into the custody of the Bishop of Durham, who repaired to Sir Thomas Parry's house to receive his charge.

Arabella's grief at the prospect of a long journey far from the city which held the beloved of her heart was intense. Her agitation was terrible to witness, and much affected the good Prelate, who used all his poor skill to comfort her, and make her submit to the royal decree by exhorting her to follow the patient example of holy saints, and that in the presence of Mr. Chancellor, Dr. Mountford, (a trusty friend of the poor prisoners,) and others. But Arabella would accept no comfort, and on the journey to Highgate, the physician was called on three times to administer cordials, so faint and sick was his fair charge.

He took upon himself next day (when after passing a miserable night at the house of Sir William Bond, Arabella woke up from a few hours' sleep in great exhaustion) to forbid her proceeding any further. The Bishop having the King's displeasure before his eyes, went to her bedside and besought her to rise, 'telling her of the sweet air, the beautiful day, and the duty of her journey.' But the good physician braved all for her health's sake, though this step entailed the necessity of a letter from Bishop and doctor too, to the Lords in Council.

James, anxious to ascertain if the illness were feigned, sent his own physician to see Arabella, and consult with Dr. Mountford, who told him plainly 'remedies were useless, and that he could warrant no amendmente of her health, or continuance of lyfe if some contentment of minde be not granted. His aim,' he said, 'was to cherish her into life.' Nevertheless cruel orders came to hurry her on her way, and during a ride of six miles, she was attacked by deadly sickness and faintness, and was carried almost insensible to the house of a gentleman named Thomas Conyers, resident at East Barnet. Letters again passed from the travellers to high quarters, and the physician wrote to Lady Shrewsbury, (Arabella's aunt,) who was most uneasy on the sufferer's account.

A respite of a month was granted. The Bishop returned to Durham, and she was committed to the care of Sir James Crofts; but her servants were removed from her side. The Bishop on his way stopped at Royston, where the Court was, and thought to benefit the prisoner's cause by most abject appeals to the King; indeed, the Bishop went so far as to say 'his cousin would willingly sweep his chamber,' which we take leave to suppose was speaking without book. At the termination of the month the lady was commanded to proceed on her way north; she was still indisposed, and she made the most of that excuse. Whenever Sir James Crofts visited her she was stretched on the bed in pain. 'She apprehended nothing but fear and anger in the most ugliest forms; the horrors of her utter ruin drive her to despair; to live out one only year in some convenient place not so clean out of the world as she termeth Durham, she could gather to herself some weak hopes of more gentle times to come.' Sir James, who like most people seems to have experienced her fascination, says again, 'the best and pleasingest discourse had no effect on her mind, but was met by tears and lamentations.' Her faithful Mountford went to London to plead for her with James, who declared 'to Durham she should go if he were King,' but at length another month's respite was granted.

Arabella had now a project in her head, and her aunt, Lady Shrewsbury, (born Cavendish,) had devoted herself to the cause of her unfortunate niece. She appealed to all the persons whom she believed to have influence at Court, and finding all other means fail, she contrived a plan of escape, and forwarded a large sum of money to facilitate the same.

The money was sent nominally for the payment of Arabella's debts, and for the commission of purchasing some needlework of Mary Queen of Scots. Crompton, her faithful man-servant, deeply attached to his mistress, managed all these transactions, prepared disguises, and communicated with William Seymour in some miraculous manner. Arabella now feigned entire submission to the King's commands, and expressed her willingness to proceed to Durham, by which means she threw her keepers off their guard; moreover, she worked on the compassion of one of her attendants (a minister's wife) to assist her.

On the 4th of June the unhappy lady assumed her disguise—'a pair of French-fashioned hose, a man's doublet, a long-locked peruke, black hat and cloak, white boots with red tops, and a rapier by her side;' and thus equipped set forth, with Markham, one of her servants, on foot. But Arabella was neither as strong of purpose, or of body as Rosalind, and she ofttimes 'disgraced her man's apparel by bearing herself like a woman.'

She turned faint ere they reached 'the sorry inne' where the trusty Crompton awaited them with saddle-horses, so much so that the hostler who held the stirrup remarked, as she languidly mounted, 'The gentleman will scarcely reach London.'

The fresh air and exercise, however, revived her, and they arrived at Blackwall in safety. This was the place of rendezvous with her husband, and some faithful followers, but in vain they waited for Seymour, till it was counted so dangerous to delay that, leaving one to communicate with him, when he should appear, she set out in a boat with a female attendant, the two men, Markham, and Crompton, following in another with her baggage. At Lee they found a vessel lying at anchor. They hailed her, and finding she was bound for Berwick, and would not change her course even for a heavy bribe, they inquired if there were not a French vessel anywhere near. Alas! these inquiries were calculated to put the bloodhounds on the track.

In describing the fugitives afterwards, the captain, having spoken of the men, said there were 'two women, one barefaced, in a black riding safeguard, and a hat; the other was so wrapped in a long cloak, and her face so closely covered, that he could not see her; but in drawing off her glove she manifested a marvellous fair white hand.' Poor Arabella, to whose beautiful hand so many courtly compliments and sonnets had been addressed!

They reached the French vessel and embarked, in despair at the non-appearance of Seymour; yet hoping for his arrival at every moment, she besought the French captain to remain at anchor at least another day; but her attendants insisted on his hoisting sail, well aware that to delay was madness. (Seymour's adventures will be related in the notice of his life.) So the French ship got under weigh, having on board for freight a heart heavy enough to sink her.

The news of her escape filled the King's mind with rage and consternation; he pictured Arabella to himself making common cause with all his enemies on the Continent; the hue and cry became general. Salisbury, who must surely in his secret heart have prayed for the escape of his old favourite, was ordered to write to the Governor of Calais to intercept Seymour and his wife, (who were supposed to be together,) on their arrival in port. Every ship was to be searched, every means taken, for the apprehension of the fugitives.

Alas! alas! the measures were too well taken (the details are needless); suffice it to say that the train was but too well laid, the track but too well followed. 'The Adventure,' one of the vessels sent in pursuit, standing for Calais, was in mid-channel when a sail was sighted. A boat was immediately lowered, as there was but little wind, and six armed men made way for the French vessel. They challenged her in vain, and fired a broadside and several volleys of musketry, giving time for the advance of 'The Adventure.'

The Frenchman stood thirteen shots before he surrendered, and then Arabella, anxious to avoid bloodshed, came on deck, discovered herself to the captain, and acknowledged there was no use in further resistance. The crew of the boat boarded the French ship, and arrested Arabella, at the same time demanding her husband. She made them a brave and noble answer, saying she had not seen him; she hoped and believed he was safe, and the joy she experienced at his escape far outweighed the sorrow she felt at her own capture.

She was then taken as a close prisoner on board 'The Adventure,' with all the rest of the passengers. The King, overjoyed at the news, lost no time; Arabella and her aunt and confidante, Lady Shrewsbury, were sent to the Tower, with several of their adherents, and others, lodged in different prisons—her faithful Crompton, Markham, the minister's wife, Sir James Crofts, and no end of arrests.

Lord Shrewsbury was kept a prisoner in his house, and the aged Earl of Hertford summoned to London, to Court. 'If he be found healthful enough to travel, he must not delay.'

The two ladies were examined before the Privy Council, and we are told that Arabella answered the Lords 'with good judgment and discretion,' while the Countess is said 'to be utterly without reason, crying out that all is but tricks and giggs, that she will answer nothing in private, and if she have offended in law she will answer in public.' A reply by no means unreasonable, although it would appear that the younger lady was calm and dignified under provocation and persecution, and the elder excited and indignant. The chief count against Lady Shrewsbury was the ready money she had advanced for her niece's escape, by which she was accused of intending to bribe the Catholic party.

The Scotch and English faction, we are informed by the same authority, were at great issue on this subject. Seymour was safe beyond seas, and James was at rest on that score, as long as the unhappy pair were separated.

In vain were appeals made in Arabella's behalf to the hard-hearted tyrant. Bishop Goodman says of her: 'She is a virtuous and good lady, of great intellectuals, and harmless, and gives no offence.' She was in all things gentle, and showed gratitude for the slightest kindness, but she was treated with great indignity,—the money and jewels found on her person seized by the King's orders, her servants denied access to her, and Lady Shrewsbury was not even allowed to have an attendant of any kind. What a contrast to the sumptuous life at Hardwicke, Chatsworth, and all the other palaces to which she had been accustomed in her mother's lifetime!

Lord Shrewsbury wrote a most pitiful appeal respecting the dilapidated state of his wife's apartments in the Tower, to Lord Salisbury, and after a time some mercy was shown her, and a servant appointed to wait on her, and, crowning grace! a copy of verses, written by Charles Cavendish for the poor prisoner's delectation, was allowed to be placed in her hands. The wretched Arabella spent her hours in weeping and mourning. Sometimes she roused herself to embroider a gift for the King, which he would not accept. Her pen was seldom idle; 'in all humility, in most humble wise,' she wrote to James, 'the most wretched, and unfortunate creature that ever lived, prostrates herself at the feet of the most merciful King that ever was.' She wrote to Lord Northampton to complain of how badly she is nourished in sickness, of how others, however poor and unfortunate, are preserved alive for charity. 'I can neither get clothes nor posset at all, nor any complement fit for a sick body in any case, when I call for it.'

Body and mind at last gave way, beneath constant suffering. Arabella showed signs of aberration of intellect, and was now moody, now despairing, now prone to fits of forced gaiety. Hearing of the marriage of her former friend and pupil, the Princess Elizabeth, the unhappy captive contrived to procure a new gown, in which she decked herself with much care. But little effect was produced at Court by the poor prisoner's gala dress, and the betrothed was too happy to waste much thought on her favourite of other days.

In the same letter, quoted above, she says 'that help will come too late,' and declares 'I do not fear to die, so I be not guilty of my own death, and oppress others with my ruin.'

Gradually but surely her intellect became undermined. She made some incoherent accusations against Lady Shrewsbury, which proved very disadvantageous to that lady, the rigour of whose captivity had been lately mitigated; but was again summoned before the Council, charged with contempt towards the King in refusing to answer questions, again replied scornfully, and pleaded the privilege of her person and nobility, and a rash vow she had made to be silent. She was remanded to the Tower, but the evident signs of insanity evinced by her unfortunate niece nullified the charges brought against her. Early in March 1613 Arabella was attacked with convulsions, and declared insane by a physician. Her humble friend Crompton had laid a second plan for her escape, but deliverance was to come in another guise.

Her husband and his father were currying favour with James, but seemed to have troubled themselves little about the poor prisoner, though by some it was believed Seymour wrote to her constantly, and that his letters were intercepted. She grew weaker in body and more feeble in mind, until on the 25th of September, says Nichols, 'that ill-fated and persecuted lady, Arabella Seymour, daughter of Charles Earl of Lennox, and cousin-german of Henry Darnley, father of King James, died in the Tower of London.'

In the dead of night the daughter of a line of kings was carried along the black river to Westminster Abbey, and there deposited in the royal vault beneath the coffin of Mary Queen of Scots. All pomp and ceremony were forbidden, the Burial Service was read by stealth as over some felon's grave, not for any fault of her own, but because 'to have a great funeral for one dying out of the King's favour would have reflected upon the King's honour.'

A sadder page can scarcely be found in England's history, and among many crimes which blacken the fame of James Stuart, perhaps the slow murder of his unhappy kinswoman is the worst.

The terrible traces of suffering and unmistakable signs of imbecility exhibited in this portrait, lead to the conjecture that it must have been painted during her confinement in the Tower.

No. 88.

JAMES DUKE OF YORK, AFTERWARDS JAMES II., KING OF ENGLAND.

By Sir Peter Lely.

BORN 1633, DEPOSED 1688, DIED 1701.

Full length. Crimson robes. Mantle. Collar and Order of Garter.

HE second son of Charles I. by Henrietta Maria. Married, first, Anne Hyde, daughter of the Earl of Clarendon, and, secondly, Maria d'Este of Modena. By his first marriage he had Mary, married to the Prince of Orange, afterward William III., and Anne, married to the Prince of Denmark, who succeeded her sister as Queen. By Mary of Modena he had Charles, who died young, James, called the Chevalier de St. George, or the Old Pretender, and three daughters.

No. 89.

ELIZABETH LADY NOTT.

Full length. Grey satin dress. Ringlets. Hand resting on table.

SHE was the sister of Sir Henry Frederick Thynne and married Sir William Nott of Richmond, in the county of Surrey.

No. 90.

ROBERT DUDLEY, EARL OF LEICESTER.

By Zucchero.

born circa 1532, died 1588.

Full length. Gold and white dress. Gorget. George and Garter. Page holding a helmet and tilting lance. Tent in background.

E was the fifth son of John Dudley, Earl of Warwick, afterwards Duke of Northumberland, by the daughter and heir of Sir Henry Guildford. He began life early. In 1551 he was named Gentleman of the Bedchamber and Master of the Buckhounds to King Edward VI., by whom he was much esteemed. But it would appear that before, or shortly after, his appointment he fell in love with Amy, the fair daughter of Sir John Robsart, over whose sad fate the 'Wizard of the North' has thrown so dazzling a glamour, though, contrary to his version of the story, it would appear that the marriage was public and took place at Court. On the death of Edward, and the failure of the scheme devised by the Duke of Northumberland to place his daughter-in-law, Lady Jane Grey, on the throne, Lord Robert Dudley was imprisoned in the Tower on a charge of high treason, and had sentence of death passed on him, and it was supposed he only escaped sharing his father's fate, by pleading guilty. Any way, he was liberated with a free pardon, and on the marriage of Queen Mary with Philip of Spain, he ingratiated himself into that Prince's favour, and 'was most serviceable to both King and Queen,' says Strype, 'by carrying messages between them, often riding post to do so.' To the Princess Elizabeth he had been playfellow in

childhood, and fellow-prisoner in the Tower, and when she came to the throne she did not forget old days.

She made him Master of the Horse, Knight of the Garter, and Privy Councillor, showering upon him grants and estates without number. Indeed, his influence with her was so great that Secretary Cecil (if we may credit that arch gossip, De Quadra, the Spanish Ambassador at the Court of London) wished Lord Robert Dudley in Paradise. The same writer says that the Queen told him that Lady Robert was very ill, and some time afterwards 'che si ha rotto il collo.' It certainly was rumoured at Court that but for the slight obstacle of a wife, the Queen would throw over all her foreign and royal suitors in favour of this handsome polished minion, as Froude calls him. The tragedy of Cumnor Hall will ever remain a mystery; but all these reports which preceded it, and the fact that Lord and Lady Robert had scarcely ever appeared together in public since their marriage, all went to strengthen suspicion against the husband.

On the other hand, no sooner did Dudley hear of his wife's death, which he said was 'the most unfortunate thing that could have happened to him,' than he caused a searching inquiry to be made, and he sent down poor Amy's half-brother to investigate the matter. On the inquest, these facts transpired: The Lady had insisted on the household leaving her to go to Abingdon Fair, and on their return she was found dead at the bottom of a staircase, without any marks of violence. By some it was suggested she might have been first suffocated and then placed in that position; others again were of opinion that she had committed suicide, seeing she had been overheard to say she prayed God to preserve her from desperation. But one of her attendants would not tolerate the idea, saying she was a good and virtuous gentlewoman. The verdict was accidental death, but the country was full of strange mutterings, the echoes of which have never died away.

A few contemporaneous documents have lately been found at Longleat which throw some fresh light on the circumstances of her marriage and domestic life. It does not appear to have been one of constrained seclusion, as commonly supposed, nor is there, in the papers alluded to, any indication of estrangement on the part of her husband, still less anything to implicate him, as accessory to her violent death, if it really were such.

In forming opinions on Dudley's moral character, it is only fair to remember that many of the stories which were spread to his prejudice have their origin in a notorious book entitled *Leicester's Commonwealth*, written by men who were his deadliest enemies in politics and religion, especially 'Parsons the Jesuit.' This was circulated in MS. for many years, a copy being extant at Longleat ; but the Queen and Privy Council published a protest against its slanders. A gorgeous funeral was decreed to the unhappy Amy at Oxford, and Dudley was free. We need not recapitulate the well-known story of Elizabeth's vacillating conduct with regard to him and her numerous suitors ; how all England believed she was on the point of selecting him as her husband; of how Mary Queen of Scots mildly remarked that the Queen of England was about to marry her horsekeeper, who had murdered his wife to make room for her ; of how Elizabeth turned round and proposed he should marry Mary, saying that if she herself intended to marry, she should prefer him to all the Princes in the world ; and contrasting him with his brother Lord Warwick, she said, ' He is rough, and lacks the delicacy of Robert.'

As far as she ever was in earnest in her constantly fluctuating matrimonial speculations, Bess really did appear to be so about the Scotch marriage, as she created her favourite Earl of Leicester apparently to fit him for a higher position ; and she remarked querulously to Melville, (Mary's confidential envoy to England,) 'You like better yon long lad,' pointing to Darnley, who bore the sword of State at the ceremony of Dudley's elevation to the peerage, and the poor 'long lad,' unfortunately for himself, became Mary's choice; and Elizabeth returned to the game of fast-and-loose with Leicester. His suit, says Froude, was never listened to more favourably than when it served to interfere with another man's, but on a sudden she was informed he was already secretly married to the widow of Walter Devereux, Earl of Essex.

Already during the lifetime of her noble husband this lady's name had been whispered in conjunction with that of Leicester, in no creditable manner, and their hasty marriage, after the sudden and mysterious death of Lord Essex, gave rise to many dark suspicions. Another scandal, too, was afloat; another secret, or pretended marriage was spoken of between Leicester and the daughter of Lord Effingham, widow of Lord Sheffield. Lodge tells us that when Dudley wished to marry Lady Essex, he compelled the unhappy woman to renounce all claim to the title of his lawful wife, by publicly espousing Sir Edward Stafford. All this transpired at a later period, when she came forward in behalf of her son, whom Lady Leicester persecuted with law-suits after his father's death. It would appear that Dudley entertained much affection for the child whom he had injured, whose legitimacy he now affirmed, now denied, and at his death bequeathed to him the estates of Kenilworth, which the bad woman who had supplanted his mother would not allow him to enjoy in peace. Lettice, Lady Leicester, survived her husband nearly half a century. Elizabeth always hated her, and would never be reconciled to her, although she was the mother of Robert Devereux, Earl of Essex, who succeeded his stepfather in the royal favour. The Queen stormed and raved on first hearing of the marriage, wept profusely, and behaved as was her wont. In 1584 she sent Leicester to the Low Countries in command of the auxiliary forces, and he joined his gallant nephew, Sir Philip Sidney, at Flushing. He lived in such state, and took so much upon himself, as to expose him to a severe reprimand from home. He returned, and went out again to Zealand with fresh levies, and was restored to greater favour than ever. In the famous speech she addressed to the troops at Tilbury, Elizabeth extolled her favourite to the skies, having already named him to the command of the army raised to oppose the expected Spanish invasion. It was reported she intended to make him Viceregent of England, but the mighty solver of many a vexed question arrested his progress. He died of fever at his house at Cornbury, county Oxford, on his way to Kenilworth, September 1588.

No. 91.

THOMAS THYNNE (TOM O' TEN THOUSAND).

By Sir Peter Lely.

SHOT IN HIS COACH, 1682.

Tawny coat. Blue mantle. Full wig. Lace collar.

No. 92.

THE HONOURABLE JAMES THYNNE.

By Kerseboom.

BORN 1701, DIED 1705.

Full length. A child seated by a fountain, pouring water from a shell. Loose white shirt. Pink and blue drapery.

A YOUNGER son of the first Lord Weymouth. He died at an early age.

DRAWING ROOM.

DRAWING ROOM.

TWO PORTRAITS OF CHILDREN OF SIR JOHN THYNNE.

ATTRIBUTED TO HOLBEIN.

No. 93.

Dressed in a dark brown frock. Sleeves of a lighter material. White pinafore. Holding in one hand a jewelled cross, in the other, two cherries. Inscription in background, 'xv. Maii MDLXXII. ætatis mens. x.'

No. 94.

An infant in a white aress, richly brocaded. Close cap and bourlet or pudding. Jewelled chain and cross round the neck. Rattle in the left hand. Inscription, 'viii. Octob. MDLXIIII., ætat. mens. vi.'

No. 95.

FRANCIS THE FIRST, KING OF FRANCE, AND HIS QUEEN, ELEANOR OF AUSTRIA.

PAINTER DOUBTFUL.

FRANCIS, BORN 1494, DIED 1547. ELEANOR, DIED 1558.

KING :—*Red and white slashed dress. Feathers and jewels in his cap.*
ELEANOR :—*Blue and white embroidered dress. Slashed cap with jewels and feathers. Holding the King's hand, and in her other a Caduceus with bells, issuing from an artichoke or pine cone. A jester in the background.*

E was the son of Charles d'Orleans, Duke of Angoulême, by Louise de Savoie. He married, first, the Princess Claude, daughter of Louis XII., and succeeded his father-in-law on the throne of France. His second wife was Eleanor of Austria, sister to Charles V., Emperor of Germany. For many years this picture has been erroneously named Francis I. and his mistress, but late researches prove the female portrait to be that of his second wife, Eleanor of Austria, and that it was painted as a commemoration picture, at the time of the marriage,—the Caduceus, the emblem of peace, recording that of Cambray, 'La Paix des Dames.'

Eleanor of Austria was the daughter of Philip, Archduke of Austria, by 'Mad Joan,' as she was called, (the daughter of Ferdinand and Isabella of Spain,) and consequently sister to Charles V., Emperor of Germany.

She was much admired at the Imperial Court, and Frederick, brother to the Elector Palatine, no sooner saw than he fell in love with her, and the affection was reciprocal; but Charles, discovering their intimacy, exiled Frederick, and hastened to give his sister in marriage.

Emanuel, King of Portugal, surnamed 'The **Fortunate,**' had governed his kingdom well, but he was ill-calculated to take the fancy of the beautiful young Princess, still less to drive out the image of a former lover. He was misshapen, and far advanced in years, but he treated Eleanor with great consideration. He did not survive his marriage above two years, leaving his widow with two children. It may easily be conjectured that the hand of Eleanor, gifted as she was with a large dower and great personal charms, was eagerly sought by many illustrious personages, but her brother appeared to favour the suit of the Connétable de Bourbon.

The wars which intervened, however, changed these projects after Francis I. had been taken prisoner by Charles V. at the battle of Pavia, the peace of Cambray was concluded between them, called frequently 'La Paix des Dames,' because negotiated by Margaret of Austria, the Emperor's aunt, and Louise of Savoy, the King of France's mother, who had been Regent during her son's absence and captivity. One stipulation was the union of the fair young widow with Francis I., and the nuptials were celebrated with great pomp. Eleanor, indeed, presided at Court as Queen in all the ceremonies, but neither her mental nor personal charms made much impression on the heart of the King, who was at that moment entirely subjugated by his mistress, the Duchesse d'Étampes. This beautiful, but bad and inordinately ambitious woman, who was designated as '**La plus belle des** sçavantes, et la **plus** sçavantes des belles,' had been one of the Queen-Mother's maids of honour. The King married her to an old courtier, and created her Duchesse d'Étampes. She was of an intriguing spirit, fostered discord, and interfered in political measures, always working counter to the Queen, who strove to keep peace, especially between her brother and husband.

The Duchess also hated the Dauphin, (afterwards Henry II.,) and between her and the famous Diane de Poictiers (already firmly established in the favour of the Prince) the spirit of rivalry raged fiercely.

When Henry II. succeeded to the throne **the all-powerful** Diane exiled the Duchesse d'Étampes, whose **downfall was complete.** Amid all the pomp of the Court, Queen Eleanor had reason to regret her quiet life at Lisbon, where she was at least admired and respected. When Francis died, his widow went to reside, first in the **Netherlands,** and then in Spain. She died at Talavera, and **was buried in** the Escurial.

No. 96.

ELEANOR OF AUSTRIA.

BORN 1498, DIED 1558.

Black and white dress and head-dress, both richly ornamented with pearls and diamonds.

SISTER to Charles V., Emperor of Germany. **Married** first the King of Portugal, and secondly the **King of France.**

No. 97
MAXIMILIAN EMPEROR OF GERMANY.
By Albert Dürer.
BORN 1459, DIED 1519.

Head. Furred dress and cap. Collar and badge of Golden Fleece. Gold diapered background.

HE son of Frederick III., Emperor of Germany, by Eleanor of Portugal. In his childhood he was nicknamed 'The Dumb,' from the difficulty he had in articulating; although in after years he was remarkable for the sweet tone of his voice. A romantic story is told in connection with him and the beautiful Princess he afterwards married.

Charles the Bold, the last Duke of Burgundy, had been much struck with the young Archduke (in an interview with the Emperor) when Maximilian was only fourteen, and made so vivid a description of his appearance and promising qualities as to interest the fancy of his fair daughter and influence her future choice. On the death of her father, Mary, (then Duchess of Burgundy,) finding herself involved in a war with France, and a series of difficulties with her Flemish subjects, felt the importance of securing a strong firm spirit, to protect and counsel her.

Amid the crowd of suitors of all nations who competed for the hand of the richest heiress in Europe, the fairest Princess in Christendom, she selected the young Archduke Maximilian.

He began his married life by a war with Louis XI. of France, but it was not of long duration. His good and beautiful wife survived her marriage but two years, dying from the effects of a fall from her horse while engaged in her favourite pastime of hawking; she left a son and a daughter.

On her death the States of Flanders, regarding the Archduke with great distrust and jealousy as a foreigner, rose in revolt, and even disputed with him the guardianship of his own children. Maximilian's life, indeed, was one of continual warfare, but though a brave, he was not considered on the whole a very successful General. He at one time formed an alliance with France against England, and at another with England against France: now friendly with, now opposed to, the Swiss, the Venetians, and others. On succeeding to the Imperial throne, he married, as his second wife, Bianca Maria, sister of Galeazzo Sforza, Duke of Milan, who brought him a large dower.

This match was most distasteful to the proud Germans, who refused to recognise the 'Bastard' as Empress, and threatened that, in the event of her having children, they should not be recognised as Princes of the blood-royal. But (perhaps fortunately for herself) Bianca was childless.

This union with an Italian led Maximilian into further warfare. He formed an alliance with the Pope, with his brother-in-law the Duke of Milan, and several States of Italy, to arrest the progress of the King of France, then marching on Naples, but this undertaking was not successful in the end. His energetic and ambitious spirit involved Maximilian, not only in constant wars, but caused him to take part in all the struggles of the day, religious and political. He was a man of remarkable vigour, learning, and skill in all martial exercises, but renowned for his extravagance, which brought him into so many straits that he gained the nickname of 'Sans Argent,' and was often without the means of defraying the pay of his soldiers. He helped to form the celebrated League of Cambray, and presided at the Diet of Worms, etc. etc.

He admired the manly and independent spirit of Luther, and showed himself no ways averse to the reform of Church abuses, although he did not survive the movement long enough to take a decided part on either side.

His health was now fast declining, and strange fancies took possession of his mind. Being dissatisfied with the construction of a palace he had ordered at Innsprück, he said, 'I will build myself another house,' and sending for a carpenter, told him to make a coffin with all speed. For four years this ghastly reminder accompanied him in all his marches and wanderings. Maximilian died at Wels, in Upper Austria, it is said his death was accelerated by eating too freely of melon! Finding his end approaching, he prepared for it, with much calmness; making his will, giving the most eccentric orders concerning his interment, and joining with fervour in the prayers for the dying which were being offered up in his presence. His body was at a later period transferred to Innsprück, where the Emperor Ferdinand I. erected a magnificent tomb to his memory. It is of white marble, representing in high relief the principal events of his most eventful life, while on either side of the mausoleum, noble statues in bronze of illustrious sovereigns, knights, and dames of all ages and nations, form a body-guard round Maximilian's last resting-place.

He had only two children, Philip, afterwards Emperor of Germany and King of Castille, in right of his wife, 'Mad Joan,' as she was called, (the only child of Ferdinand and Isabella,) by whom he had Charles V., and Ferdinand, who both succeeded to the Imperial throne. Maximilian's only daughter, Margaret, was sent on the death of her mother to France, to be educated with the children of Louis XI., who designed the little heiress as bride for the Dauphin Charles. The betrothal took place with great pomp and ceremony when Margaret had attained the advanced age of three years. But in 1491, Charles, who had then succeeded his father as King of France, resolving on an alliance with Anne, heiress of Brittany, sent his little child-wife back to her father, an indignity which Maximilian resolved to wipe out in French blood.

Margaret afterwards married John Infant of Spain, and secondly Philibert Duke of Savoy, and she eventually became Governess of the Netherlands.

Albert Dürer was much esteemed not only by the Emperor Maximilian, but by his successors Charles and Ferdinand.

LARGE UPPER CORRIDOR.

LARGE UPPER CORRIDOR.

No. 98.

THOMAS WENTWORTH, EARL OF STRAFFORD.

AFTER VANDYCK.

BORN 1594, EXECUTED 1641.

In armour. Holding a baton.

HE eldest son of Sir William Wentworth, of Wentworth Wodehouse, county York, by Anne Atkinson, of Stowel, county Gloucester. Educated at home, and afterwards at Cambridge, where he gained an excellent reputation for conduct and study. His father dying when Thomas was twenty-one, he found himself at that early age the Master of Wentworth, of large estates and property, the husband 'of a fair wife,' (the daughter of Francis Earl of Cumberland,) and the guardian of a flock of young relatives, yet he found time not only for the diligent pursuit of study, but for the relaxations of 'hunting, hawking, and fishing;' in fact, for all the varied business and pleasures of a country life.

But he was not long allowed to remain in the privacy of Wentworth, being elected member for York, and Custos Rotulorum. This was in the place of Lord Savile, who had been compelled to resign for misconduct. But Sir Thomas had not held the office long before the Duke of Buckingham requested him to retire, that Savile might be reinstated, a proposition which so nettled his high spirit that he couched an indignant refusal in terms that made a lifelong enemy of the haughty favourite.

Sir Thomas was for some time a silent member in the House of Commons, although warmly espousing the Liberal side in politics, and making a vigorous stand against the encroachments of the Court party, a course he pursued after the accession of Charles I. The hatred of Buckingham was not likely to be appeased by such conduct, and through his instrumentality Wentworth had the office of High Sheriff thrust upon him in order to disqualify him from voting, and soon afterwards he was summarily dismissed from the post of Custos Rotulorum. He received the Royal despatch while sitting on the bench of magistrates, and reading it aloud with pardonable indignation, observed, 'It might easily be believed by what means I could retain my post, but that would cost too dear. Yet I know of no fault in myself, or virtue in my successor, that would justify such a step.'

In the ensuing year he stoutly refused to contribute to a loan levied without the consent of Parliament, and was summoned before the Council, where, while animadverting on the conduct of the 'Court vermin,' Wentworth took the opportunity of expressing his devoted loyalty to the person of Charles I., and his desire to serve His Majesty in any manner compatible with his own sense of patriotism. Nevertheless he was sentenced to be imprisoned in the Marshalsea, an act of injustice which did not prejudice him in favour of his persistent enemy the Duke of Buckingham and his party.

On his release Wentworth became a vigorous leader of the opposition, 'and took the field,' as it was said, 'with the Pyms and the Prynnes' against the King's Government, supporting with all the eloquence of which he was master, the memorable Petition of Rights to which the King was compelled to give a tardy, but full consent. Then Sir Thomas Wentworth adopted that sudden line of conduct, which has been so differently judged, so differently described, by different historians. He declared his conviction that the nation might now be well content with the concessions made by the Crown, bade adieu 'to the Pyms, the Prynnes,' and their policy, walked over to the other side of the House, went through the form of a reconciliation with the Duke of Buckingham, and proffered his services, head, heart, and sword, to the Royal cause. The opposition (above all the 'Puritan party') was worked to a pitch of fury, and heaped opprobrium on his name,—'an apostate, a traitor, a time-server;' while the Royalists upheld the conduct of a man who chose the moment of impending danger to rally round the unsteady throne and the unpopular Sovereign.

Charles naturally received him with open arms, and the honours which were heaped upon him increased the ire of his enemies. His former ally, Pym, meeting him one day at Greenwich, uttered these ominous words: 'You are going to leave us, but I will never leave you while you have a head upon your shoulders,' a promise too cruelly redeemed. The murder of the Duke of Buckingham removed every obstacle to the advancement of Sir Thomas Wentworth; he was raised to the Peerage by the titles of Baron and Viscount Wentworth, and being appointed to the arduous post of Lord Deputy, and Commander-in-chief in Ireland, he sailed for that 'distracted country' with a code he had drawn up for his own government in his pocket, from which he never swerved.

Lord Wentworth's administration of Irish affairs, his transient popularity, his reforms in all matters, civil, military, and religious, his quarrels with the Irish nobles, punctilio in matters of form and etiquette, his hurried voyages to and from England, are all subjects of deep interest, but too lengthy to be discussed here. It would have been well for him if he had taken the advice of his life-long friend and correspondent, Archbishop Laud, and 'curbed his impetuosity, and avoided prosecutions, and the like.'

The correspondence between these two remarkable men, (whose friendship, in the spirit of their joint motto and watchword, was 'Thorough',) although treating, for the most part, of grave and important subjects, was interspersed (more especially on the Prelate's part) with playful raillery and constant allusions to the sports of the field, in which they both delighted. The Lord Deputy had gained great odium in consequence of a severe sentence passed by him, in a court-martial, upon an Irish Peer, as failing in his duty as an officer, and the cry was so great against him that Wentworth judged it best to go and tell his own tale to the King of England.

On his return to his government a harder task than ever awaited him. Finding that the disaffection of the Scotch to the Crown had produced a baneful influence on the sister country, he set himself to work to counteract that influence, and his prompt and vigorous measures made him (already too well provided with enemies) an object of detestation to the greater part of the Scottish nation. In 1639 he again crossed to England, where he received the long-coveted Earldom of Strafford, was nominated Lord-Lieutenant of Ireland, taken into the King's full confidence, and became for a time virtually Prime Minister. War with Scotland, Parliaments summoned in England and Ireland, and subsidies demanded,—these were some of Strafford's proposed measures. From his own privy purse he contributed (as an example) £20,000 towards defraying the expenses of the coming campaign.

To make use of a homely proverb, 'The grass was never allowed to grow under' Strafford's feet. He crossed to Ireland, called a Parliament, obtained large subsidies, summoned a council of war, raised a large body of men to serve under his command in Scotland. Then he took a painful farewell of his beloved children,—'those dear young whelps, God bless them! for the old dog there is less matter,' and all this in the space of one fortnight.

Borne down as he was by continued ill-health and increasing bodily infirmities, Lord Strafford was so anxious to return to England that he insisted on crossing in a storm which daunted the sailors, and he had nearly died at Chester; yet, in spite of all expostulations, he resolved to proceed to London, and caused himself on his arrival to be carried into the Council-chamber in a litter, to all appearance in an expiring condition.

But too much remained for him to do, and the spirit was victorious over the body. On the dissolution of Parliament, Strafford accepted a military command, (against the Scots,) under the ostensible command of the Earl of Northumberland, who, however, was either too sick, or feigned to be so, to prove efficient, and the real duties fell to Strafford's share. He came up with the King at York, and found the army in a sad plight—'hope and spirit fled, and the Royal cause in the dust.'

Unable to walk, scarcely able to sit upright on his saddle, his energy was indomitable. He rallied the troops, upbraided the sluggishness of the leaders, and set a brilliant example to the whole army. But the King stayed his hand, and thwarted the vigorous tactics of his General, the command was in fact taken from him, although Charles was eager in his praises, and gave Strafford the Garter at York. He, moreover, insisted that they should travel together to London—two victims hastening to their doom.

Strafford was averse to the plan, foreseeing the danger which menaced him at the opening of Parliament, and his presentiment was realised, for a few days after the commencement of the session Pym began his long-meditated attack.

The bloodhounds were on the track, the hunt was up!

Lord Strafford was in the House of Lords, when Pym appeared at the bar to impeach him of high treason. He was allowed but a short time to say a few words, and was compelled to listen to the charge on his knees, then given into custody, and lodged in the Tower.

We deeply regret the limited space which forbids us to do more than glance at the circumstances of Strafford's trial and defence, though in truth it is a well-known tale.

A Scotchman, and an enemy, gives a most graphic description of the noble scene which Westminster Hall presented on the occasion, crowded to the roof—the King, the Queen, the whole Court and nobility of England, ladies of the highest rank, whose tears flowed copiously, and who were unanimous in their verdict in favour of the illustrious prisoner.

It was well said by the elder D'Israeli, 'that Strafford's eloquence was so great as to perpetuate the sympathy which it received in the hour of his agony.' He had, indeed, need of eloquence. Every obstacle was thrown in his way, especially in the matter of summoning witnesses in his favour, while his personal enemies were invited from all parts of England, Scotland, and Ireland. His confidence was betrayed, his words perverted; the proceedings were unlawful and unprecedented; but the Solicitor-General overruled such arguments by declaring that for 'wolves and wild beasts of prey' no law could be given, and that the prisoner ought to be knocked on the head.

Whereupon with difficulty a bill of attainder was provided, and some members who gave negative votes had their names posted up in the city as 'Straffordians.' The two Houses had passages of arms on the subject; but the vultures were hovering round, and would not be disappointed of their prey. Thus Thomas Earl of Strafford was declared guilty of high treason.

We will not dwell on the sad passage in Charles's sad life.

He had pledged his royal word, 'You shall not suffer in honour, in fortune, or in life.' Feeble attempts at intercession with the dreaded power of the Parliament, hesitation and delay, and then he signed the death-warrant of his devoted friend, weeping as he did so—yet he signed, laying up for himself hours of deep remorse, during the few years that he survived. The generous captive indeed wrote to his master to absolve him from his promise, but when he learned that he must prepare for death, he raised his eyes to heaven, exclaiming, 'Put not your trust in princes, or in any child of men.'

During the short interval between the sentence and the execution, the prisoner, 'resigned and at home with his own fate, experienced in full all that inward strength which had grown up with the unconscious religion of a noble life.'[1]

He busied himself with his religious duties, with the settlement of his worldly affairs, and in writing wise, tender, and pathetic letters to his relatives, particularly to his eldest son. He petitioned to be allowed an interview with his well-loved friend and fellow-prisoner, Archbishop Laud, but was cruelly refused, and only permitted to send him a message, asking his prayers, and entreating that he would wave him a blessing as he passed to execution.

Accordingly on the 12th of May 1641, Strafford, on his way to the scaffold, raised his eyes to the window of the cell where Laud was confined, and perceived the Prelate's aged and trembling hands extended through the bars, in token of a solemn farewell.

So overcome was Laud by grief and emotion, that he fell backwards on the floor of his dungeon in a swoon.

The avenues to the Tower were lined with thousands of eager spectators, and the lieutenant hurried his prisoner into the carriage lest he should be torn in pieces. Strafford smiled, and said 'it mattered little to him whether he died by the

[1] Mozley.

hands of the executioner or by those of the people.' He had
'faced death too often to fear it in any shape.'

The mob glared on him as he passed, but offered him no
indignity, for he marched, says a spectator, 'like a general at
the head of his army, bowing with lofty courtesy to the gazing
crowd.' His friend Archbishop Usher and his brother Sir
George Wentworth were already on the platform when he
came, as he said, 'to pay his last debt to sin, which was death.'
He submitted to the judgment with a contented mind. He
affirmed that his whole aim through life had been the joint
and individual prosperity of the King, and the people, although it had been his misfortune to be misconstrued: 'right-
eous judgment,' he said, 'shall be hereafter.'

He stoutly denied the charges of upholding despotism
and Popery, asked forgiveness of all men whom he had
offended, and prayed that 'we may all live to meet eternally
in heaven, where all tears shall be wiped from our eyes, and
sad thoughts from our hearts.' Then he prayed for some
time, concluding with the Lord's Prayer; bade farewell to
those near him, and embracing his brother, delivered the most
pathetic messages to different members of his family, to his
sister, his wife, with admonitions to his eldest son 'to fear
God, be a good subject to the King, and faithful to the
Church of England,' etc. etc.; forbidding him to harbour any
feelings of revenge. 'Give my blessings also to my daughters,
Anne, ('the sweet little Mistress Nan, his loved companion,
the image of her dead mother,') to Arabella, named after the
dear saint, to the little infant who cannot speak for itself—
God speak for it. One stroke,' he said, 'will make my wife
husbandless, my children fatherless, my servants masterless,
and separate me from my dear brother and all my friends.
But let God be to you, and to them, all in all.' About to take
off his doublet, he thanked God he could do so as cheerfully
as ever he did when going to bed. And then he looked

round and forgave the executioner and all the world. It was indeed an imposing scene: Strafford apparently restored on that momentous day to all the energy of health and vigour; his tall and symmetrical figure, his regular features, with a complexion 'pallid, but manly, black, like polished armour that had received many a hack and bruise in the battle of life.'

Once more he knelt in prayer, between the Archbishop of Armagh and the minister, tried the block, and finally having warned the executioner that such would be the sign, he stretched forth his white and beautifully formed hands, those hands which Vandyck has immortalised, which Henrietta Maria, his sworn enemy, had pronounced 'the finest in the world,' and one stroke from the cruel axe ended the mortal career of Thomas Earl of Strafford. Yet his name still continues a firebrand, between contending parties, in religion and politics. His faithful and devoted friend, Sir George Radcliffe, pays a most touching tribute to his memory in a well-sketched mental portraiture, and among many noble traits he mentions 'that my Lord was not angry when told of his weaknesses, though let it be remembered that by nature he was of a hot and hasty spirit, for he was a man and not an angel, yet such a man as made conscience of his ways, and did endeavour to grow in virtue and victory over himself.'

He was thrice married, first, as we have already said, to Lady Margaret Clifford, who died childless; next to the Lady Arabella Holles, daughter to the Earl of Clare, by whom he had one son, his successor; Anne, married to Lord Rockingham, and Arabella, married to the son of my Lord Clancarty.

Of Lord Strafford's second and best loved wife, Radcliffe writes: 'She was a lady exceeding comely and beautiful, and yet more lovely in the endowments of her mind.'

There was a mystery attending his third marriage, (which was clandestine,) with Elizabeth, daughter to Sir Godfrey Rhodes. They parted almost immediately after the ceremony, and he was some time before he would acknowledge her openly. Their correspondence was singular, in one letter he promises to be a good husband; in another, he reminds her that she is the successor of two of the noblest ladies of the time. Laud, in writing his congratulations, is rather jocose on the subject, but it does not quite appear whether the doubt existed as to the lady's character, or to the fitness of her birth and breeding. Her husband's letters to her during his trial are couched in affectionate terms. She bore him several children, one of whom alone survived him.

Of his connection with that beautiful schemer, Lady Carlisle, the 'Erinnys of politics' (born Percy), there can be no doubt, and the undue influence she exercised over him,—she who (says Sir Philip Warwick) changed her gallant from Strafford to Pym, going over to his deadly enemy.

But there were many other names coupled with his, apparently without any reason, save the love of slander.

No. 99.

CHARLES THE FIRST, KING OF ENGLAND.

AFTER VANDYCK.

BORN 1600, SUCCEEDED 1625, EXECUTED 1649.

Robes, Collar and Order of the Garter.

THE second son of James the First by Anne of Denmark. Married Henrietta Maria of France. Dethroned and beheaded by his subjects.

No. 100.
THREE CHILDREN OF CHARLES THE FIRST.

AFTER VANDYCK.

CHARLES, PRINCE OF WALES, AFTERWARDS KING.
Light dress. Lace collar.

JAMES DUKE OF YORK, AFTERWARDS KING.
White frock. Lace cap.

PRINCESS ROYAL, WIFE TO THE PRINCE OF ORANGE, AND MOTHER TO WILLIAM THE THIRD.
Two dogs beside the children.

No. 101.
HENRIETTA MARIA, QUEEN OF ENGLAND.

AFTER VANDYCK.

BORN 1607, DIED 1669.

Blue dress, with flowers in her lap.

DAUGHTER of Henry IV., King of France, by Marie de Medicis, and wife of Charles the First, King of England.

No. 102.

WILLIAM, SECOND DUKE OF HAMILTON.

After Vandyck.

Born 1616, died 1651.

Mantle, Ribbon, and Star of Garter.

ECOND son of James, second Marquis of Hamilton, by Anne, daughter of James Conyngham, seventh Earl of Glencairn. Educated at the University of Glasgow, and afterwards travelled in foreign countries. His brother, who was ten years his senior, was the friend and companion of King Charles I., who raised him to a Dukedom. William, in returning home after his tour, reckoned on his brother's influence for promotion at Court, and applied for the post of Master of the Horse to the Queen. The refusal he met with, although founded on the plea of a previous promise to another, so angered young Hamilton that he announced his intention of going back to France, and it was with difficulty he was dissuaded from so doing by prospects of speedy advancement. He had not long to wait. In 1639 he was created Baron Polmont and Machanshire, and Earl of Arran and Lanark, and the following year Secretary of State for Scotland, honours which must surely have satisfied this ardent and ambitious spirit, although Scotland was at that moment in such a state of fermentation that the direction of her affairs was far too arduous for a young man totally unacquainted with public business. Lord Lanark therefore looked to his brother as a man of ability and experience for advice and guidance. The mother of the two Hamiltons, a determined and energetic woman, had early instilled into the mind of her first-born the religious tenets in which she had been educated by her father, a staunch Covenanter; and the elder had no difficulty in imparting his views to the younger brother, and the two young men conceived, says Lodge, 'the impracticable scheme of uniting and reconciling the actual monarchy with a Calvinistic Church.'

For two years Lord Lanark strove, on the one hand, to persuade the King to make all manner of humiliating concessions to the Covenanters, while on the other he used fruitless endeavours to stem the tide of the rebellious outbreak; and naturally he was unsuccessful in both instances. Charles's partiality for the house of Hamilton was no help to him in his troubles north of the Tweed. In 1642, the Scotch having called a Parliament without the royal sanction, the King wrote,—' If, notwithstanding our refusal, and the endeavours of our well affected subjects and servants to hinder it, there shall be a Convention of the Estates, we wish all those who are right affected to us should be present at it, but do nothing but only protest against their meeting and actions.' The Hamiltons accordingly took their seats, but were silent members on most occasions. Their conduct in several instances was most inconsistent, and when the Scotch Parliament, following the example of their English brethren, levied troops in the King's name to make war on Charles himself, Lanark actually affixed the royal signet to the proclamation for the levy!

Such behaviour naturally incensed all true-hearted Royalists, and the Duke of Montrose especially was so disgusted that he hastened to Oxford, where the Court then was, to denounce the brothers. They on their part, discovering his intention, thought it wisest to follow him, but were arrested and imprisoned on their arrival. Lanark soon found means to escape to London, and afterwards to Scotland, where he recommenced his temporising policy, professing all the while deep attachment to the King, which did not prevent his joining the Covenanters against the Duke of Montrose. So contradictory a proceeding led to the rumour that he acted in obedience to secret orders from the King himself, who soon afterwards received him back into favour, and reinstated him in the Secretaryship of which he had been deprived. Charles's conduct with regard to the Duke was inexplicable, for when that nobleman, who had been for some time a prisoner in Pendennis Castle, Cornwall, (whence he was released by the chances of war,) joined the King at Newcastle, he was received without the slightest signs of anger. Neither did Charles resent the manner in which Lanark endeavoured to enforce the bitter terms proposed by the Scottish Parliament, although he resolutely refused to submit to such conditions. This was in 1646, when the idea was entertained of delivering up the person of the King to the English Commissioner. Lanark, however, was roused on this occasion, and exclaimed indignantly, 'As God shall have mercy on my soul at the great day, I would choose rather to have my head struck off at the Market Cross of Edinburgh than give my consent to this vote.' He was now in constant attendance on the King, who treated him with great confidence. The Duke of Hamilton placed himself at the head of an army of Scottish Royalists, and made an irruption into England, but was defeated by Cromwell's forces and taken prisoner. His trial and execution followed shortly after that of the King himself; and about the same time, Lanark, being deprived of his public offices and proscribed by the Government, fled to Holland.

It was not, indeed, till his arrival in that country, Clarendon says, 'that he knew he was Duke Hamilton by the slaughter of his brother;' Charles II. received the new Duke with affection and sympathy. Lanark had loved his brother with a blind affection, which led to his following him on many occasions against his own views.

He said his condition had been very hard, for having been bred up in the Church of England, for which he had a great reverence, he had been forced to comply with the Covenant, which he perfectly detested. Charles gave him the Garter, and took him in his suite to Scotland, where, not being permitted to enter the capital, he retired to the isle of Arran, whence he was recalled by the King's orders.

At the commencement of the ensuing year he raised a body of men for His Majesty's service, and distinguished himself at their head against the English Roundheads in Scotland, and was appointed Lieutenant-General of the Scotch army under orders to cross the Border. Hamilton's inclination was to march on London, but his wishes were overruled by the King. Cromwell came up with the Royalist troops, and gave them battle at Worcester—a sad day for England's nobles, when so many fell. Bishop Burnet tells us how devoutly and piously the Duke passed the vigil of his last battle. Stationed at his post at an early hour, he saw with dismay (shortly after the commencement of the action) his own regiment in retreat, and rashly galloped forward to rally the fugitives. A shot in the leg shattered the bone, and the brave General fell into the hands of his enemies. But the wound (though it proved mortal) saved him from the fate that had attended his brother. He only survived eight days, the surgeons quarrelling all the time over the question of amputation. There is a tradition in Worcester that the body of the Duke was buried provisionally, under the hearthstone, in the room of a hospital, (now a Blind School,) called the Commandery, before it was transferred to the Cathedral. Lord Clarendon says of Duke William: 'He was much to be preferred to his brother, a wiser, but less cunning man, an accomplished person; and though he had been led into some unwarrantable actions, it was evident it was not through his own inclination. In his death he showed a great cheerfulness, that he had the honour to die for the King, and thereby wipe out the memory of his former transgressions, which was odious to himself.' Burnet says from a child he could never on any temptation be made to lie.

His faults seem to have been greatly owing to a blind adherence to the proceedings and opinions of his brother. The Bishop describes William Duke of Hamilton 'as of middle stature, complexion black, but very agreeable, and his whole mien noble and sprightful.' He married in 1638 Lady Elizabeth Maxwell, eldest daughter and co-heir of James Earl of Dirleton, in Scotland, and by her had one son who died an infant, and five daughters.

No. 103.

MARTIN LUTHER.
BORN 1483, DIED 1546.

Black gown and cap.

THE biography of 'the day-star of the Reformation' belongs to the history of the world, and we have no space for a notice of the principal events of his life. He was the son of a miner, originally intended for the study of civil law, but being struck by lightning, his mind took a strong religious turn, and he eventually became a priest. It is well known how his indignation was aroused by the sale of indulgences, and other abuses of the Church of Rome, and with what indomitable courage and energy he upheld and promulgated his opinions, enduring persecution, danger, and imprisonment for conscience' sake. He married Catherine von Bora, who had been a nun, a step which gave great offence in many quarters.

He is one of those men whose name is a history in itself.

No. 104.

CHARLES PRINCE OF WALES, AFTERWARDS KING CHARLES THE FIRST.

After Vandyck.

Full length. In armour. Red and gold trunks. Riding boots, one top turned down to show the Garter. Helmet on the ground.

No. 105.

HENRY THE FOURTH, KING OF NAVARRE, AND OF FRANCE.

BORN 1553, MURDERED 1610.

Full length. In armour, with a white scarf, blue ribbon, and Order. Boots and spurs. Helmet on the ground.

E was the son of Anthony de Bourbon and Jeanne d'Albret, Queen of Navarre. Brought up by his mother in the strictest principles of the Protestant faith, whose champion he became, defending it by speech and sword. He was heir to the throne of France, as well as Navarre, in right of descent from Louis IX., called St. Louis. On the death of Henry III. he succeeded him as King, and it was then he embraced the Roman Catholic faith, although he watched over the interests of his former friends as far as was consistent with the policy of his government.

The Edict of Nantes in 1595 was most advantageous to the Huguenots. Henry was for some time involved in foreign warfare, but peace was at length established. Though having at heart the improvement and the well-being of his subjects of all conditions, yet parties ran so high that his life was constantly attempted. It was reserved for the hand of a fanatic, one Ravaillac, (a monk, whose ill conduct had caused him to be expelled from his convent,) to terminate the valuable life of this great and noble Prince. He was twice married, first to Margaret de Valois, sister to Charles IX., the King and Queen-Mother having elected to make the terrible massacre of St. Bartholomew one of the features of rejoicing for these ill-starred nuptials. From her he was divorced, and married as his second wife Marie de Medicis.

No. 106.

EDWARD STAFFORD, DUKE OF BUCKINGHAM.

After Holbein.

EXECUTED 1521.

Brown vest, blue sleeves. Red mantle with fur. Black cap, and jewel.

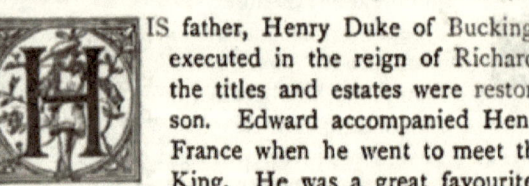

IS father, Henry Duke of Buckingham, was executed in the reign of Richard III., but the titles and estates were restored to his son. Edward accompanied Henry VIII. to France when he went to meet the French King. He was a great favourite with his Sovereign, which caused him to be an object of jealousy at Court, and his downfall was planned by influential foes, amongst whom Wolsey was accounted the chief. Buckingham was the last to occupy the post of Lord High Constable of England, an office of great power and emolument. Accused of high treason, his enemies went so far as to say he aspired to the Crown, it having been prophesied by one

Hopkins, a monk, that King Henry would die without male issue. The Duke was found guilty on very insufficient evidence, and beheaded on Tower Hill. His name and memory are endeared to us, through the inspired pages of Shakespeare—the eloquent description of his character given by the King himself, even while he promised him no mercy, and the appeal of Queen Katherine, pathetic, but unavailing, 'that the Lord Cardinal should deliver all his evidence in charity.'

No. 107.

HENEAGE FINCH, EARL OF NOTTINGHAM.

By Sir Peter Lely.

BORN 1621, DIED 1682.

Robes and badges of office.

SIR Thomas Finch, Privy Councillor to Queen Elizabeth, holding many lucrative offices under the Crown, had an only daughter, Elizabeth, by his wife, the daughter of Sir Nicholas Poyntz, of Acton Poyntz, county Gloucester. Sir Thomas left his heiress a very large fortune, and she married Sir Moyle Finch, and was the grandmother of the first Earl of Nottingham of that name. Sir Moyle died in 1614, and his widow was created Viscountess Maidstone in 1623, and in 1628 further advanced to the grade of Countess of Winchilsea. Her fourth son, Heneage, was a celebrated lawyer, Speaker of the House of Commons, and the friend of Bacon. He married the daughter of Sir Edmond Bell of Beaupré, county Suffolk, and their eldest child was the subject of this memoir.

He was born at his father's beautiful estate of Eastwell in

Kent, but passed most of his youth at Kensington, which property, it may here be observed, was purchased by William III. of Finch's grandson, and has remained in possession of the Crown ever since.

Heneage received a good education at Westminster and Oxford, and went to Christ Church in 1645, where he was steady and studious; but the sudden death of his father, from whom he inherited a large fortune, called him away from the University before he had taken his degree. Rich as he was, it did not suit the young man's taste to remain without a profession; **and he began to study law in the Inner Temple,** where he soon gained **a name for fluency of** speech and readiness of reply, and **was called to the bar** before the usual time in consideration of his proficiency.

During the Protectorate Finch contented himself with an extensive private practice, and having married Elizabeth Harvey, daughter of a London merchant, lived a happy domestic life with his 'pretty and dearly-loved wife.' He came of too loyal a family, and shared their opinions too truly, to be popular with the powers that then were, or to seek their favour.

His kinsman, Sir John Finch, (Speaker of the House of Commons,) had made himself so obnoxious to the Government that he had found it advisable to fly the country, while another cousin was in actual attendance on the King's person.

At the time of the Restoration, Heneage Finch contrived to ingratiate himself with His Majesty by getting up a memorial, signed by the principal inhabitants of his county, to show forth that none of 'the men of Kent' had had any participation in the ' murder of Charles the Martyr.' At all events, it was not long after his Restoration that the King summoned him from his retreat, named him Solicitor-General, and gave him a Baronetcy. In return for these honours perhaps it might have been that Sir Heneage pursued the prosecution of the regicides with great violence, and would willingly have brought John Milton to condign punishment on account of his political tendencies.

He served in several Parliaments for Canterbury, Oxford, etc., but never gave up his profession, and as a true Templar he acquired great '*kudos*' (in 1601) by an eloquent course of lectures, which he delivered, in his capacity of Reader, at the Temple. Surely that time-honoured pile had never witnessed such a brilliant concourse as flocked to listen to the law and learning of the future Lord Chancellor. All the dignitaries of London, in the robes of their respective callings, municipal, clerical, commercial, legal, and the last day of the course many Peers of the realm, members of the royal household, in barges of State, attended by servants in scarlet and white doublets, the King's own Majesty, accompanied by the Duke of York, Prince Rupert, and numerous grandees. This was but the shadow of coming honours.

Sir Heneage continued in Parliament for some time, now gaining, now losing, popularity with his constituents, for voting as he thought fit on important measures.

In 1670 he became Attorney-General on the death of Sir Jeffrey Palmer, having exercised the duties of the office for some time past. His ambition, however, suffered a temporary disappointment, when, on the removal of Sir Orlando Bridgeman, he saw his rival, Lord Shaftesbury, elevated to the Woolsack in his despite.

But he had not long to wait for his enemy's downfall. At the end of 1673 the Great Seal of England was consigned to him, and the beginning of the next year saw him Lord Keeper, with the title of Baron Finch of Daventry, in the county of Northampton, and other dignities.

In 1677 he sat as Lord High Steward of England on the trial of Philip Earl of Pembroke, and in 1680 on that of William Howard, Viscount Stafford, where his speech, in which he passed sentence on that unfortunate nobleman, (accused of plotting against the King,) was pronounced a model of eloquence, but scarcely of justice. Burnet, who found great fault with him in many ways, testifies to his probity, yet other writers insinuate that he consulted the royal wishes on many points of law, at least before he had attained to the heights of his ambition.

Be that as it may, he was very firm on all matters where the interests of the Reformed Church were concerned. In his latter days Lord Finch became so great a sufferer from gout that he was for some time incapacitated from attending his duties in public, and he did not long survive the last mark of royal favour, dying within a year after the Earldom of Nottingham had been conferred on him.

This great lawyer, who has been called 'the Father of Equity,' and 'Finch the Silver Tongue,' died at his house in Queen Street, Covent Garden, and was buried at Ravenstone, near Olney, county Bucks, where a grand monument assigns him every virtue under the sun. He had fourteen children, of whom the eldest son was the ancestor of the present Earl of Winchilsea and Nottingham, and the second of the Earl of Aylesford.

Lord Nottingham was a liberal patron of literary men, and encouraged rising talent. As Bishop Warburton quaintly expresses it, (in a letter to Lady Mansfield, Nottingham's granddaughter, and wife of the celebrated Judge,) 'He was elegantly ambitious to give the last polish to his country by patronage of learning and science.'

In the distribution of Church preferment he was very conscientious, and often said, 'God knows, I would not willingly appoint one unworthy.' He was by no means of a grasping disposition, and having a good private fortune, gave up of his own accord £4000 a year, which was allowed him in his official capacity for the expenses of the table.

In 'Absalom and Achitophel,' Dryden contrasts him, (by the name of Amri,) in most complimentary terms, with Lord Shaftesbury.

Alluding to the English laws, the poet says he had fathomed them all :—

> 'No Rabbin speaks like him, their magic spell,
> So just, and with such charms of eloquence ;
> To whom the double blessing does belong,
> With Moses' inspiration, Aaron's tongue.'

Worth says, that 'the business, rather than the justice of the Court, flourished exceedingly under Finch.' Another opinion has it that 'he was a formalist, and took much pleasure in encouraging and listening to nice distinctions of law, instead of taking a broad view of the equity of each case.' So do historians differ. It was said he had such fear of thieves stealing his wand of office, that he used to sleep with the mace under his pillow.

No. 108.

GEORGE MONCK, DUKE OF ALBEMARLE.

By Sir Peter Lely.

BORN 1608, DIED 1670.

Gold armour. Mantle, collar, and badge of Garter. Left arm akimbo. Right hand holding a truncheon.

A NATIVE of Devonshire. When a youth of seventeen he became involved in some local quarrel, where, says the *Biographie Universelle*, 'par excès d'amour filial, il maltraita le sous-Sheriff d'Exeter.' He was sent to sea, and served at one time under the Duke of Buckingham. In 1629 he entered an English regiment in Holland, where he studied the art of war with great diligence, and was remarkable for his steadiness of conduct, and the discipline he maintained among the soldiers, treating them at the same time with uniform kindness. In 1639 he returned to England; and in Charles I.'s disastrous expedition to Scotland, Monck displayed great skill in command of the artillery, though productive of no good results. He then went to Ireland on promotion, where he did considerable service, and was made Governor of Dublin; but the Parliament intervening, he was suspended from the office; and on the conclusion of a treaty (by the King's command) with the Irish rebels, he once more returned to England.

On his arrival he found that doubts of his fidelity had been implanted in Charles's mind, but on joining him at Oxford, he completely cleared himself, was promoted, and ordered to relieve Sandwich, where he was taken prisoner by the Roundheads and sent to the Tower. During the two years of his captivity Monck steadily refused all overtures made to him by the Protector, and occupied his leisure hours in making notes on military and political subjects. Cromwell entertained a high opinion of his soldier-like qualities, and offered him the alternative of prolonged imprisonment or a command to put down the Irish rebels under O'Neill. Monck accepted the latter, but was ill supported by the Government at home, so much so that he was reluctantly compelled to sign a truce with the insurgents. For this he was called to account on his return to England, but he was too useful that Cromwell should afford to quarrel with him again; and so he was despatched to Scotland, where he did much service. The Protector at the time was well aware of the General's loyal proclivities, and wrote to him shortly before his death: 'There be those that tell me there is a certain cunning fellow in Scotland called General Monck, who is said to lie in wait there to introduce Charles Stuart. I pray you to use your diligence to apprehend him and send him up to me.'

The share which Monck took in the Restoration is too well known to be repeated here. Charles called him his father, gave him the Garter, created him Baron Monck, Earl of Torrington, and Duke of Albemarle, and appointed him Lieutenant-General of the forces of the United Kingdom, with a large income.

In 1653 he married or acknowledged his marriage with Anne, daughter of John Clarges, who had long resided under his roof,—'a lady,' says Guizot, 'whose manners were more vulgar and less simple than those of her husband, and who was the laughing-stock of a witty and satirical Court.'

The French historian speaks disparagingly of the great General, but in the time of the plague, when the King and Ministers left London, the Duke remained to watch over the necessities of the wretched inhabitants, to save families from pillage, and to alleviate the sufferings of the poor. He was afloat when the fire occurred, and the general cry was : ' Ah, if old George had been here, this would not have happened.'

He died in his sixty-second year, leaving an enormous fortune to his spendthrift son Christopher, and was buried in Westminster Abbey with great splendour, Charles II. attending the funeral. Guizot says: 'C'etoit un homme capable de grandes choses, quoiqu'il n'eut pas de grandeur dans l'âme.' His jealousy of his noble comrade Lord Sandwich seems to bear out the French historian's opinion in some measure. In his last illness he was much occupied in the arrangement of the alliance of his surviving son Christopher (the death of the elder had been a terrible blow to him) with the heiress of the wealthy Duke of Newcastle. His death was peaceful : he expired in his arm-chair without a groan.

HENRY BENNET, EARL OF ARLINGTON.

By Sir Peter Lely.

born 1618, died 1685.

Black dress, white sleeves. Sitting holding a letter. Black patch on his nose.

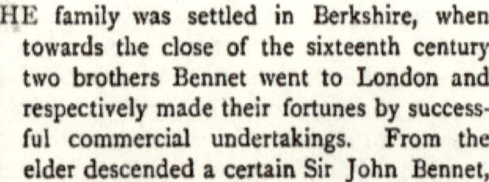

THE family was settled in Berkshire, when towards the close of the sixteenth century two brothers Bennet went to London and respectively made their fortunes by successful commercial undertakings. From the elder descended a certain Sir John Bennet, living at Dawley, county Middlesex, who married Dorothy, daughter of Sir John Crofts of Saxham, county Norfolk. The subject of this notice was their second son. He was carefully educated under the paternal roof, but went to Oxford, and was entered a student at Christ Church, where he took his degree as B.A. and M.A., and was much esteemed both as scholar and poet. He remained some time at the University, where he was still a resident when the Court arrived in 1644.

He was presented to King Charles, and soon after entered the army as a volunteer. Lord Digby, then Secretary-of-State, took a fancy to young Bennet, and appointed him Under-Secretary. But this post did not interfere with his military duties, he was ever in the field 'when honour called,' and was so severely wounded at Andover, in an engagement near that town, as to be invalided for a long time. He was indeed dangerously ill, and there is little doubt that it was in one of these encounters, that he received the scar by which he is so well known in all his portraits.

Deeply attached to the Royalist cause, on the termination of the war Bennet went to France, and on into Germany and Italy, never losing sight of the hope of once more joining and serving the house of Stuart. In 1649 he was summoned to Paris by James Duke of York, to fill the post of private secretary.

King Charles, writing to his brother, says: 'You must be very kind to Harry Bennet, and communicate freely with him, for as you are sure that he is full of duty and integrity to you, so I must tell you that I shall trust him more than any about you, and cause him to be instructed in those businesses of mine, when I cannot write to you myself.'

Charles's letters to Bennet also plainly show the terms of intimacy and trust which existed between them.

This was especially remarkable as regarded the affairs of Spain; and in 1658, Sir Henry Bennet, Knight, was sent as Ambassador to Madrid. Clarendon says the step was at the instigation of Lord Bristol, but at this time there was strife between the new Ambassador and his former patron. Henry Bennet, with all the zeal that usually characterises a recent convert to Catholicism, was very anxious that his royal master should make his profession to the same faith, whereas Digby, or rather the Earl of Bristol, (as he had become,) though himself a Roman Catholic, considered that such a step would be ruinous to Charles's interests, and opposed it stoutly. Great bitterness in consequence existed between Bristol and Bennet, increased by the jealousy excited in the mind of the former with regard to Bennet's mission, being under the impression that he himself was far better fitted for the post.

Sir Henry, however, seems to have pleased most parties in his diplomatic capacity; and at the Restoration he was sent for by the King, who gave him the office of Privy Purse, and made him his constant companion. Bennet was well calculated to suit the taste of the Merry Monarch. Burnet tells us he had the art of observing the King's humour, and managing it, beyond all the men of his time; and Clarendon gives us a clew to one of the reasons, when he mentions that 'Bennet filled a principal place, to all intents and purposes, at the nightly meetings,' (alluding to the King's jovial suppers in Lady Castlemaine's apartments,) added to which, he was most lively and sparkling in conversation.

In 1662 Charles bribed Sir Edward Nicholas to resign his Secretaryship of State, (and that with a considerable sum,) that he might bestow the vacant post on his favourite. The contrast between Bennet's entire submission to the Royal will and the honest rectitude of the Chancellor (Clarendon) increased the King's dislike to that worthy servant of the Crown, on whose downfall Bennet rose still higher.

In 1663 he was raised to the Peerage as Lord Arlington, whereupon Clarendon threw some ridicule on the choice of the title, taken from an obscure village in Middlesex, which had once belonged to Bennet's father, but was now in the possession of another family.

While at the head of public affairs, no measures of any importance were undertaken, with the exception of the first Dutch war.

In 1670 was formed the famous Cabal Ministry (spoken of more fully in our notice of Lord Shaftesbury) which Arlington consented to join, and of which his title formed one of the initials.

So notoriously now did he consult the King's wishes rather than the public good, that he was rewarded in 1672 by the dignity of Baron Thetford and Earl of Arlington, and later invested with the Garter. Being sent on an embassy to Utrecht, in company with the Duke of Buckingham and Lord Halifax, (which was productive of no good results,) he afterwards turned his attention to the overthrow of the Cabal, in the breaking up of which he was most instrumental. He however fell into great disrepute with both Catholics and Protestants about this time, the Duke of York (on the passing of the Test Act) loading him with every kind of abuse, while the opposite side charged him with endeavouring to introduce Popery.

The Duke of Buckingham was loud in censure of Lord Arlington, who was impeached, and, after making a long defence, acquitted by a small majority. He held office for a short time longer, and advocated a treaty of peace with the Dutch, but soon after resigned office, having received (it was said) a douceur from his successor of several thousands.

In 1674 he was named Chamberlain of the Household in recompence (so ran the Royal declaration) 'of his long and faithful services, and particularly of his having discharged the office of principal Secretary of State to his Majesty's entire satisfaction.'

Lord Arlington's wish to be again employed in public affairs was not gratified till 1675, when he once more went on a diplomatic mission to Holland, in company with the Earl of Ossory. Lady Arlington and Lady Ossory were sisters, and members of the house of Nassau. This was his last appearance in public life. Burnet says that 'Arlington entirely mistook the character of William Prince of Orange,' with whom he had to deal; speaking to him in a dictatorial manner, which was not at all agreeable to that Prince, although he was then young in years. Arlington still held a place in the royal household, but he had fallen into disgrace, and the King encouraged and enjoyed any jest, or ridicule, at the expense of his former boon companion. Nothing delighted Charles more than to see some of his courtiers put a black patch upon their noses, and strut about with a long white staff, in imitation of 'Harry Bennet.'

James II. on his accession did not remove Arlington from his post in the household, but he only survived a few months, dying in July 1685.

He was buried at Euston, in Suffolk. He married Isabella, daughter of Lewis de Nassau, Lord of Beverwart, in the United Provinces, by whom he had an only child, Isabella, married, in 1672, to Henry Fitzroy (son of Charles II. by Barbara Villiers), who was created Earl of Euston and Duke of Grafton.

No. 110.

THE HONOURABLE HENRY THYNNE.

BY SIR GODFREY KNELLER.

BORN 1675, DIED 1708.

Blue coat. Full wig.

HE eldest son of the first Lord Weymouth, by Lady Frances Finch, daughter of the Earl of Winchilsea. He was of a studious and literary turn of mind, and delighted in the companionship of his father's guest, Bishop Ken, in conjunction with whom he formed a pleasant coterie of cultivated spirits at Longleat. Henry Thynne was a good linguist, and, as we have mentioned in the notice of Bishop Ken, gave lessons in French and Latin to the young poetess afterwards known as Elizabeth Rowe. He married Grace, daughter and sole heir of Sir George Strode of Leweston, county Dorset, by whom he had two daughters, Frances Countess of Hertford, and Mary, married to William Greville, Lord Brooke, who died in the nineteenth year of her age. Lady Hertford inherited her father's taste for literature, and became a patron and friend of divers authors, many of whom are well known to fame, while others were only local bards. For instance, Pope and Thomson were her guests, while she patronised and befriended Stephen Duck, known by the title of 'The Wiltshire Thresher.' Henry Thynne died before his father, at the age of thirty-three.

No. 111.

WILLIAM CAVENDISH, DUKE OF NEWCASTLE.

By Abraham van Diepenbeke.

BORN 1592, DIED 1676.

He is dressed as a Roman warrior in armour, leading his wife by the hand. She wears a yellow robe, and has a white veil on her head. Several children in fantastic costumes. Horses. One of the children is mounted on horseback.

HE was the son of Sir Charles Cavendish, (who was brother to the first Earl of Devonshire of that family,) by a daughter and co-heir of the last Lord Ogle. Educated at home, and then at Cambridge, he was made Knight of the Bath when Henry (son to King James I.) was created Prince of Wales. He accompanied Sir Henry Wotton on his embassy to Savoy, who writes of him as 'a young man nobly bred, and of great expectations.' The Duke of Savoy took a fancy to Cavendish, offered him a high post in his army, and loaded him with valuable presents when he returned to England.

In 1620 he was created Lord Ogle and Viscount Mansfield, having already succeeded to the paternal estates. Charles I., after his accession, further created him Lord Cavendish of

Bolsover and Earl of Newcastle, and subsequently Governor to the Prince of Wales, with a seat in the Council.

Newcastle was much liked at Court. 'The King esteemed him highly, as did Wentworth, but Buckingham was jealous of him.' His manner of living was splendid; indeed, it was said of him later in life, that he went to battle in a coach-and-six. He entertained the King and Queen at his dwelling-houses of Welbeck and Bolsover in so sumptuous a manner as to make a great noise.

When the war broke out with the Scots, he was one of those loyal nobles who contributed large sums towards levying troops for the Royal service, and he raised a regiment at his own expense, which he named the Prince of Wales's Own. It was on account of a question of precedency for this regiment, (in which many members of the Cavendish family held commissions,) that Newcastle quarrelled with Lord Holland, General of the Horse, and no sooner was the army disbanded, than he sent that General a challenge, but the King having gained intimation of the impending duel, prohibited the same, upon which some of Newcastle's enemies accused him of avoiding the encounter from want of personal courage, a statement ill borne out by his proverbial valour.

Shortly after this he resigned his post at Court, and retired **to his** own estates; but, on the breaking out of the Civil War, **he** once more buckled on his armour, and resumed the military career for which Clarendon tells us ' he had neither talent nor inclination, but pursued from sheer loyalty.' Collins gives a very different version, enumerating manifold victories which Newcastle was mainly instrumental in gaining, in the north of England, more especially the battle of Bradford, where the rebels were defeated, and where he took twenty-two great guns, and many colours.

In 1642 he met the Queen at Burlington, when she landed with supplies, and escorted her to Oxford, where the

King then was, for which and other services he was made Marquis of Newcastle and Knight of the Garter.

In 1643 his first wife died. Newcastle had a stormy time of it in that most stormy period, not only through the vicissitudes of war, not only in the battlefield, but through bickerings and jealousies in the army, and 'slanderous pens,' which often tempted the Marquis to throw up his command in disgust. This design he carried into effect, immediately after the battle of Marston Moor, where he commanded the right wing of the Royal army. He took ship at Scarborough, and, accompanied by several relatives and friends, sailed for Hamburgh. He spent many years on the Continent, frequently visiting his royal master Charles II. in Holland, and when the King was invited to Scotland, his faithful servant asked permission to attend him, but was refused by the Scots. While abroad the Duke and Duchess of Newcastle (for he had married a second time) were in most straitened circumstances, and were often compelled to pawn their clothes to procure the necessaries of life, the English Parliament having seized upon most of his estates and revenues, and cut down his timber, which caused the Duchess to go over to England, as we shall presently see. The noble exiles, after many wanderings, had settled in the City of Antwerp—'my Lord choosing it for the pleasantest and quietest place to retire himself and his ruined fortunes in.' It was here he wrote that splendid work on Horsemanship which adorns most of our finest libraries, and by which the name of the Marquis of Newcastle will ever be remembered.

At the Restoration they returned to England, when he received a dukedom, but he resolved to have no more to do with public life, and retired to the shade of the few ancestral trees his enemies' axes had spared him. The Duke's remaining years were spent in the society of his beloved wife and valued friends, and in the pursuit of his favourite occupations. He died at an advanced age, and was buried in Westminster Abbey, where stands a monument to him, on which are represented the forms of William, Duke of Newcastle, the 'loyall Duke,' and his wife, side by side. He was brave and accomplished, loved riding, dancing, singing, and was so devoted to poetry, that he was said to have made Sir William Davenant his Lieutenant-General of Ordnance, more on account of his proficiency as a poet, than for any knowledge of military affairs. 'His courage,' says Sir Philip Warwick, 'was invincible, but his edge had too much of the razor in it.' He was a strong upholder of monarchy and the Church, though not very nice as to points of creed. We have no room for one hundredth part of the eulogiums pronounced on him by his Duchess, but of his exterior she tells us that 'his shape was exactly proportioned, his stature of a middle size, his complexion sanguine, his behaviour a pattern to all gentlemen, courtly, civil, and fine, without formality,' and so forth; while another account of him was, 'a fantastic general and a virtuoso on horseback!' From the heading of one of the chapters in his book, it is evident he was very proud of his proficiency as an equestrian, for he says, 'Some, seeing, imitate, and imagine they ride as well as I do.'

His first wife was Margaret Basset of Blore, county Stafford, relict of Henry Howard, son to the Earl of Suffolk, by whom he had a very large family, and of whom her successor records that 'she was a kind, virtuous, and loving lady, who blessed her husband with dutiful and obedient children, who did all in their power to relieve and support their father in his banishment.'

Margaret Lucas, Newcastle's second wife, is better known to fame. Her epitaph says 'she was youngest sister to Lord Lucas of Colchester, a noble familie, for all the brothers were valiant, and all the sisters virtuous. This Duches was a wise, wittie, and learned lady, which her manie books doe testifie. She was a most loving, virtuous, and careful wife, and was with her lord all the time of his banishment and miseries, and when he came home, never parted from him in his solitary retirement.' She was a voluminous writer in a quaint and high-flown style, and a great favourite of Charles Lamb's, whose mention of her in Elia causes her perhaps to be better known than her own literary merits may lay claim to. Elia says, 'where a book is good and rare, such a book, for instance, as the life of the Duke of Newcastle, by his Duchess, no casket is sufficiently durable to honour and keep safe such a jewel.'

In 1643, the year in which Lord Newcastle lost his first wife, Margaret Lucas went to the Court of Henrietta Maria, where, she tells us, her gravity, reticent, and virtuous timidity, which ill assorted with the courtly manners of the period, caused her to be regarded as a simpleton. She did not relish the life, but remained on, by her mother's wish; and when the Queen fled to France, Margaret Lucas accompanied her.

In 1645, Newcastle, being in Paris, saw, and loved the Maid of Honour, who became his wife. The union was most happy. They loved each other truly, and had many pursuits and tastes in common, notwithstanding which a story is told that the Duke, being once complimented on the talent of his wife, replied, 'Sir, a wise woman is a very foolish thing.'

The Duchess was of graceful person, reserved, and reticent. Her piety, generosity, and charity, were proverbial, and, as we have before observed, when her husband's affairs were involved, she went to England, where she spent a year and a half, endeavouring with the help of her brother and brother-in-law to get some compensation for the property seized by the Parliament. 'Then I made haste to return to my Lord, with whom I had rather be as a poor beggar, than to be mistress of the world, absented from him.' And they were happy, 'though fortune did pinch their lives with poverty.'

It would seem that this picture must represent Margaret Lucas, since the first wife was never Duchess; the introduction of the horses, too, would surely imply that the portraits were painted after, or at the time, the book on Horsemanship was published; when we surmise also that Newcastle made the acquaintance of the painter Diepenbeke at Antwerp, though he accompanied the Duke to England.

No. 112.

SIR THOMAS OVERBURY.

By Zucchero.

BORN 1581, POISONED 1613.

Oval. Black coat. Red and white sash. Lace collar. Pointed beard.

AS of a good family in Warwickshire. Born at Compton Scorfen, the home of his maternal grandfather. Entered Queen's College, Oxford, as gentleman commoner, where he studied logic and philosophy, and afterwards went to the Middle Temple.

His father, having been bred to the law, wished he should pursue the same calling, but Thomas preferred the study of polite literature, and the allurements of a Court life.

After a brief tour on the Continent he went to Scotland, where he became acquainted with Robert Carr or Kerr, then page to the Earl of Dunbar, and, forming a close friendship, they travelled to London together. Writers appear to be at variance as to the date when King James I. saw, and took a fancy to young Carr; and the story of his falling wounded from his horse, in a tilting-match, at the King's feet, requires confirmation.

But there was no doubt that he soon stood high in the royal favour, and Carr was one who well knew how to improve his opportunities, being of a time-serving disposition, and no way above flattery. His education had been neglected, and the 'royal pedant,' as James has so often been called, undertook to teach the youth Latin. Whether he prosecuted his studies with much zeal we do not know, but he was an adept in the art of self-aggrandisement; and, believing in Overbury's disinterested friendship, he consulted him on every step he took. Interceding with the King for his friend, he gained the honour of knighthood (for honour it was indeed esteemed in those days) for Thomas, and managed that the father Overbury should be made a judge. This was about 1608.

Carr himself was raised to the peerage by the title of Viscount Rochester. He became enamoured of the Countess of Essex, (wife to the third Earl of the Devereux family, and daughter to Howard, Earl of Suffolk,) then but eighteen years of age, 'of a sweet and bewitching countenance, hiding a wicked heart.' She was headstrong into the bargain, and her passion for Carr knew no bounds. She hated her husband, her father, and all who expostulated with her on her shameless conduct, and smiled on no one but her lover and 'sweet Mistress Turner,' her go-between.

It has been adduced against Overbury, that he at first encouraged the intrigue, but when the question of a divorce arose, he left no stone unturned to dissuade Rochester from the attempt to procure one, which brought down upon him the lasting hatred of the beautiful termagant. Overbury warned his friend, that it would be destructive to his future fortunes to marry a woman whose husband was still living; moreover, that her conduct was infamous, and would brand them both with ignominy. Peyton (Sir Thomas's servant) describes the quarrel which took place between his master and my Lord of Rochester on the occasion.

Overbury waited 'in the chamber next the privy gallery' for the return of Rochester, who did not appear till three in the morning. High words passed between them, my Lord asking angrily what Sir Thomas 'did there at that time of night;' Overbury replying by the question,' Where have you been? Will you never leave the company of that bad woman?' But all his warnings and admonitions were thrown away, and only insured him the deadly enmity of both lovers. The King, who was not likely to be deterred by any sense of rectitude from the weak pleasure he found in complying with any demand that Rochester might make, not only connived at the passing of the divorce, but created **Carr** Earl of Somerset, as he was not considered of sufficiently high rank to marry one who had been a Countess. The lovers now turned their thoughts to the ruin of their quondam friend. It was easy in those days to procure a commitment to the Tower, and Sir Thomas Overbury soon found himself within those dreary walls, Somerset pretending all the while the greatest friendship for the prisoner.

Overbury's father wrote him a pleading letter in behalf of his son, but Sir Thomas was not allowed to see any friends. There can be no doubt of the fact that his food was drugged, and he fell into bad health; but his constitution was strong, and he languished for some time.

The perfidious Somerset sent him a white powder that he was 'convinced would be efficacious. He might,' he said, 'take it without fear, even if it produced sickness, which sickness may be a plea for your release.'

The unfortunate man's release was by the hand of death. He died from the effects of strong poison administered to him medically, and was buried with indecent haste. Ugly rumours were abroad, and the names of Lord and Lady Somerset were in many mouths, but few cared to come forward as accusers while the mantle of Royal protection was thrown over them.

But 'Robie' was supplanted at Court by 'Steenie,' or in other words, by George Villiers, afterwards Duke of Buckingham; and when his star was in the ascendant, then the mouths of many were opened. About this time too, a curious incident occurred which helped to confirm the suspicions concerning Overbury's mysterious death.

One day that Lord Salisbury was entertaining at the same time, at dinner, Sir Gervase Elwes (Governor of the Tower at the time of Overbury's death) and Sir Ralph Winwood, Secretary of State, his lordship recommended the former to the patronage of the latter, upon which Winwood said how much he wished Elwes could clear himself of the imputation of murder that had been cast upon him. Whereon he (Elwes) spoke out, and confessed all, together with the share that the Earl and Countess of Somerset had had in the terrible transaction, and so it came about that the guilty pair were arrested with the consent of the King.

The hypocritical James, taking leave of his ex-favourite, embraced him with every show of affection; but no sooner had he left the apartment, than he cried out: 'The devil go with thee, for I will never see thy face again.'

The trial of persons so high in position, and so well known in royal circles, caused a great sensation, and the Court was crowded with ladies and great personages. Lord Somerset wore a dress of black satin, and a gown of uncut velvet, his ruff and cuffs were of cobweb lace, neither had he forgotten to wear his George and Garter, or have his hair carefully curled. His handsome face was very pale, and he pleaded not guilty. 'He trusted to the justice of the Lords to acquit him.' He denied everything, even his own letters, which he said were 'counterfeit.'

The lady was arraigned next day, and her demeanour, which we are told by a contemporary was 'sober,' was altogether different from that of her husband. She pleaded guilty with a low obeisance. She several times covered her face with her fan, during evidence given, but she confessed everything. She shed (or made a show of shedding) some tears divers times. Her deportment, says the same authority, 'was more curious and confident than was fit for a lady in such distress.'

Yet it is also said of her that her voice was scarce audible from fear, when she hoped the Lords would intercede for her. The verdict was, that the Earl and Countess of Somerset, with several accomplices, were guilty of devising and compassing the murder of Sir Thomas Overbury.

The King, fickle and cruel as he was, appeared very uneasy during the trial, even going so far as to lose his appetite for dinner and supper; but he did not like the idea of signing the death-warrant of the two people at whose wickedness he had connived; so he signed their pardon, and they were committed to the Tower—the lady not being taken thither till after her confinement, when it is said she shed a few tears over her new-born daughter, and was removed to prison.

The accomplices, Elwes, Weston, and the beautiful but infamous 'Mistress Turner,' Lady Somerset's go-between in her amours, and abettor in the murder of Overbury, with others, were all executed.

An eye-witness speaks of the bewitching appearance of the fair Mistress Turner on the scaffold. 'I saw her die,' says the letter alluded to—'her powdered hair, her yellow bands, her starched ruff;' and a poem that was written, called 'Overbury's Vision,' speaks of the cruel cord that did 'misbecome her comely neck; yet by man's just doom had been her death.' 'Sighs and tears and Court vanities,' etc. etc.

Lord and Lady Somerset lived together in the Tower till 1622, when an order from the King in Council set them at liberty, prescribing for them, however, a place of residence. James intended to restore their property, which was forfeited, but died before the fulfilment of his promise, and Charles I. did not see fit to ratify the same. They were in consequence reduced to great poverty, and the passion which had led them to such fatal extremes turned to loathing; so that, although residing under the same roof, Lord and Lady Somerset lived as strangers, and the miserable woman died of a most painful disease, crying out in her last moments on the name of the husband she had so basely injured: 'Oh, Essex! Essex!'

A touching incident is told of their daughter, the wife of the Earl of Bedford. Her portrait by Vandyck is well known, and her sweet fair face and lovely form live in more than one gallery. Lord Somerset dearly loved his only child; the affection was mutual, and she reverenced his memory; but one sad day, as the lovely Lady Bedford sat reading by the window, she came accidentally across a pamphlet which opened her eyes to the complicated guilt of both her parents. The shock was too much for her, and the next person who entered the room found her in a swoon on the floor, with the open book beside her.

We have perhaps afforded too much space, in a notice purporting to be a life of Sir Thomas Overbury, to the story of Somerset and his wife, but the lives are so intimately connected, that we hope to be held excused. Overbury had a reputation for wit and talent, and wrote several pieces in prose and verse.

No. 113.
THOMAS, SECOND MARQUIS OF BATH,
WHEN YOUNG.
BY HOPPNER.
DIED 1837.
Maroon-coloured coat. White waistcoat.

No. 114.

JOHN RUSSELL, SIXTH DUKE OF BEDFORD.

BORN 1766, DIED 1839.

Seated in a red chair. Black coat. Wig.

E was the second son of the Marquis of Tavistock, by Lady Elizabeth, daughter of the second Earl of Albemarle, of the Keppel family. Lord Tavistock was killed by a fall from his horse in 1767, and his widow died of grief. Of their three sons the two eldest succeeded to the Dukedom and estates, and the third (posthumous), Lord William, was murdered by his valet Courvoisier in 1840. In 1786 John Russell married Georgiana Byng, second daughter of the fourth Lord Torrington, who died in 1801, and two years afterwards Lady Georgiana, daughter of the fourth Duke of Gordon, which lady died in 1853. The Duke had children by both marriages.

No. 115.

SIR KENELM DIGBY.

OLD STONE, AFTER VANDYCK.

BORN 1603, DIED 1665.

Black dress. Pointed beard.

ON of Sir Everard Digby, born at Gothurst or Gayhurst, county Bucks, the property of his mother, daughter and sole heir of William Mulsho.

He was but a child when his father suffered death, as one of the conspirators in the Gunpowder Plot. The Crown laid claim to the estates and revenues of the family, but the widowed Lady Digby, a woman of great energy and determination, not only saved her own dower, by her strenuous efforts, but rescued a few hundreds for her son out of the wreck, and, although a rigid Roman Catholic, she suffered her boy to be educated as a Protestant from prudential motives. The romance of the loves of Kenelm Digby and Venetia Stanley, which made such a noise at the time, and has been the subject of curiosity and controversy ever since, whenever their names are mentioned, began at a very early age. Sir Edward Stanley of the noble house of Derby lived at Tong Castle, county Salop. He married the daughter and co-heir of the Earl of Northumberland, who brought him two daughters, 'the divine Venetia' being the youngest. Her mother died when she was a few months old. The widower gave himself up to grief, shunned all society, and could not even derive comfort from the society of his children. He sent them therefore (or at all events Venetia) to the care of a relative, who was a neighbour of Lady Digby's. Thus began the acquaintance, and Sir Edward's beautiful little girl and Lady Digby's lovely boy met constantly, and played at love-making, jealousy, rivalry, coquetry, quarrels, reconciliations,—in fact a perfect rehearsal of all the drama that was to be enacted in good earnest, a few years later. The marriage of the Princess Elizabeth with the Palatine, afterwards King of Bohemia, called Sir Edward to London. With a violent wrench he tore himself away from his beloved seclusion, and sending for Venetia carried her with him to the Court of King James, then the scene of great festivity.

In all these gaieties, according to Digby's account, the juvenile beauty took part, and was the centre of admiration. In the meantime her young lover pursued his studies under the care of Laud, Dean of Gloucester, subsequently Archbishop of Canterbury, and afterwards with Dr. Thomas Allen, an eminent scholar, at Oxford.

Digby distinguished himself at the University, where he remained two years, but whenever he returned home for the vacation, the flirtation with his fair neighbour was resumed. He wrote a strange and wild romance respecting her, in which it is impossible to disentangle truth from fiction, but some of the adventures are too marvellous for belief, and the whole narrative disagreeable, and tedious in to the bargain.

His jealousy seems to have been excited by a certain courtier, whose suit, he affirms, was favoured by Venetia's governess. Lady Digby was too wise a mother to smile on such a precocious courtship, even if she disbelieved the reports which had already begun to circulate, detrimental to mistress Stanley's reputation.

She despatched her son on foreign travel, but before his departure the lovers had met and plighted their troth. According to the traveller's own account he made a conquest of the French Queen when in Paris *en route* for Italy.

A report of his death having been accidentally or purposely circulated, Venetia's conduct on the occasion was differently represented to her absent lover, some declaring she was inconsolable, others that she lent a willing ear to the suit of the very same courtier who had before excited Kenelm's jealousy.

Nothing can be more bombastic and high-flown than the language in which he describes the fluctuations of his passion for Venetia, his implicit trust in her constancy in one page, his doubts and suspicions in another.

It seems more than probable that the prudent Lady Digby intercepted her son's love-letters, and did all in her power to prevent a marriage she thought most undesirable, and she was doubtless delighted when Kenelm accompanied his kinsman, Lord Bristol, to Spain, where he was then negotiating the Prince of Wales's marriage with the Infanta at Madrid. Kenelm became himself attached to the Prince's suite, and took an active part in diplomatic transactions.

In this land of romance it may well be imagined that the handsome and accomplished Englishman ran the gauntlet of many adventures among the dark-eyed daughters of the south, nor does he omit to allude to innumerable conquests; indeed, he went so far as to have a portrait of himself painted with an effigy of one of his victims in the background, but he incessantly boasted of his constancy to the absent loved one. On his return to England with the Prince of Wales, he was knighted by the King at Hinchingbrook, and immediately flew to his lady-love in spite of maternal prohibition. Then followed recriminations, explanations, trials of her faith and virtue, challenges, duels—a stormy suit, indeed, according to his own testimony.

Respecting the date of their marriage, there is great difference of opinion. At all events, Kenelm insisted on its being kept secret, nor was poor Venetia allowed to announce it, even when a fall from her horse brought on a premature confinement, which nearly cost her her life.

King James admired Sir Kenelm for his great erudition, and complimented him on his essays on Sympathetic Powder, Alchemy, and other subjects bordering on the supernatural, On the accession of Charles I. Sir Kenelm Digby was made gentleman of the privy chamber, commissioner of the navy, and governor of the Trinity House, shortly after which, he was appointed to the command of a naval squadron, sent to the Mediterranean against the Venetian fleet, and the Algerine pirates.

In this voyage he was eminently successful, bringing the Venetians to terms, chastising the pirates, and releasing a large number of English slaves. It is said that on the eve of his embarkation, a second son being born to him, he had permitted his wife to declare their marriage, and had consigned her to the care of his kinsman, Lord Bristol, during his absence from England. About this time, his faithful old friend, Thomas Allen, bequeathed to him a splendid library, which he made over to the Bodleian.

In 1633, after his return, his beautiful but far from happy wife died, and the mystery which had shrouded Venetia's whole life hung like a dark cloud over her death, and reports of all kinds were current.

There is no doubt that Sir Kenelm had been in the habit of making chemical and alchemical experiments on Venetia for some time past, and the tradition of the concoction of snails which he had invented as a preservative of her naturally brilliant complexion is still extant at Gayhurst, where it is said the somewhat rare breed of large 'Pomatia' is still to be found.

By Digby's desire, his wife's head ('which contained but little brain') was opened, and he decided that she had taken an overdose of viper wine. But spiteful women declared she had fallen a victim to a viper husband's jealousy, though Aubrey, who tells sad tales of Venetia before her marriage, says she was a blameless wife.

There is more than one portrait of her, with allegorical emblems of Innocence, Slander, and the like. Her name had often been coupled with that of the Earl of Dorset, and some said he had settled an annuity on her, which was paid up to the time of her death. Be this as it may, Sir Kenelm and Lady Digby always dined once a year with my Lord Dorset, who received them courteously but formally, only permitting himself to kiss the beauty's hand with great respect.

Venetia was buried in a church near Newgate, in a tomb of black marble, with long inscriptions, surmounted by a copper-gilt bust, all destroyed in the great fire. Numerous epitaphs were written in her honour. Ben Jonson calls her 'A tender mother, a discreet wife, a solemn mistress, a good friend, so lovely and charitable in all her petite actions, so devote in her whole life,' etc.

Whatever Sir Kenelm's real feelings were, his outward grief

was extreme. He retired to Gresham College, lived like a hermit, studied chemistry, wore a long mourning cloak, and left his beard unshorn. Although it was generally supposed that his secession from the Protestant faith took place when he was in Spain, it was not until 1653 that he wrote to his friend Laud (whose admirable answer is extant) to announce the fact. He was a firm adherent of Charles I., and greatly esteemed by Henrietta Maria; but his loyalty got him into trouble with the Parliament, and he was exiled to France. Returning in a few months, he was imprisoned in 1640 for nearly three years, and was supposed only to have regained his liberty through the intercession of the French Queen, who had loved him twenty years before. His release, however, was conditional. He was forbidden to take part in any public affairs, and he therefore gave himself up to literary and scientific pursuits, and engaged in a polemical correspondence with his quondam tutor, Laud, whom he is said to have tempted to change his faith, by the bait of a Cardinal's Hat. Sir Kenelm returned to France, and frequented the Court of his old flame, the Queen-Dowager, where his noble appearance, almost gigantic size, his handsome features, agreeable conversation and manners, his learning, and last, but perhaps not least, his predilection for the occult sciences, made him an universal favourite. On the death of his eldest son, killed on the Royalist side at the battle of St. Neot's, Sir Kenelm returned to compound for his estates, but was not suffered to remain in England. He went back to Paris, where Henrietta Maria made him her Chancellor. And he was then intrusted with a mission to Pope Innocent X., who welcomed him at first, but after a time the 'Englishman grew high, and hectored at His Holiness, and gave him the lie.'

Once more in England, after the dissolution of the Long Parliament, Cromwell took him into his confidence, hoping by his mediation to gain over the Roman Catholics.

His conduct in these circumstances has been praised by some and censured by others, as may well be imagined, according to religious and political bias. He travelled through France, Lower Germany, and the Palatinate, always seeking and being sought by men of letters; and 1660 saw him once more back in his native land.

Charles II. showed him but little favour. He was **nominated F.R.S.**, and resided (1663) in a fair house **in Covent Garden, where he** had a laboratory. 'Philosopher, theologian, **courtier, soldier**; polite, amiable, handsome, graceful.' Lord Clarendon's testimony is, 'eccentric, vain, unstable in religion, a duellist.' These are the counterbalancing portraits of Sir Kenelm Digby. He desired **to be buried** near Venetia. His epitaph was as follows:—

> 'Under this tomb the matchless Digby lies,
> Digby the great, the brilliant, and the wise;
> This age's wonder, for his noble partes,
> Skilled in six tongues, and learn'd in all the artes!
> Born on the day he died, th' eleventh of June,
> And that day bravely fought at Scanderoon:
> It's rare that one and the same day should be
> The day of birth, and death, and victory.'

He had four sons and one daughter.

No. 116.

SIR WILLIAM LYNCH.

IN PASTEL.

DIED 1785.

Blue coat. Red collar and cuffs.

SON of Dr. Lynch, Dean of Glastonbury, friend of the first Lord Bath's. Was Member of Parliament for Canterbury and other places.

No. 117.

ARCHBISHOP JUXON.

By Vandyck.

BORN 1582, DIED 1663.

In Bishop's robes.

THE son of Richard Juxon of Chichester, in Sussex, where he was born. Educated at Merchant Taylors' School, and in 1598 elected a Fellow of St. John's, Oxford. Destined for the bar, he studied civil law at the University, and took his degree of B.C.L. in 1603, having already entered as student at Gray's Inn.

He changed his mind, however, and read divinity with much diligence, took Orders, and was granted a living by his College,—St. Giles's, Oxford; but he removed in 1614 to Somerton, in the same county. In the east window of this church is his paternal coat of arms.

He kept up his connection with the University, and was much esteemed by Laud, afterwards Archbishop of Canterbury. This remarkable man, destined to play so conspicuous a part in public life, was then President of St. John's College, an office which he resigned in 1621, and it was chiefly owing to his exertions that Juxon was chosen to succeed him. In the same year Juxon became Doctor of Laws, and later on Vice-Chancellor of the University. Laud, who was first Bishop of Bath and Wells, and then of London, and high in favour with Charles I., interested the King in Juxon's preferment. He was appointed Chaplain-in-Ordinary to His Majesty,

Dean of Worcester, and Prebendary of Chichester, and, at Laud's particular request, Clerk of the Closet. This was in 1632, and Laud's object in the choice was said to have been his 'desire to have some one he could trust near the royal person, should he himself grow weak or infirm.'

New honours crowded on Dr. Juxon. He was elected to the Bishopric of Hereford in 1633, and made Dean of the King's Chapel, but before consecration was translated to the See of London, Laud having become Primate of England. Laud, it seems, had made himself unpopular in the diocese with many of its members, but the mild and genial temper of the new Bishop gained him much respect and kindly feeling. The Archbishop of Canterbury desired above most things the aggrandisement of Churchmen, and their preferment to public offices of State, and for that aim he worked both for himself and his friend.

Dr. Juxon was, through his influence, raised to the office of Lord High Treasurer, a post which had not been filled by a Churchman since the reign of Henry VII., and this step was much cavilled at by the greater part of the nation, especially by many members of noble families who considered themselves (from their position at least) better fitted for the situation than a clergyman hitherto little known beyond the precincts of his College, and only two years in the possession of a mitre. Loud and angry were the invectives poured on the Government, but more particularly on the Primate,—the Puritans, Laud's bitter enemies, being most violent on the occasion.

Juxon, in the meanwhile, by his wisdom and discretion, and the excellency of his administration, disarmed the anger of most of those who were so averse to his nomination, and, says Chalmers, 'when the Republican party ransacked every office for causes of impeachment, sequestration, and death, they found nothing to object to in Bishop Juxon.'

In 1641 he was one of the few manly and generous-hearted

Englishmen who defended the cause of Strafford. On the passing of the bill of attainder, which he had strenuously opposed, the Lord High Treasurer resigned his office, and retired to his palace at Fulham, where he remained quietly for some time, unshaken in his loyalty to the King, and often visited by persons of distinction, many of whom consulted him and valued his advice. Charles paid him this tribute: 'I will say, I never got his opinion freely in my life, but when I had it, I was ever the better for it.'

By consent of the Parliament, Juxon waited on the King at the treaty in the Isle of Wight, 1648, and by Charles's particular desire, at Cotton House, in Westminster, in January of the following year, at the commencement of the trial.

He now never left the King, who found in this excellent Churchman the greatest comfort and support. He stood beside his royal master on the scaffold, and when the last moment was approaching, 'There is, sir,' he said, 'but one stage more, which, though turbulent and troublesome, is still a very short one. It will soon carry you a great way: it will carry you from earth to heaven, and there you shall find, to your great joy, the prize to which you hasten—a crown of glory.'

'I go,' said Charles, 'from a corruptible to an incorruptible crown, where no disturbance can be.'

'You are exchanged,' said Juxon, 'from a temporal to an eternal crown—a good exchange.'

In taking his last leave of his faithful and devoted friend, Charles looked at him earnestly and said, 'Remember!' delivering at the same time his diamond George, to be given to his son.

The King's last word brought down upon the Bishop the wrath and curiosity of the regicides. They insisted on knowing what it signified.

They insisted also on Juxon's betraying the confidence of

his Sovereign, by detailing all his last conversations. So far the Bishop answered, that the King had charged him to instil into his son's mind the necessity of forgiving his murderers, and that the word 'Remember' had reference to this admonition; but this did not satisfy the suspicions of the inquirers. He accompanied the body to Windsor, where the cruelty of those in power forbade him to read the Funeral Service over the beloved remains. The Commonwealth deprived Juxon of his bishopric, and he retired to his private estate of Little Compton in Gloucestershire, where he remained for some time without molestation, occasionally indulging in the relaxation of field sports, to which he, in common with his Grace the Archbishop, was much addicted.

At the Restoration he was raised to the Primacy, and at the Coronation he placed the crown on the head of Charles II. During the short period of his Archbishopric, Juxon enlarged and improved Lambeth and Croydon Palaces, and greatly ameliorated the clerical state of the See. He died of a painful disease in 1663, and was interred with great pomp in St. John's College, Oxford, near the tomb of his friend and patron, Archbishop Laud. He left considerable sums to be laid out in Fellowships for his favourite College, and many charitable bequests. His reputation for moderation, piety, learning, and unswerving loyalty can scarcely be questioned. Not many of his genuine writings are extant.

No. 118.

WILLIAM LAUD, ARCHBISHOP OF CANTERBURY.

By Vandyck.

BORN 1573, BEHEADED 1645.

In Bishop's robes.

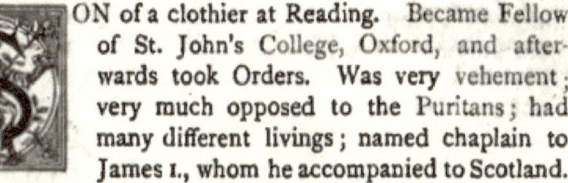

SON of a clothier at Reading. Became Fellow of St. John's College, Oxford, and afterwards took Orders. Was very vehement; very much opposed to the Puritans; had many different livings; named chaplain to James I., whom he accompanied to Scotland. Was Prebendary of Westminster; consecutively Bishop of St. David's, Bath and Wells, and London, and subsequently Prime Minister, and Archbishop of Canterbury. In 1622 he held a famous conference with Fisher the Jesuit, in the presence of the Duke of Buckingham and his mother, who were wavering in their allegiance to the Protestant faith, and were fixed therein by the eloquence of Laud. Yet it was said of him that he was more than once tempted to abjure his religion by the offer of a Cardinal's Hat; each time, however, he gave an emphatic denial. He was very strict respecting the revision and licensing of published books by high ecclesiastical authority, and was concerned in several prosecutions of the Star-Chamber against Bishop Williams, the Master of Westminster School, etc. etc. When the Parliament was abruptly dissolved in 1639, Laud was attacked in his palace at Lambeth by the mob. He had indeed made himself unpopular with the people at large, and with the House of Commons; and on the accusation of Sir Henry Vane, he was sent to the Tower in 1641, where he was detained three years, and treated with great severity. In 1644 he was tried, and though the treasonable charges were not proved, the bill of attainder was passed. He made an eloquent defence; but all in vain. The execution of Strafford was the forerunner of his own, and he suffered death on Tower Hill, displaying great courage. Clarendon says: 'Such learning, piety, and virtue have been attained by few, and the greatest of his infirmities are common to all men.'

Of all the prelates of the Anglican Church, Lord Macaulay says, Laud departed furthest from the principles of the Reformation, and nearest to Rome. He hated Calvinism, loved forms and ceremonies, and advocated celibacy among the clergy, all of which opinions made him an object of abhorrence to the Puritans, and there was no love lost. Every corner of the realm, every separate congregation, nay, it was said the private devotions of individuals, were subjected to the supervision of his spies. Unfortunately for himself and the country, Charles was influenced in all public matters by the precepts of the Primate. He was a staunch friend, a genial companion, shrewd and witty, and fond of field sports. In fact, all his tastes and qualities endeared him to Lord Strafford, as we have mentioned in the notice of that remarkable man.

BEDROOM A.

BEDROOM A.

No. 119.

PHILIP, FOURTH EARL OF PEMBROKE.

BY VANDYCK.

DIED 1649-50.

Tawny coat. Blue bows. Ribbon, Collar, and Order of Garter.

E was the second son of Henry Herbert, Earl of Pembroke, by the beautiful and talented Mary Sidney, the 'Sidney's sister, Pembroke's mother,' of 'rare Ben Jonson,' or, as Spenser describes her, 'the gentlest shepherdess that most resembled both in shape, and spirit, her brother dear.' Surely those who trace the inheritance of maternal qualities of mind in the child, are at fault in this instance. Philip received his education at New College, Oxford, but he was so illiterate that he could scarcely write his name. He went to Court at an early age; Rowland White, that amusing gossip, calls him 'Little Master Philip Herbert,' and three years afterwards says, ' he is the forwardest courtier that ever I saw, for he had not been here (at Court) two hours than he grew as bold as the best.'

The young man was at that time engaged in seeking a wife, and sued (unsuccessfully) the daughter, first of his kinsman, Sir William Herbert, and afterwards of Sir Arthur Gorges. In 1604, however, he espoused Susan, daughter of Edward de Vere, Earl of Oxford, the ceremony being performed with great pomp and magnificence. The King himself sent a fine present.

Sir Thomas Edmonds, in a letter to Gilbert Earl of Shrewsbury, (whose daughter, the Countess of Pembroke, was sister-in-law to Philip Herbert,) says, 'The gifts of gloves and garters alone amounted to wellnigh a thousand pounds.' The same authority, speaking of Herbert's growing favour with James I., says, 'he is desirous to doe all men goode, and to hurte no man.' But another contemporary seems nearer the truth when he observes, 'Sir Philip is intolerable, choleric, and offensive, and did not refrain to break wiser heads than his own.' He was constantly involved in some quarrel through his arrogance and insolence; and once being at some races at Croydon, he so raised the ire of Ramsay, afterwards Earl of Holdernesse, that the enraged Scot inflicted personal chastisement on Herbert, in the sight of the whole course.

But James made him Privy Councillor, and in 1605 Baron Herbert of Hurland, Isle of Sheppey, and Earl of Montgomery. He was already a Knight of the Bath, and shortly afterwards he received the Garter. Other dignities followed, and on the accession of Charles I., that King continued to distinguish this most unworthy man.

He was made Chamberlain, and Warden of the Stannaries; he is said to have beaten one Thomas May with his Chamberlain's staff in the banqueting-hall at Whitehall, and to have so far tyrannised over the people of Devon and Cornwall as to have endangered a rising in those counties. Charles I., whose kindness of heart so often betrayed him into culpable weakness, bore with Lord Montgomery's misconduct for some time, but after a disgraceful scene in the House of Lords between him and the Earl of Arundel, in which blows are said actually to have passed, the King availed himself of this opening to choose another Chamberlain.

Indeed both Lords were committed to the Tower for a time, and from that moment the Earl of Pembroke (for he had succeeded to the ancestral honours on the death of his brother) forsook the master who had laden him with benefits. He ranged himself with the King's bitterest enemies, and in 1642, being appointed one of the committee that waited on His Majesty at Newmarket, he urged (and that in so unbecoming a manner) that the King should relinquish the control of the militia to the Parliament, that Charles exclaimed indignantly, 'No, by God! not for an hour. You have asked that of me, was never asked of a king before.' Lord Pembroke was employed several times in negotiating between the King and Parliament; he became Chancellor of the University of Cambridge, where he was deservedly unpopular. He spoke in the House in a most intemperate and even absurd manner, and in 1649 accepted a seat, as representative for the county of Berks, in Cromwell's House of Commons. In the January following he died. By his first wife he had seven sons, of whom the fourth, Philip, succeeded him in his titles and estates, and three daughters. His second wife was the celebrated Anne Clifford, daughter and heir of George, third Earl of Cumberland, and widow of Richard Sackville, third Earl of Dorset. He treated her shamefully, endeavouring to force her to give her daughter Lady Isabella Sackville in marriage to one of his younger sons, striving hard to get possession of the young lady's portion. In a letter to her uncle, the Earl of Bedford, Lady Pembroke says, 'I dare not venture to come up without his leave, leste he should find occasion to turne mee out of this house, as he did at Whitehalle.'

She fortunately survived her tyrant many years. Lodge gives at length a most amusing lampoon, purporting to be Philip Earl of Pembroke's last will and testament. It was attributed to Samuel Butler.

We have only space for a few extracts :—'*Imprimis*, for my

soule, I confesse I have heard a great deal about souls, but what they are, and what they are for, God knowes, I knowe not. They tell mee of another worlde, I knowe not one foot of the way thither. When the King stood I was of his religion, then came the Scot and made me a Presbyterian, and since Cromwell I have been an Independent. I will not be buried in the church porch because I was a Lord. I will have no monument, because then I must have an epitaph, and verses, and all my life long I have had too much of them. *Item*, I give nothing to the Lord Say, because I knowe he will bestowe it on the poore. To the two Countesses, my sister and wife, I give leave now to enjoy their estates. *Item*, I give fifty pounds to the footman who cudgelled Sir Harry Mildmay, whom I threatened but did not beat. *Item*, As I restore other men's wordes, I give to Lieutenant-Generall Cromwell one worde of mine, because hitherto he never kept his owne, etc. etc. I give up the ghoste.'

No. 120.

ELIZABETH, QUEEN OF BOHEMIA.

By Honthorst.

BORN 1596, DIED 1662.

Black and gold dress.   Ruff.   Small crown.   Fan in her hand.

THE eldest daughter of James I. by Anne of Denmark, born in the Palace of Falkland, North Britain. On the accession of her father to the English Crown, the young Princess was intrusted to the care of the Countess of Kildare, daughter to Charles Howard, Earl of Nottingham, Lord High Admiral of England, James himself taking pleasure in occasionally presiding over

his daughter's studies. She afterwards went to reside with Lord and Lady Harrington at Combe Abbey, county Warwick, where she was very happy in the society of genial companions. Lord Harrington had two children—a son, who became the chosen friend of Henry Prince of Wales, and a daughter, Lucia, (afterwards Countess of Bedford,) whose beauty and learning inspired the muse of Dryden, Donne, and other poets. Lord Harrington's niece, Anne Dudley, was, however, the Princess's favourite playmate, and remained her fast friend in all her wanderings. The only drawback to Elizabeth's residence at Combe Abbey seems to have been the separation of brother and sister, for dearly did she love the Prince of Wales, and a touching little note is extant, written by her to Henry when he was only eight years of age: 'Most dear and worthy brother, I most kindly salute you, desiring to hear of you. From whom, though I am now removed far away, none shall ever be nearer in affection, than your most loving sister, Elizabeth.'

While staying at Combe, the Princess was treated most royally on all occasions, and there is a picturesque account of her first visit to Coventry, when only eight years old:—

'She was sufficiently expert in horsemanship to have headed the procession, but the degeneracy of the age was attested by their substituting a line of coaches, in one of which sat the gracious child, who bore her part bravely with the Worshipful the Mayor, the burghers, etc. etc.'

Even at that tender age Elizabeth was remarkable for that winning gentleness of manner and sweet courtesy, which, in after times, gained for her the title of 'Queen of Hearts;' but we have no space to linger over the details of the childhood of one whose after life was so eventful. When about sixteen, several overtures of marriage were made and rejected; amongst others, the hero, Gustavus Adolphus of Sweden, sought her hand.

Her parents were at variance on the subject, the Queen declaring her daughter should marry none but a Sovereign, while James, though loving her dearly, was less ambitious.

Frederick Elector Palatine had made himself acceptable to the King of Great Britain by his staunch support of the Protestant faith. He came to England as a suitor to the Princess Elizabeth, saw, loved, and was beloved in return. The Queen was much disgusted at her daughter's choice, and sneered at her as 'Goody Palsgrave,' but Elizabeth, backed by her father and her brother, was proof against ridicule, and declared she would rather marry a Protestant Count than a Catholic Emperor. A deep sorrow was in store, not only for the Royal family, but for the whole nation, in the death of Henry Prince of Wales, the idol of his father's subjects, but to Elizabeth the loss was irreparable. The marriage, however, took place on Valentine's Day 1613, with much pomp, and the union was very popular in England in spite of the Queen's ill-temper, James's vacillating humour, and the new Prince of Wales's milder dislike to the bridegroom. In a letter to the Duke of Buckingham he says: 'Steenie, I send you herewith two letters for my sister, and brother. I place them so, because I think the grey mare the better horse.'

Nor was he quite singular in his opinion.

The bride was accompanied by a goodly retinue of countrymen and countrywomen on her voyage, and many of them remained in her service, and shared her chequered fortunes. The newly-married pair took up their abode at Heidelberg, the capital of the Palatinate. Elizabeth's reception in her new country was, indeed, one calculated to delight her imagination, and gratify her heart. Frederick and his people planned all sorts of picturesque surprises, to which the lovely scenery of the Rhine formed a charming background, while his excellent mother and sisters vied with each other in extending a cordial welcome to the English Princess. At

Heidelberg they passed many happy years, leading useful and contented lives, doing good in their generation, beautifying and improving all within their reach, and welcoming to their Court not only the distinguished men of the country, but such old friends as Lord and Lady Harrington, the poet Donne, and others.

Frederick took great delight in planning and carrying into execution a beautiful garden, on the slope which surrounds the castle, for his wife's delectation, where her sweet spirit seems still to hover, at least to the English pilgrim who visits the shrine of which she was once the idol.

Alas for the ambition that lured them from this happy home! 'that preferred to eat bread at a kingly board rather than feast at an electoral table,' though, doubtless, the zeal of both husband and wife for the Protestant cause weighed in their decision.

Schiller has told the story better than we can. We shall therefore only remind our readers, as briefly as possible, of the principal incidents in which the Elector and his wife were implicated. The kingdom of Bohemia, hitherto elective, had just been made hereditary, but the king, Ferdinand, was a strong Papist, and therefore most unpopular with the Bohemians, who were staunch Reformers.

They revolted, formed a Provisional Government, offered the Crown (which was refused) to the Dukes of Savoy and of Saxony, and finally to the Elector Palatine, who accepted it.

The King of England tried to dissuade his son-in-law from this step, but his mother and her family and his beloved wife added their persuasions to his own half-formed decision, and Frederick and Elizabeth were crowned King and Queen of Bohemia. The ceremony took place in the beautiful city of Prague, with all the pomp and circumstance of secular and religious magnificence. The Emperor Ferdinand now issued a ban, proclaiming Frederick a traitor, depriving him at the same time of his Electoral dignity, while he made preparations to march on Bohemia.

The English people were eager to assist their favourite Princess, but James ignored the newly-gained title, and refused supplies, although his daughter wrote earnest appeals for help. The battle of Prague, on the 9th of November 1620, was one of the most decisive and memorable of the war in question; the newly-made Sovereigns were compelled to fly, and a hard journey through the winter's snow (partly on horseback, and partly in a coach) was heroically endured by Elizabeth, then many months gone with child.

The fugitives went first to Breslau, but were hunted from one place to another, till they took refuge in Holland. Indeed, it was to the liberality of the Princes of Nassau, combined with casual supplies from private parties in England, that they were indebted for their support.

It was a sad and humiliating position for the daughter of a line of kings, and vulgar satire and petty spite were of course directed against her in her misfortunes. A print, published at Antwerp, is we believe still extant, representing this Queen (at least in name) as a poor beggar-woman, with dishevelled hair, her baby at her back, and her husband carrying the cradle. But though fortune frowned on her, Elizabeth never wanted for friends. Her courage, her dignity, and her genial warmth of heart made her the object of respectful but devoted affection.

The Knights, so to speak, who wore her colours were numerous, and mostly illustrious in military fame,—the hero Gustavus Adolphus, Duke Christian of Brunswick, Count Thurn, and above all, her faithful and lasting friend, Lord Craven, whose heart, sword, and purse were always at her disposal. No one ever merited better that Crown of an elective monarchy, the only one that now remained to her, for even among the common soldiers of the army she was known and acknowledged as Queen of Hearts. The accession of her brother to the Crown of England brought back a gleam of hope that the Palatinate at least might be recovered. But Charles's exertions in his sister's behalf were only half-measures. Not so the zeal displayed by the noble King of Sweden, whose services were only terminated with his life; he died a hero's death at the battle of Lützen in 1632, Frederick surviving him but a few months, to mourn his loss. That unfortunate Prince died at Mentz in the thirty-sixth year of his age, absent from his beloved wife, whom he consigned with his dying breath to the care of Henry of Nassau, a Prince whose affection for the exiles had been cemented by his union with Amelia of Solms, a chosen friend of Elizabeth's amongst the ladies of her Court.

The unhappy widow addressed a memorial to the States of Holland, in which she says: 'It has pleased Almighty God to call from this scene of woe my ever and most entirely beloved consort, and what renders the calamity more overwhelming is, that it followed immediately that of his ally, the glorious, the invincible King of Sweden, and on the eve of our triumph.'

Poor Elizabeth, whose sanguine disposition had held out so long! She was not alone in her distress; her children mourned their father with passionate sorrow, while the aged Princess, the Electress Juliana, strove to restrain her own feelings, in order to administer comfort to the widow of her beloved Frederick.

Elizabeth resided for some years at The Hague, busying herself with the care and education of her sons and daughters. Her family was so numerous, and their several destinies so varied and eventful, that we have no space to attempt any details.

Charles I., it will be remembered, invited two of his nephews over to England, of whom the younger, Prince

Rupert, became naturalised, and did his uncle gallant service in the field.

The ex-Queen employed her time in conversation, and in correspondence with men of literature and science, taking also great delight in the exercise of hunting, being a fearless horsewoman. The management of her household she intrusted to her devoted friend, Lord Craven, who entered the service of the States in order to be near her, and it has commonly been believed that they were privately married.

So fervent was her attachment to the Reformed faith, that on her brother's sending Sir Harry Vane, to persuade her into compliance with his proposal that her eldest son should go to Vienna, and espouse an Austrian Princess, which step would entail his becoming a Catholic, she indignantly replied she would rather kill him with her own hand.

This same son treated his mother most unkindly, and refused her all pecuniary aid in her distress.

Charles II., on his Restoration, invited his aunt to return to England, and she landed at Margate. How wonderful was the contrast between her return and her embarkation from that same place on the occasion of her marriage!

In the meanwhile the King had raised Lord Craven to an earldom. This unwavering and loyal friend conducted Elizabeth to his own home, called Drury House, surrounded by a delightful garden, where she took up her abode.

Drury Lane Theatre was built on the site of the garden, but a tavern existed near Craven Court, called 'The Queen of Bohemia,' on the door of which was an equestrian portrait of Lord Craven. The building was standing as late as 1794. It would appear that Elizabeth did not go to Court, although Pepys mentions her accompanying the King to the theatres, sometimes attended by Lord Craven. But at his house she had a little Court of her own, and all that hospitality, generosity, and the most refined consideration for his royal guest, wife, or friend, could suggest, was lavished upon her by her noble-hearted host. Here too she was once more united to her favourite and dutiful son, Prince Rupert. In the autumn she changed her residence, and went to Leicester House, belonging to Lord Leicester. But her health, which had been slowly undermined, now gave way; she prepared for the end, and made her will, leaving her books, pictures, (a most interesting collection may be seen at Combe Abbey,) and papers to Lord Craven. She died on the 13th of February 1662.

Lord Leicester, in speaking of his 'royal tenant,' says with some flippancy, 'It is a pity she did not live a few hours more, to die on her wedding-day; and that there is not so good a poet as Dr. Donne to write her epitaph, as he did her epithalamium unto St. Valentine.'

She was interred with much pomp in Westminster Abbey; Lord Craven was occupied at that time in constructing a house for her reception at Hamstead Marshall, county Berks, which was destined to be a miniature Heidelberg, but it was burnt to the ground before it was completed. The gate-posts, which are all that remain of the building, bear an Electoral Crown, entwined with the coronet of an English Earl, carved thereon.

It is strange to reflect that Elizabeth, who was deprived of her titles of Electress and Queen, should be the ancestress of every crowned head in Europe at this moment.

No. 121.

FRANCIS BACON, BARON VERULAM, AND VISCOUNT ST. ALBANS.

BORN 1561, DIED 1626.

Black dress. Ruff. Cloak. High hat.

THE second son of Sir Nicholas Bacon, by Anne, daughter of Sir **Anthony Cooke**, sister-in-law to Lord Burghley. Nicholas was Keeper of the Great Seal to Queen Elizabeth, who, visiting him one day at Gorhambury, observed that the house was too small for him. 'No, Madam,' replied the courtier, 'it is you who have made me too big for my house.'

The Queen had a great liking for little Francis, and delighted in asking him questions, which the boy generally answered pertinently.

'Come hither,' she said to him one day, 'and tell me how old you are.'

'Just two years younger than your Majesty's happy **reign**.'

The reply pleased Elizabeth, who in these early days dubbed the child jestingly 'My Lord Keeper.'

Francis Bacon was educated at Trinity College, Cambridge. He accompanied **Sir Amias** Powlett on his embassy to Paris, and was employed in several diplomatic missions, but the sudden death of his father brought him back to England. Finding himself unprovided for, he studied the law with great zeal at Gray's Inn; but he did not succeed for some time in getting any official employment, which was his aim. He formed a close friendship with Lord Essex, which displeased his relations of the Cecil faction, who in consequence were not willing to exert themselves in his behalf, save perhaps by obtaining the reversion of the office of Registrar-General. He also sat in the House of Commons.

In 1596, the post of Solicitor-General being vacant, Lord Essex endeavoured to obtain it for Bacon, but, failing in this attempt, was much disgusted, and, we are told, went over from Richmond to his friend at Twickenham to tell him so. The particulars of this interview are related by Bacon himself —Lord Essex expressing the anger he felt towards the Queen for denying his suit, and thanking Bacon 'for that you have spent your time and thoughts in my matters,' pressed on his acceptance a piece of land, *i.e.* Twickenham Park, with a delightful house denominated 'The Garden of Paradise.'

Essex also strove, but with the same lack of success, to assist Bacon in his design of forming a wealthy matrimonial alliance. Lady Hatton, (born Cecil,) granddaughter to Lord Burghley, and therefore a cousin of Bacon's, was the rich widow of Sir William Hatton, nephew and heir to the Lord Chancellor. The lady was witty, capricious, violent in temper, and of a worldly spirit, but all these qualities were thickly gilded, and Francis Bacon was needy.

Lord Essex once more stood his friend, and wrote to the lady's father and mother, to the effect that 'were she my sister or daughter, I would as confidently resolve to further the match as I now persuade you.'

But the wayward fair one had fixed her fancy elsewhere, and instead of her handsome and accomplished cousin—a rising man between thirty and forty—she preferred crabbed old Sir Edward Coke, a widower of advanced age, 'to whom there were seven objections—himself and his six children.' She induced her elderly lover (the future Chief-Justice) to elope with her, and the marriage was performed in so irregular a manner, that the newly-married pair were summoned before the Ecclesiastical Court.

Not content with running off with Bacon's mistress, Sir Edward Coke gained the post of Solicitor-General—thus bearing away the two prizes. But if Francis Bacon had any revengeful feelings against his rival in love and law, he might be consoled by learning that Sir Edward had a sad life of it with his rich wife, till she left him, his very children being taught by her to neglect and disobey him.

Bacon did not prove grateful for the friendly attempts, however unsuccessful, which Essex had made to serve him.

When the favourite fell into disgrace, he came forward to plead against him at the bar, and, not contented with so doing, published a pamphlet accusing the prisoner of treason, and the like. It was supposed that he hoped by so doing to ingratiate himself with the Queen, in which aim he failed, and finding he was much censured, he prepared an apology for his conduct, which he addressed to the Earl of Devonshire, the attached friend of the Lord Essex. Disappointed in his hopes of public employment, our philosopher now devoted himself to scientific studies, and to the prosecution of those labours and those writings which have rendered his name immortal and gained for it a world-wide fame.

The next Sovereign was more propitious, for James I. was a great admirer of Bacon's genius and learning, while he on his part was very useful to the King in the House of Commons. He became Solicitor-General, Attorney-General, etc., Baron Verulam, Viscount St. Albans, and Lord Chancellor of England. But troublous times were in store for the new peer. He was now very unpopular in the country, and all the more so for his adherence to the falling fortunes of the Duke of Buckingham, while Sir Edward Coke proved a dangerous enemy. He was first charged with corruption in having accepted large bribes from two suitors in Chancery, an accusation that was fully proved; and although the Upper House, to which he had just been admitted, showed a willingness to deal leniently with him, fresh and startling disclosures of the same nature, followed fast one upon another. James evinced much sympathy for Lord St. Albans, and thought to serve him by procuring an adjournment of Parliament, which only gave his enemies time to gather more evidence against him. The accused deemed it the most prudent course to make a full confession of his guilt, which he did in a letter universally cited as a model of style and eloquence.

The letter was presented by Henry Prince of Wales, but was of no avail. Lord St. Albans was deprived of the Great Seal, and sentenced to a fine of £40,000, or to be imprisoned in the Tower; also to be declared incapable of holding any public office or sitting in Parliament for the future.

James, however, soon released him, and remitted the whole of the sentence, with the exception of the Parliamentary prohibition. Lord St. Albans never again succeeded in obtaining any employment, although his means were so necessitous that he did not disdain to apply for the Provostship of Eton College, and was much mortified by receiving a flat denial. The remainder of his life was given to study, but the most important of his works were, curiously enough, written during the years of his official life.

The great philosopher was no true lover. He wrote in slighting terms of the tender passion, such as: 'Amongst all the great and worthy persons, of whom the memory remaineth, either in modern or ancient times, there hath not been one man transported to the mad degree of love, which shows that great spirits and great business do keep out this weak passion.' Might one dare to call in question the validity of so great a man's opinion?

We have seen what strenuous efforts he made to marry an unamiable woman for her wealth, and late in life he sought the hand of Alice Barnham, daughter to a rich London alderman—'pour les beaux yeaux de sa cassette' alone.

The marriage was most unhappy. They lived for some time together on wretched terms, and at length separated, the husband, in his last will, revoking every bequest he had made in his wife's favour, and only leaving her what she might claim by settlement. Seldom could the line of 'the ruling passion strong in death' be more appropriately applied than in the case of Bacon, who indeed fell a victim to his love for scientific research.

Journeying from Gravesend to Gorhambury with the King's physician (a congenial spirit) in winter, they fell into a discussion which caused them to set about making the experiment whether snow and ice would prove efficient substitutes for salt in the preservation of dead flesh.

The two companions immediately began to search for snow, and having found a sufficient quantity, they entered a cottage, and purchased a fowl, which Lord St. Albans stuffed with snow with his own hands.

The weather was intensely cold, and he was shortly taken with a shivering fit, and became so alarmingly ill that he could not prosecute his journey, but was conveyed to a house in the neighbourhood, belonging to Lord Arundel. A splendid house, as it appears, and the servants placed their noble guest in the state bed, but alas! the room was cold, the sheets damp, and the consequences fatal.

In his last moments he seems to have found consolation in likening himself to the elder Pliny, who fell a victim to his scientific ardour, being suffocated by the fumes of Vesuvius from having approached too near the raging crater, in order to investigate the phenomena of the eruption. Bacon—we call him by the name he generally bears as an author—died on Easter Day, in the arms of Sir Julius Cesar. He was of middle height, limbs well formed, but not strongly built, ample forehead, bright eyes and genial smile, with deep lines of thought on his face, as became a philosopher. His manners were attractive. He was fond of the country and rural pursuits, and found a relaxation from profound study in gardening and planting.

His faithful secretary erected a noble monument to his beloved patron in St. Michael's Church, at St. Albans, with an excellent portrait of the great philosopher sitting in a chair, his head resting thoughtfully on his hand. He appears to have been in constant pecuniary difficulties, having once been actually arrested for debt, and dying insolvent. He deplored his childlessness, for though children, he said, increase the cares of life, they mitigate the remembrance of death—laying, however, the flattering unction to his soul, that great men have no continuance.

No. 122.

FREDERICK, KING OF BOHEMIA.

By Honthorst.

BORN 1596, DIED 1632.

Brown and gold slashed dress. Blue mantle. Blue ribbon. Ruff.

THE family history of Frederick, Elector Palatine, afterwards King of Bohemia, bears so materially on the public history of the time, and the events of the Thirty Years' War, that we must be held excused if we go back some three generations to notice circumstances which tended not only to shape the career of this Prince, but to influence the destinies of all Germany.

Jacqueline de Longwy, wife of Louis de Bourbon, Duke of Montpensier, was secretly but deeply devoted to the Reformed faith, and she contrived, contrary to her husband's wishes, to effect a union between her eldest daughter and the Prince of Sedan, a zealous Calvinist.

Enraged beyond measure, the Duke forced his youngest daughter Charlotte into a convent, but not before the girl (then only eighteen years of age) had, at her mother's instigation, signed a protest against this compulsory step, at the same time declaring her strong predilection for the religion of her mother. Charlotte remained for seven years (during which time the Duchess of Montpensier died) at Jouarre in Normandy, where she became Lady Abbess.

In 1572 hostilities commenced between the Catholics and Protestants, and the gates of Jouarre, in common with those of many other religious houses, were thrown open by the latter party. Charlotte, finding herself free to follow the faith in which her mother had reared her, gladly availed herself of her liberty, taking refuge first with her sister, the Princess of Sedan, and afterwards going to reside at Heidelberg, under the guardianship of the Elector Palatine, where she openly abjured the creed of Rome.

Charlotte was an enthusiast in all things, and a hero-worshipper, and even before they had ever met, the fame of the Protestant champion, William 'the Silent,' Prince of Orange, had inflamed her fancy.

His valour, his religion, his patriotism, all rendered him an object of admiration in her eyes. She was desirous to consecrate her life to one whose every feeling and opinion were in harmony with her own; nor was the Prince insensible to the preference of a woman distinguished alike for nobility of character and birth, as well as for courage, while the fame of her personal charms might be supposed to weigh somewhat in the scale. William had divorced his first wife for her infidelity, and married the daughter of Maurice of Saxony, on whose death he asked the hand of Charlotte de Montpensier. But there were those who objected to the match on the plea that his first consort was still living. Charlotte's vows of celibacy were also adduced as an impediment, although they had been compulsory, and her change of faith had made them null and void by a decree which was confirmed by the Parliament of Paris.

The lovers now eagerly sought the consent of the Duke of Montpensier, who not only bestowed the paternal benediction, but enhanced its value by a considerable dower, and so, three years from the time Charlotte de Montpensier left her convent, she became the bride of the Prince of Orange.

Their happiness was complete, and for a while uninterrupted, but mischief was pending. The Spanish tyrant, Philip II., had set a large sum on the head of the patriot Prince, and a miscreant was found willing to attempt his life. As William was sitting, surrounded by his family, in the palace at Antwerp, a shot was fired in at the window, which wounded him severely, though not mortally.

The shot that was aimed at the husband, may well be said to have entered the wife's heart. She swooned away, and though she rallied sufficiently to nurse him as he lay for some time between life and death, yet the shock to her system, from the alternations of hope and fear, fatigue and excitement, proved too much for her strength. She lived to kneel by William's side in the thanksgiving service for his recovery, but she drooped gradually, and died gently, with the beloved name on her lips, mourned not only by her husband and family, but by the whole nation.

In Louisa, daughter of the Admiral de Coligny, the Prince of Orange gave his children a kind and judicious stepmother, who reared them with tenderness, and presided carefully over their education.

Juliana, Charlotte's eldest daughter, was destined to take an important part in the religious struggles of Germany. She was a woman of remarkable energy, wisdom, and courage, and (following in the footsteps of her illustrious parents) devotedly attached to the Reformed Faith. She married the Elector Palatine, and was the mother of Frederick, afterwards King of Bohemia. On the death of her husband, the widowed Electress was named Regent and co-guardian with her young kinsman the Duke de deux Ponts, who usually deferred to her matured judgment in matters both public and private. She managed the affairs of the Palatinate with masculine energy, always making the interests of the Reformed Church her principal object. While yet in their respective cradles, Juliana had, in her own mind, betrothed her first-born to the Princess-Royal Elizabeth of England, and she now devoted her thoughts to giving her son the best education within her reach. The Duke de Bouillon had married Juliana's sister as his second wife, and at Sedan they held a small Court, which was the resort of the flower of the Protestant youth of France, Switzerland, and Germany. Here the young men were not only encouraged to shine in military exercises and courtly manners, but they were invited to pursue their academical studies, strengthened in the tenets of the Reformation, both by precept and example.

In this wholesome atmosphere the young Elector Palatine passed his early years, much beloved by his relations, the Duke and Duchess de Bouillon, and doing honour to their fostering care. His studies completed, Frederick returned to Heidelberg, and was received with pride and joy by his mother. Singularly handsome, of polished manners, skilled in all the athletic exercises and the accomplishments which were considered indispensable in the education of a royal prince, the young Elector added to these gifts a piety, earnestness, and gentleness of heart which made Juliana believe him fitted to captivate the fancy of the most noble among the princesses of Christendom. She had relations and connections on all sides, but especially in the house of Nassau, who were willing and capable to assist her in her schemes for the happiness of her son, and the advancement of the Protestant religion, and we have already seen, in the notice of Elizabeth, daughter of James I., how successful was the Elector's suit. On his return to Heidelberg with his bride, they lived an almost ideal life of domestic happiness, until the offer was made to Frederick to accept the crown of Bohemia, and place himself at the head of the Protestant party, the Bohemians having revolted from the Emperor.

Frederick is said to have hesitated to break up the happy life which contented his affectionate and unambitious nature, but the two women he loved best, Juliana and Elizabeth, were urgent in their persuasions, and successful.

Frederick was not only driven from Bohemia by the imperial army, but placed under the ban of the Empire, and stripped of his hereditary dominions, which were afterwards recovered by his son. An exile, a wanderer, a mere soldier of fortune, the chief consolation of Frederick's sad life was the love of his wife and children, from whom, however, he was constantly separated. His health gave way under the pressure of sorrow of all kinds, aggravated by the untimely death of his eldest son, who was drowned before his eyes.

Frederick, having again joined the army, was in no fit state to bear with composure the news which reached him while still suffering from fever, of the death of his illustrious ally and devoted friend, Gustavus Adolphus, King of Sweden, who fell at the battle of Lützen in the moment of victory. At a distance from his wife and children, Frederick's last thoughts were of their welfare, and he implored the continued friendship and kindness of the Nassau Princes; entreating the King of England also to watch over his beloved Elizabeth.

Thus died the ex-King of Bohemia at the Castle of Mentz in the thirty-sixth year of his age. How many sad events had been crowded into that short space of time! His brother caused him to be interred within the boundaries of his paternal home, but, dreading lest the sanctity of the grave might be violated, he afterwards directed that the body should be removed to Sedan. Thus the scene of Frederick's happy and careless youth became his last resting-place.

No. 123.

CHARLES GERARD, EARL OF MACCLESFIELD.
By Dobson.
DIED 1693.

Head in oval. Green dress. Tagged shoulder-knot. Dark hair.

LOYALIST. Was created Baron Gerard of Brandon by Charles I., 1645, and Earl of Macclesfield by Charles II., in 1672. He was succeeded by his son, who died childless, as did his successor in turn; when the title became extinct in the Gerard family.

No. 124.

ALGERNON PERCY, EARL OF NORTHUMBERLAND.
By Sir Peter Lely.
BORN 1602, DIED 1668.

Black dress. Blue ribbon.

THE third son of Henry Percy, ninth Earl of Northumberland, by Dorothy, daughter of Walter Devereux, Earl of Essex. Educated at Christ Church, Oxford, under Robert Hughes, the celebrated mathematician, and in 1616 was one of the youthful Knights of the Bath, at the creation of Charles Prince of Wales.

On the accession of that Prince to the Throne, he was called by writ to the House of Peers (his father being then alive) as Baron Percy.

He afterwards, as Privy Councillor, attended the King to Scotland for his coronation, having by that time succeeded to his father's titles and estates.

In 1636 he had the command of a noble fleet, the largest, says Lodge, since the death of Queen Elizabeth.

Lord Northumberland was much commended for his services in the expedition against the Dutch fishery, making advantageous terms for the King of England, after which he turned his time and thoughts to reforming many abuses then prevalent in the navy.

In 1637 he was named Lord High Admiral, and in 1639 commander of the troops marching against the Scots, but was prevented—so he pleaded—from joining the army by illness, when the real command devolved on the Earl of Strafford. Clarendon says, 'Lord Northumberland was chosen for ornament.' It appears by a letter to his brother-in-law (Lord Leicester) that he had most gloomy forebodings as to the result of the enterprise, which, 'it grieves my soul to be involved in.' An incident occurred shortly afterwards, which does not redound to the credit of the Earl of Northumberland.

We will give an abridged account of Lord Clarendon's version. Henry Percy, a zealous Royalist, brother to the Earl of Northumberland, was on his way to France, on the King's service, just at the time that the Commons had petitioned Charles to prohibit any of his servants leaving England. Striving to embark, he was attacked and wounded by the people of the Sussex coast, and narrowly escaped with his life to a place of concealment, whence he wrote to his brother in a private and confidential manner. Northumberland carried the letter to the House of Commons (which had already voted an impeachment of high treason against Henry Percy), and laid the document upon the table. Clarendon makes but a lame defence for this conduct on the part of the elder brother, who was, he said, 'in great trouble how to send Henry in safety beyond seas, when his wound was cured, he having taken shelter at Northumberland House.'

But the end of the matter was, that Henry did escape from England, and there was enmity between the brethren from that day forth. This was the first time in which Northumberland 'showed his defection from the King's cause, and Charles had been a good friend to him, and laden him with bounties.'

He acted in direct opposition to the King's commands, when he obeyed those of the Parliament, to equip the royal navy, and to appoint the Earl of Warwick Admiral of the fleet.

In 1642 he resigned his commission of Lord High Admiral, and openly abandoned his allegiance, siding with the Parliamentarians, and though their faith was rather shaken in him on one occasion, he was too valuable an ally to quarrel with.

Northumberland was appointed head of the Commissioners employed to negotiate with the King, in the several treaties of Oxford, Uxbridge, etc., and was intrusted with the custody of the royal children, which he retained until the King's death. It would appear that he had at least the grace to facilitate their interviews with their unhappy and loving father, and that he cared for the wellbeing of his royal wards. They were subsequently committed to the guardianship of his sister, the Countess of Leicester, and were removed to her Lord's house of Penshurst in Kent.

Words, in truth, Lord Northumberland used to prevent the execution of the King, but his deeds had hastened the catastrophe. We are told he 'detested the murder.' Immediately after Charles's death Northumberland repaired to his seat at

Petworth, in Sussex, where he remained until 1660, when he joined Monck in his exertions to bring about the Restoration. He held no public office under Charles II. excepting the Lord Lieutenancies of Sussex and Northumberland. Clarendon, in a long character of him, says: 'His temper and reservedness in discourse got him the reputation of a wise man. In his own family no one was ever more absolutely obeyed, or had fewer idle words to answer for;' and, alluding to his defection from the Royal cause: 'After he was first prevailed upon not to do that which in honour and gratitude he was obliged to, he was with the more facility led to concur in what in duty and fidelity he ought not to have done, and so he concurred in all the counsels which produced the rebellion, and stayed with them to support it.'

He took great delight in his gardens and plantations at Petworth, where he resided in the summer, but in the winter he was much in town, attending to his Parliamentary duties. He had two wives; the first was Lady Anne Cecil, daughter to Thomas, second Earl of Salisbury. On her death we hear Lord Northumberland 'is a very sad man, and his sister (Lady Leicester) has gone to comfort him.' By Lady Anne he had five daughters. His second wife was the second daughter of Theophilus Howard, second Earl of Suffolk, who brought him in Northumberland House in London, originally called Northampton House. Sion House had been granted by the Crown to the ninth Earl. Evelyn went to see it, and thought it 'pretty, but the garden more celebrated, than it deserved.'

By Lady Elizabeth Howard, who long survived her husband, he had an only son and heir, and a daughter, who died unmarried. Algernon Earl of Northumberland was buried at Petworth, in Sussex.

No. 125.

HELENA, PRINCESS RAGOTSKI, OR RACOZI, WIFE OF COUNT EMERIC TEKELI OR TÖCKOLI.

Three-quarters length. In widow's weeds. Black wimple. The right wrist is concealed by a handkerchief. Letter lying on the table. Castle burning in the background.

HIS beautiful woman, whose life was a series of romantic adventures, misfortune, and privation, was the daughter of Count Serini, or Zrini, Ban of Croatia. He had involved himself in the struggles of the day, and was in arms against Leopold, the Emperor of Austria, in defence of Hungarian privileges. His associates in the undertaking numbered most of the noble names in Hungary, Count Nadasti, a high officer of State, Frangipani, a young nobleman of great promise, Trauttenbach, Governor of Styria, and others. Zrini's daughter Helena (or as she is called in a contemporaneous novelette, purporting to be an account of her early adventures, 'Aurora Venetia') was of exceeding beauty, and had many suitors; but the fair one was reckoned cold and coy, and she showed no preference until the Count Emeric Tekeli entered the lists. So decided was her predilection in his favour, that she persuaded her father to give his consent to their betrothal, but Zrini had at heart to gain over Prince Francis Ragotski (whose father had been a staunch upholder of Hungarian liberty) to the same cause, and he in consequence broke his daughter's engagement to the penniless Count, and gave her hand to the rich Prince.

Francis's father had died at Waradin from the effects of a wound received in a battle against the Turks. On the point of gaining the victory, his helmet falling off, a heavy sabre-cut brought him almost lifeless to the ground. His men, panic struck, bore their disabled general from the field, and left the day to the Turks.

On the death of Ragotski, his widow, who was in the stronghold of Mongatz with her son, guarding the family treasures, thought it advisable to enter into a treaty with the Emperor. She accordingly delivered up to him certain fiefs, which had long been coveted by the Turks, on condition that Austria would garrison them against the Ottoman troops. But she was a courageous and resolute woman, and when Leopold sought to encroach on some other of her son's possessions, she withstood him stoutly. Indeed so zealously did she watch over the family treasures in her fortress, that on a subsequent occasion, when Prince Francis (her son) appeared before the walls with the intention of assisting some of the patriots (whose finances were greatly reduced) from the family coffers, the Châtelaine ordered the guns to be pointed against her own son. But she managed matters between him and the Emperor so well, that he was pardoned his share in the rising, while several of his colleagues were degraded, their estates confiscated, their right hands struck off, and some of them finally executed for high treason.

But to return to Prince Ragotski, the husband of Helena: He did not long survive his marriage. He left two sons, of whom the eldest (his namesake) took great part in the affairs of Hungary on arriving at man's estate.

Count Tekeli no sooner heard that the woman to whom he had been deeply attached was free, than he turned his eyes in the direction of the beautiful widow. The old Princess Ragotski, a rigid Roman Catholic, set herself to oppose the union, and sent troops to harass Tekeli, and it was not till after the old lady's death that the marriage was brought about, as was supposed, by the intervention of young Zrini, Helena's brother, who had been taken prisoner. The nuptials were celebrated with the greatest pomp and magnificence.

Helena was eminently fitted to be a soldier's wife. She not only gloried in her husband's feats of arms, but she constantly instigated him to fresh enterprises, panting for revenge (as she was) on the destroyers of her father and kinsmen.

Tekeli was reputed to be an indifferent stepfather, neglecting his wards' comfort and well-being, but we must remember that he had many detractors. His wife, at all events, loved him dearly, exulted in his valour and successes, mourned for him in misfortune, and nobly did she defend the citadel of Mongatz for upwards of two years against the imperial troops, and that at a time when her husband was absent.

Once when, straitened for want both of food and ammunition, the garrison showed an inclination to capitulate, Helena rallied the soldiers in person, cheered them with the hope that Tekeli would shortly come to their rescue; and such was the influence of her courage and beauty that the men enthusiastically renewed their vows of fidelity. The elements too ranged themselves on her side, for the constant rains had made the ground so soft as to render the Austrian General's outworks useless, while they replenished the cisterns of the besieged, just as the enemy thought to cut off their supply from the river.

Over and over again did the Austrian commanders try to bring Helena to terms; threats, reports of her husband's imprisonment, advice that she should submit, were all in vain. The intrepid Châtelaine made proud replies to all these messages; she said it was not much to the Emperor's credit to make war upon women and children; that as guardian of Prince Ragotski's sons, she was bound to defend their possessions and interests; but at length, seeing all hope was over, and the only alternative was starvation for herself, her children, and her faithful defenders, she consented to capitulate, after having held out, off and on, for two years, and more than once obliged the enemy to raise the siege.

The Emperor wrote her a letter (doubtless the one lying on the table beside her) in which he offers her honourable terms, but she would not be dictated to, even in her hour of distress, and she added many stipulations of her own, before she abandoned the fortress, which she had so long and so valiantly held. Amongst other conditions, she was to take with her whatsoever she wished of property, furniture, etc., and an amnesty was to be proclaimed for her garrison and people. The fortress of Mongatz was to be given up to the Emperor, who was to undertake the guardianship and education of the young Ragotskis.

Two days after the treaty was concluded, Countess Tekeli and her two boys proceeded on their road to Vienna, where, on their arrival, Leopold broke almost all the conditions. He took her children from her, forbade her to write to her husband, treated the defenders of Mongatz with severity, and at last consigned the heroine to a compulsory retreat, in the Convent of the Ursuline Nuns. The education which Leopold bestowed on the young Princes did not (at all events in the case of the eldest) bring forth the fruits of submission he anticipated, as Francis in after years distinguished himself as an upholder of Hungarian liberty. Helena's freedom was granted her at length, in exchange for an Austrian General, and she immediately joined her husband, living a chequered life of alternate luxury and poverty in the East.

His latter days were full of privation, which she shared without a murmur, and closed a career of heroism, misfortune, and fidelity, by dying two years before Tekeli, in 1703.

There is a strange tale which is told by La Mottraye, but we recommend that it should be taken *cum grano*.

The writer had a profound admiration for the fair exile, when he visited the Count Tekeli at Constantinople, and tells us that Helena had relinquished almost all the money and jewels which Prince Ragotski had bequeathed her, to her second husband, with the exception of four thousand ducats; but this sum, and a few remaining jewels, she had locked in a little strong-box, and deposited in the custody of the reverend fathers, the Jesuits at Galata.

A devoted Roman Catholic, she had designed the treasure to defray the expenses of a pilgrimage to Jerusalem, should her life be prolonged, or to be expended in masses for her soul, in the event of her death, keeping the key in her own hands, and—so said the good fathers, her spiritual advisers—all this, without the knowledge of her husband. Her reason may be well imagined, for he, being a Lutheran, 'and fearing no pains between death and paradise, and having so much occasion for money in temporal affairs, would have dissuaded her from being at so much expense for spirituals.'

Only one of her servants knew her secret. Him she sent from time to time, to fetch a priest of the order, to celebrate mass, hear her confession, and administer communion to the exiled lady.

When her life was despaired of, the servant in question told the Count's secretary of the treasure with the Jesuits. The secretary immediately told his master, and they held a council together, the result of which was, that they should send the servant, who would not be suspected, with a message purporting to be from the Countess, to the effect that they should send her the box, she wishing to make some additions thereto, and that in three or four days one of the priests should go to her for it.

Bribed by the promise of a large reward, the servant is said to have undertaken the business, but the secretary judged it more prudent to follow, and watch the messenger.

By the time he returned with the treasure, the Countess had breathed her last, and when the father-confessor arrived two days after, he found the lady buried already; and instead of the box he had intrusted to the servant, another was presented to him, containing Countess Tekeli's heart, which she had bequeathed to the holy fathers in her last moments, and to which they gave distinguished funeral rites.

The secretary offered the priest a hundred ducats, which he refused, demanding the whole contents of the casket, for masses to be said for the soul of the departed. The Count refused, observing that, though his wife might have required the money to travel to the earthly Jerusalem, she could not possibly need it to go to the heavenly Jerusalem. The secretary—we still quote La Mottraye—who was also a Protestant, laughed irreverently in his sleeve at the disappointment of the holy men.

There are duplicate pictures of the Count and Countess in the possession of a lady in London. The curious manner in which the Countess conceals her hand with a handkerchief led to the conjecture that the beautiful insurgent might have suffered the penalty of amputation, so frequent at that time, as in the case of her father, and his friends; but the lady who owns the companion picture to Lord Bath's gave me another version of the story.

She had some time ago an old German master who was a Hungarian, and much interested in the portrait of his fair compatriot. His tradition was, that the picture was painted to commemorate the valiant manner in which the Countess behaved, when, writing a letter in her tent, a stray cannonball shattered her right hand.

No. 126.

COUNT EMERIC TEKELI OR TÖCKOLI.

BORN 1658, DIED 1705.

Three-quarters length. Richly-embroidered costume. Leopard's skin. Holding an axe. Crescent in cap. Troops crossing a bridge in the background.

THE Hungarian subjects of Leopold I., the Emperor of Austria, disgusted with his violation of the promises of civil and religious liberty which he had made them on being proclaimed King of Hungary, and which he ignored on ascending the Imperial throne, revolted in large numbers.

Many of the highest in the land headed the malcontents; and, as we mention in the notice of the Countess Tekeli, her father Count Zrini, Counts Frangipani, Nadasti, and Trauttenbach, suffered death in defence of the privileges of their native land, in 1670-71.

Count Stephen Tekeli, the friend and comrade of these chiefs, a Lutheran of vast possessions, and obnoxious to the Emperor on all these counts, was besieged in his own castle by Leopold's orders, and died before it surrendered.

His son Emeric, the subject of this notice, then a youth, made his escape in the disguise of a girl, with some friends during the night, and sought refuge at the Court of Poland. Finding the King of that country unable to assist him, he repaired to Transylvania, the Waiwode of which country, Prince Abaffi, his father's greatest friend, welcomed the young Emeric, made him Prime Minister, and despatched him with the troops, which he was sending to the relief of the Hungarian malcontents. Very shortly afterwards the Count was promoted to the grade of Generalissimo, with the title of Prince and Protector of the Kingdom.

Emeric Tekeli was at that moment in the full vigour of youth and beauty, for which he was very remarkable. His presence was majestic, and his undoubted courage and ardent patriotism gave him great influence. Innumerable volunteers flocked to his standard, bearing the sacred device, '*Pro aris et focis*,'—the persecuted Lutherans, the mourners whose relatives had been cut off by the bloody hand of the executioner, panting for revenge. The discontented of all classes fixed their hopes on the hero, who had risen so suddenly to eminence. Tekeli published a manifesto promising to defend the liberties of Hungary; his army increased daily; and at the head of these irregular troops, he held his own for three years against the Imperial army.

In the life of the Countess Tekeli will be found the account of his marriage. He had been affianced to her before her union with Prince Ragotski, whose suit her father preferred to that of the handsome but then penniless Count.

After Ragotski's death Tekeli marched on Mongatz, where his former love resided with her two children, and her mother-in-law, who was most averse to the union with Tekeli. There is a romantic story told of how on one occasion the lover contrived to penetrate into the fortress in the disguise of a pedlar, and being ushered into the presence of Princess Helena, he drew from his bosom the miniature she had given him of herself some years before. But it is difficult to sift fact from fiction in the loves of these remarkable people, and to fix the dates of their adventures. The marriage did not take place till after the death of the Princess-Dowager, and 'war's alarms' soon called Tekeli from the side of his beautiful wife. She was not one indeed to damp his military ardour, or to detain him from the field. He marched into Moldavia, and continued his campaign, resisting and distrusting the frequent overtures made him by Leopold's ministers. But at length he deemed it politic to call in foreign aid, and applying to the Sultan, Mahomet IV., he obtained from him, with the title of Prince, an auxiliary of Ottoman troops, under the Grand Vizier Caram Mustapha.

The campaign of 1683 was marked by the most revolting cruelty; and, terrible to say, the Christian commander seemed to vie with his Pagan allies in acts of violence and rapacity. He was a strange mixture of the fine gentleman and the barbarian, affecting great luxury and magnificence in his dress, military appointments, arms, accoutrements, and the arrangement of his tent.

There is a story extant respecting the head-dress he wears in his portrait. On his arrival at Buda, he was conducted with much ceremony to the Pasha, who received him with honour, and taking off Count Tekeli's cap placed it on his own head. Count Tekeli's cap was replaced by another after the Turkish fashion, by some called a diadem, richly studded with precious stones, and ornamented with heron's feathers.

Tekeli was present at the famous siege of Vienna, and at Pressburg, where the cruelties practised will not bear description. The town was rescued from his hands by the Prince of Baden; but Tekeli and Mustapha now fell out, and branded each other with recriminations, so that the Hungarian, who was no better indeed than a tributary of the Porte, thought it politic to go to Constantinople in person to make his own defence against Mustapha's accusations. He did so, but not long after his arrival he was seized at the table of the Seraskier, loaded with chains, and imprisoned by order of the Sultan, on some frivolous pretext. This conduct so disgusted the Count's Hungarian friends, that they broke their alliance with the Turk, and submitted to Austria under promise of an armistice. Then the Sultan relented, set

Tekeli free, and gave him large sums of money. He also nominated him Waiwode of Transylvania.

Surely no one man ever had so many empty titles bestowed on him as Emeric Tekeli. He made war in Slavonia and Servia against the Prince of Baden and Count Piccolomini, but much after the fashion of a guerilla. In 1696 he was with the Sultan in the defence of, and the battle of Orlach, where the Turks were defeated.

Tekeli then retired to some mineral baths in Anatolia to recruit his shattered health and strength, when he was informed that the Sultan had declared a renewal of hostilities, and proclaimed him King of Hungary!

Into that country the Ottoman troops had already penetrated, and the poor titular Sovereign was dragged off to join them, in spite of his failing health. He advised the Sultan to avoid an encounter with the Imperial troops, and rather to march on Transylvania, which was undefended; but his counsels were unheeded, and the Turks were completely routed in an engagement with Prince Eugene.

A story was told on this occasion to the disparagement of the Count, namely, that he remained in the Ottoman camp after the flight of the army, and possessed himself of all the available treasures his friends had left, before the reconstruction of a bridge enabled the enemy to come in for their share.

It was reckoned a shabby trick, but all is fair, we are told, in love and war, and if the Turks had not fled so soon, they might have carried off their own property. The peace of Carlowitz put an end to a terrible war, terminated the campaign, and concluded Count Tekeli's military and political career. By this treaty, in which the Count's name was not even mentioned, Turkey ceded most of the disputed territories to Austria, completely ignoring the man whom she had invested with so many titles appertaining to these provinces.

Once more Tekeli proceeded to Constantinople, in spite

of all this treatment, to renew his offers of service to the Sultan, on the breaking out of a fresh war. But on arriving near the city he was met by a high officer, who desired him not to enter. It appears that our English Ambassador, Lord Paget, had had an interview with the Sultan, to warn him against harbouring Tekeli. He was therefore ordered off, to a kind of sumptuous banishment, at a delightful country house at Nicomedia, whither a few Hungarians and Transylvanians followed the man who had been their Sovereign in name. His faithful wife joined him the moment she regained her liberty; and here Count de la Mottraye visited him, spending eight days, as he says,—'where I was nobly entertained, till I was tired, with pheasants and wild-fowl, which were found there in prodigious plenty.'

Towards the end of 1703 the Count and Countess removed to another country-house called The Field of Flowers, and here died the brave, noble, and devoted, Helena Princess Ragotski, Countess Tekeli.

For the strange story of the hundred ducats, we refer the reader to the notice of her life. Be that true or false, there is no doubt Tekeli was treated with ingratitude, neglect, and caprice; his revenues stopped, and he himself obliged to gain a scanty subsistence by carrying on the trade of a vintner: the Prince, the Prime Minister, the Generalissimo, the Waiwode, the King of Hungary! Monsieur de la Mottraye visited him a second time at The Field of Flowers, and alluding to the affair of the ducats, he says: 'The Jesuits made many visits to the Count in the hope of converting him to their creed, but he remained a steadfast Lutheran.' Other writers testify to his having embraced the Roman Catholic faith; but this is the testimony of one who saw him in his latter days, and thus describes him :—

'He was sitting in an elbow-chair, according to his usual custom, with a carpet over his knees, much afflicted with the gout. His beard had grown greyer, and new troubles, especially the death of his Countess, seemed to grieve him much. He complained that France had promised him large sums of money for expenses in the war, and had not sent him two-thirds, and since his misfortunes had not sent him ten ducats. I observed that it had to pass through too many hands on its way to Turkey.'

The same writer tells us 'Count Tekeli had the most taking countenance, and one of the finest tongues, also that he spoke good Latin fluently,' but that is an accomplishment shared by most of his countrymen. His personal beauty was acknowledged even by his enemies, who gave him the sobriquet of Absalom.

Poor Tekeli was (as La Mottraye observes) as ill treated by the gout as by fortune. He survived his faithful wife only two years, and was interred in the Greek cemetery at Constantinople. Emeric Tekeli, from his wild adventures, his romantic history, and all his curious vicissitudes, became a marked man, the observed of all observers, and there are very curious books extant, with squibs, some in Italian, some in German, as also caricatures of a rude kind of pleasantry, representing him in prison beating against the bars, and bewailing his sad fate.

'So lohnt der Turk denen die ihm trauen,
Man sollt' die Trauerspiel recht anschauen,' etc. etc.

No. 127.

ELIZABETH SEYMOUR, AFTERWARDS COUNTESS OF AILESBURY.

As a girl. White dress. Scarf and pearls. Holds a wand.

HE was the daughter of Henry Lord Beauchamp, by Mary Capel. She married Thomas Earl of Ailesbury, to whom, on the death of her brother William, third Duke of Somerset, she brought large estates in Wilts (Savernake being one of them) and other counties.

No. 128.

JOHN LOWTHER, VISCOUNT LONSDALE.

BORN 1655, DIED 1700.

Buff coat. White sleeves. Cuirass. Red mantle. Long wig.

E succeeded his grandfather, as Baronet, in 1675; sat in Parliament for Westmoreland in 1678-9, and when the House dissolved was re-elected, at the next meeting. It is a matter of history, how often Parliament was prorogued and dissolved in those troublous times; suffice it to say that Sir John distinguished himself by his zeal for the Protestant cause, and his opposition to the Duke of York's succession; yet when that event took place he again served in Parliament, as likewise in that called the Convention, which settled the Crown on the heads of the Prince and Princess of Orange.

In fact, in every session, until called to the Upper House, he was strong in favour of King William III., and gained over the counties of Westmoreland and Cumberland to his cause, for which services he was made Vice-Chamberlain, Privy Councillor, Lord-Lieutenant of the county, and in 1696 he was created Baron Lowther and Viscount Lonsdale, county Westmoreland.

He was twice one of the Lords Justices for the government of the kingdom during His Majesty's absence in Holland, and in 1700 he died, and was buried in the church at Lowther. He married the youngest daughter of Sir Henry Frederick Thynne of Longleat.

No. 129.

CHARLES THE FIRST, KING OF GREAT BRITAIN.

Black coat, slashed sleeves. Ruff. Ribbon and George.

No. 130.

CATHERINE VISCOUNTESS LONSDALE.

By Michael Wright.

DIED 1712.

Drab dress. Blue mantle. Seated. Her hand resting on the back of a dog.

CATHERINE was the youngest daughter of Sir Henry Frederick Thynne, by the daughter of Keeper Coventry, and therefore sister to Thomas Lord Weymouth. She married John Viscount Lonsdale, by whom she had three sons and five daughters. She was buried at Lowther, by the side of her husband.

No. 131.

WILLIAM SEYMOUR, THIRD DUKE OF SOMERSET.

BORN 1651, DIED 1671.

Drab dress. Red mantle. White wand in his hand. Painted when a boy.

HE was the son of Henry Earl of Beauchamp, by Mary, eldest daughter of Lord Capel. He succeeded his grandfather in 1660, but did not long survive him. He was buried at Great Bedwyn, county Wilts, when the honours devolved on his uncle, Lord John Seymour.

BEDROOM B.

BEDROOM B.

No. 132.

HENRY, PRINCE OF WALES.

By Zucchero.

BORN 1594, DIED 1612.

Garter on the leg. Mantle, Collar, and George of the Order. Red velvet surcoat. White satin trunk hose, braided with gold. White shoes and rosettes. Jewelled sword-belt and glove. Hat on table.

HE eldest son of James VI., King of Scotland, afterwards I. of England, by Anne of Denmark; born at Stirling Castle, and consigned when an infant to the joint care of the Earl of Mar, and the Countess his mother, who had been nurse to His Majesty. The lady was of an austere temper, though conscientious, and between her, her son, and the Queen, many quarrels ensued. Neither James nor his wife liked the trouble of educating or bringing up their own children, the younger members of the family being sent out to board and lodge at the houses of different noblemen. But James loved pomp, and appointed a household for his eldest son, when still an infant. Besides the Earl of Mar, his Governor, the illustrious babe had a Gentleman of the Bedchamber, in the person of Sir David Murray, who attended him into England, and

remained with him till his death. When between five and six, Henry was removed to the custody of Adam Newton, a learned Scot, on whom James, on his accession to the English throne, bestowed the Deanery of Durham (although a layman), and a Baronetcy. This was probably a reward for translating a work of the royal pedant's into Latin. The Pope was anxious himself to superintend the education of the heir-apparent to the English Crown, but the proposal was not smiled upon!

No sooner did the little Prince arrive in England than a residence was allotted him in one of the royal palaces, and a splendid household appointed, with numerous attendants—the celebrated Inigo Jones named Comptroller of the Works.

Henry was of a mild, loving, gentle disposition, combined with high courage, and a passion for military exercises of all kinds; dutiful and respectful to a bad father, religious, and truthful in the extreme, he was indeed a gracious Prince. He never pronounced the name of God but with the deepest reverence, and abhorred the practice of swearing, to which James was so strongly addicted. On one occasion when out hunting, his sport was spoiled by a butcher's dog setting on the stag, and killing him. A courtier who was present observed, had His Majesty been there, he would assuredly have sworn. 'Nay, sir,' said the Prince, 'all the pleasure in the world is not worth an oath.'

The Ambassador of Henry IV. of France, writing to his Sovereign, says,—'None of his pleasures savour of a child. He loves horses and hunting, is fond of games, especially tennis; usually plays with those older than himself. He studies for two hours every day, but loves better to toss the pike, leap, shoot, etc. etc. He is kind and faithful to his dependants. Is never idle. He is already feared by those who have the management of affairs, especially my Lord of Salisbury, who seems to fear the Prince's ascendency.'

Be it remembered, this testimony is of a boy of thirteen years of age. He governed his large household, as he grew in years, with a discretion and a justice which argued well for the kingdom it was vainly hoped he would one day govern.

'He loved, and did mightily strive,' says Cornwallis, 'to do somewhat of everything, and to excel. He walked fast and far to prepare, in case long marches should be required of him. He greatly delighted in art, science, and mechanism.'

Did ever Prince seek to educate himself more thoroughly, or strive to render himself worthy to govern a great country? By nature haughty, he subdued what might have been arrogance into proper dignity. He took as great an interest in naval as in military affairs, and his political opinions were in every way opposed to those of his father; but he was a most dutiful son, extremely reserved, the result of his early education. He was a zealous Protestant, and steadily refused marriage with all the Catholic Princesses suggested to his choice, saying, if he must marry one, it should be the youngest of them all, as there would be more hope of her conversion.

He formed few friendships, Sir John Harrington being one of those singled out by him. He showed great partiality for his cousin Arabella Stuart, and strove to befriend her several times. His sister Elizabeth he loved dearly, from his early boyhood; and the correspondence between the royal children, although partaking of the formal style of the day, was marked by tenderness.

Most of the contemporary writers concur in the opinion that the Prince's heart was not susceptible, but there were whispers abroad, that he was a victim to the charms of the beautiful and wicked Lady Essex, and that his dislike to Lord Somerset was enhanced by rivalry.

Neither of his parents was worthy to possess the blessing of such a son. The Queen tried in vain to gain some influence over his mind, but she loved him not, and James, it was easy to imagine, was jealous of the adoration with which his English subjects regarded his son and heir. Moreover, Henry, though always respectful to his father, silently rebuked him by the contrast in their way of life and general conduct. Amongst the different suitors for the hand of his beloved sister, the Prince of Wales favoured the young Elector Palatine, more especially on account of his strong Protestant tendencies.

It was in the midst of the preparations for the marriage of the Princess Elizabeth, that the hope of the nation was seized with sudden and almost unaccountable illness. Different causes were assigned :—**he had,** when over-exerted by too frequent swimmings in the **Thames, ridden** hastily to and from Belvoir Castle, to wait on the King's Majesty, etc. etc. The illness, pronounced by the physician to be putrid fever, appears to have been aggravated by injudicious medical treatment. He was lying at St. James's, where his father, mother, and sister visited him in the early days of his illness. But James soon took fright for his own safety, and retired to Theobalds. Delirium with fearful convulsions now set in, with lucid intervals, when Henry displayed all the courage **and** gentle patience which might well be expected from so good and **noble** a Prince. His illness lasted about a fortnight. We quote the words of Richard Earl of Dorset on this deeply-deplored death: 'Our rising sun set; it had scarcely shone, and with him all our glory lies buried.'

The news which plunged the **whole** nation in sorrow, the King received with much indifference, and issued an order forbidding the people to wear mourning, on the plea of the approaching nuptials of his daughter. He also directed that the arrangements for the Christmas festivities should in no wise be interrupted.

A report was now circulated which accused Lord Rochester of having poisoned the Prince of Wales, a suspicion which doubtless gained more credence when that unworthy man was found guilty of the murder of Sir Thomas Overbury. Bishop Burnet says that Henry's brother Charles never wavered in his belief that such was the case, although the Court physicians denied it.

The description which Sir Charles Cornwallis gives us of Henry's appearance is as follows: 'He was of a comely stature, about five feet eight inches high, strong, straight, and well made, as if Nature in him had showed all her cunning; with somewhat broad shoulders and a small waist, of an amiable and majestic countenance; his hair auburn, long-faced, and broad forehead, piercing grave eye, a most gracious smile, with a terrible frown.'

The beautiful house at Bramshill, Hants, now the property of Sir William Cope, was said to have been built as a residence for the Prince of Wales, likewise the picturesque old house of Charlton, in Kent.

SMALLER CORRIDOR UP-STAIRS.

SMALLER CORRIDOR UP-STAIRS.

No. 133.

THE HONOURABLE LADY THYNNE.

Head oval. Brown dress. White scarf, fastened in front with a jewel. Ringlets.

SHE was the daughter of Lord Keeper Coventry, and the wife of Sir Henry Frederick Thynne.

No. 134.

ADMIRAL CAVENDISH, THE CIRCUMNAVIGATOR.

BY ZUCCHERO.

DIED AT SEA 1593.

Light brown hair. Clean shaven. Embroidered vest. Band of pearls over the shoulder. Dark cloak. Right arm akimbo.

THOMAS CAVENDISH was the son of a gentleman of fortune in Suffolk. He had an early fancy for the sea, which was strengthened by circumstances. At the age of twenty-one he had already dissipated the chief part of the property left him by his father, through gambling and other pleasures.

England was at this time at war with Spain, and it was considered fair play for 'amateur buccaneers' on the high seas to attack any vessel, or take possession of any settlement, in any part of the world, belonging to that nation.

In this manner Cavendish thought to retrieve his fortunes, and he accordingly, in 1585, equipped a stout bark at his own expense, and accompanied Sir Richard Grenville on his voyage to Virginia, Florida, the West Indies, etc. etc. The expedition was very successful on the whole, though naturally the English met with some reverses. Cavendish returned with his income much replenished; but he went to the Court of 'the maiden Queen,' where he lived in splendour, and indulged in great extravagance, so that the dollars did not remain long in his purse. He determined to go afloat once more, but he had to sell or mortgage the remainder of his estates to enable him to fit out three vessels, and, fired by the example of Sir Francis Drake, he resolved to visit some of the spots where that famous sailor had been so successful. He first steered for Sierra Leone, where he landed, and pillaged and burned the town, ostensibly as reprisals for a wound inflicted on one of his crew by a native. Proceeding to South America, he touched at many points as he coasted along, giving English names to the places which took his fancy. One beautiful bay, glistening with golden sands, he called 'Elizabeth,' after his royal mistress, although it did not enjoy a good reputation, being inhabited by cannibals who had feasted largely on the unfortunate Spaniards. He landed frequently whenever there was a prospect of gain, and attacked the Spaniards in their settlements, burning, destroying, and plundering, often with considerable loss on his own side; but he was never daunted, and his success outweighed his reverses. He took many Spanish barks, but his chief prize was the 'St. Anna' galleon laden with rich merchandise, specie, jewels, etc. etc. He marked her for his own, lay in wait for her, and in spite of fearful odds as to numbers of the respective crews, he boarded and took possession, with all the invaluable freight. He then proceeded on his voyage round the world, which he performed most successfully, and returned to Plymouth, being the second Englishman who had circumnavigated the globe, and the first who had achieved the voyage in so short a time.

Cavendish was received at Court with great favour; the Queen knighted him, and he found England ringing with his fame, which in no wise displeased him. He wrote to Lord Hunsdon in a style of self-complacency, describing all he had done and seen, especially laying stress on the fact that he had shown no mercy to the Queen's enemies, and that he had lost no opportunity of pillage. He had indeed done very good service to navigation by the improvements he had made in charts, and the like, the exact log he had kept, and the observations he had taken as he sailed along, besides discoveries made.

He pointed out especially the resources and advantageous position of the fertile island of St. Helena, hitherto little frequented excepting by the Portuguese. We have not space to recount all his wonderful escapes and adventures. Cavendish had, as we have before observed, a great taste for magnificence of all kinds, and when at Court he was remarked for the splendour of his dress. He was also very nice in the decoration of vessels, and was said to have had one of them adorned with a mainsail of costly damask. But in all his wanderings he had not learned prudence. A third time he found his money all gone, and it was no longer in his power to raise a sufficient sum for the fitting out of any more ships. A joint-stock company was formed for the purpose of effecting this, and Cavendish was engaged in their service; but he found himself very soon in a most humiliating position, under the orders of men who were entirely ignorant of navigation, and who constantly interfered and took share in the command, instead of listening to the advice of this experienced Admiral.

Quarrels and bickerings ensued, and not long after the small fleet weighed anchor, storms and tempests set in, and disasters of every kind were encountered. The brave spirit gave way at length, being broken down by ill-health, disappointment, and perplexity, the crowning point being the mutinous conduct of the sailors towards one who had hitherto been paramount on his own quarter-deck. Cavendish had not proceeded far on his return to England, which he was never destined to see again, when he died at sea, after a life of storm and adventure such as few had experienced even in those stirring times.

No. 135.

PORTRAIT UNKNOWN.

No. 136.

LADY MARGARET HARLEY, AFTERWARDS DUCHESS OF PORTLAND.

By Mercier.

DIED 1785.

As a girl. Full length. Dressed as a shepherdess. Hat and crook. Dog and lamb beside her.

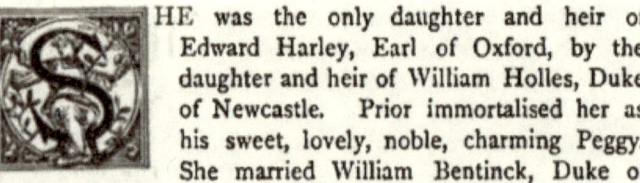

SHE was the only daughter and heir of Edward Harley, Earl of Oxford, by the daughter and heir of William Holles, Duke of Newcastle. Prior immortalised her as his sweet, lovely, noble, charming Peggy. She married William Bentinck, Duke of Portland, by whom she had several children. The eldest daughter became the wife of the first Marquis of Bath.

No. 137.
JOHN GRAHAM OF CLAVERHOUSE, VISCOUNT DUNDEE.

By Vandyck.

BORN 1643, KILLED IN ACTION 1689.

In armour. Laced band. Broad red sash. Holding a baton.

HE eldest son of Sir William Graham of Claverhouse, county Forfar, N.B., by Jane, daughter of John Carnegie, first Earl of Northesk. The family was a branch of the noble house of Montrose, descended from William Lord Graham of Kincardine, by his second wife, Margaret, daughter of Robert III., King of Scotland.

John Graham studied at the University of St. Andrews, but went to France to finish his education, where he entered the army of the Great Monarch as a volunteer. Having resolved on the career of a soldier, he left France, and obtained a cornetcy in the Horse Guards of William Prince of Orange, by whom he was promoted to the command of a troop in 1674, in consideration of his bravery at the battle of Seneffe, in which engagement, indeed, he saved the Prince's life.

Some time afterwards, Graham applied for the command of one of the Scotch regiments in the Dutch service, but being refused, the young soldier was so disgusted that he threw up his commission and went to England.

Now, although it did not suit the Prince of Orange to grant Graham's request, he gave him the warmest recommendation to Charles II., who immediately made him commander of a body of horse just levied in Scotland to oppose the rising of the Covenanters, nominally under the orders of the Duke of Monmouth. Graham found himself vested with full power to act as he thought fit, and history and historical romance alike testify to the severity, and even cruelty, with which he carried out his measures.

He entertained a personal hatred to the Whigs, and his hot temper made him vindictive in public as well as private matters. He had no toleration for the opinions, or mercy for the disaffection, of these enthusiasts, numbers of whom he forced, at the point of the sword, to take an oath hateful to their consciences. In 1679, one of their conventicles having been attacked, the peasants rose and defeated a detachment of his troops with considerable loss. Exasperated beyond words at what he considered a disgrace, the General gave vent to his fury, massacring the unfortunate 'hillside folk,' who were unarmed; putting to death without a moment's respite those who refused the test, and making for himself a road of carnage and desolation wherever his march was directed. Who can wonder that he gained for himself the name of 'Bloody Claver'se'?

The Crown, however, rewarded his zeal by making him Sheriff of Wigtownshire in 1682, captain of a troop in the Royal Regiment of Horse, Privy Councillor in Scotland, together with a grant of the castle of Dudhope, and the office of Constable of Dundee.

Notwithstanding his cruelty to their countrymen, he was much favoured by the Scotch Episcopalians, until his marriage with the granddaughter of the Earl of Dundonald, 'a fanatic,' brought him into temporary disrepute.

On the accession of James II., the King was persuaded (on the plea of this marriage) to remove Claverhouse from his seat in the Council; but he was soon reinstated, and successively promoted to the rank of Brigadier and Major-General, and in 1688 created Viscount Dundee and Baron Graham of Claverhouse in Scotland. At the time of his elevation to the Peerage, Dundee was in attendance on the King in London, vainly endeavouring to prevail on the unhappy monarch to make a stand against the Prince of Orange, offering to collect 10,000 of the disbanded troops, and at their head to stem the torrent of invasion. But James was deaf to these manly and vigorous counsels, though one of the last acts of his Government was to intrust Dundee with the management of all military affairs in Scotland.

Thither Claverhouse (for by that name he is best known) repaired, and on arriving in Edinburgh took his seat at a Convention of the Estates then sitting. Here he endeavoured to carry matters with too high a hand, and finding that some of his arbitrary requests were refused, he left Edinburgh in dudgeon, at the head of a large body of horse. Prompt and energetic in all his measures, the General repaired to Stirling, called a parliament of the friends of the expatriated King, and considerably harassed and hampered the movements of his adversaries.

Receiving intelligence of the approach of a force sent by the Convention to seize his person, he retired to Lochaber, where a gathering of the clans soon placed him at the head of a large number of Highlanders, all enthusiastically devoted to his person and the Royal cause.

Dundee now made a fresh appeal to James, then in Ireland, entreating him to cross over to Scotland, where his presence would 'fix the wavering and intimidate the fearful, and where hosts of shepherds would start up warriors at the first wave of his banner on the mountains.'

But once more his advice was thrown away. James sent him a small store of arms and ammunition, together with some feeble promises and faint words of praise.

Claverhouse had not only the qualities of a great commander, but in his cooler moments possessed the requisites for a ruler and administrator of justice.

On one occasion, at Inverness, he found the inhabitants of that town in arms against a body of neighbouring chiefs, to decide a quarrel respecting some question of debt. He sat in judgment on the matter, severely reproved both parties for drawing their daggers on each other, instead of uniting to support the cause of their royal master; and then, to the surprise and delight of the litigants, he drew the amount of the debt from his own purse and paid it on the spot. In an ecstasy of enthusiasm and gratitude the two adverse parties joined in hearty fellowship, and enlisted with one accord under his banner. Indeed, his influence throughout the country was wonderful, and he entered on a system of communication with all those whom he considered likely to advance the cause for which he worked so zealously. It is unnecessary to recount all his efforts to win adherents, but perhaps the most remarkable of his successes in this particular occurred in the case of a band of Highland vassals raised by Lord Murray on the estate of his father, the Earl of Athole.

While Murray was in the act of reviewing them they quitted their ranks, hastened to a neighbouring brook, filled their bonnets with water, drank the health of King James, and, with pipes playing, marched off to join Dundee. William III. now thought it time to take some decided measures, and he despatched General Mackay (who had distinguished himself in Holland) with a considerable force into Scotland, while James sent orders to his General to avoid a battle until the arrival of fresh reinforcements from Ireland. For these supplies the eager-spirited soldier had to wait two months in the mountains, keeping, however, (according to modern parlance,) his hand in during that time by spirited attacks and retreats. The delay must have been displeasing to the man of whom it was said that the first messenger of his approach was the sight of his army, and the first intelligence of his retreat that he was beyond the enemy's reach.

No sooner did the raw and ill-provided recruits who formed the promised reinforcement arrive than Claverhouse prepared for active measures. Hearing that Mackay was marching on Blair Castle, in Athole, a fortress of much importance, he resolved to intercept him. Accordingly, when William's General arrived on the plain at the mouth of the Pass of Killiecrankie, he found Dundee on the surrounding hills awaiting his arrival. He did all he could to incite the enemy to immediate action, but it suited the Scotch commander to delay for some hours.

As the sun of July the 27th, 1689, sank slowly to rest, the word was given, and the Highlanders, whose eager spirits had been controlled for so many hours, dashed down the hillside with even more than their usual impetuosity. It was but the work of a moment: William's army was routed as if by magic. Dundee, who had fought on foot in the onset, now leaped on his horse and galloped to the mouth of the Pass to intercept the enemy's retreat. In his hot haste he outstripped his men, and looking round, found himself almost alone, and he waved his sword to motion his men forward, when a musket-ball struck him in the arm-pit. He fell fainting from his horse, and was carried off the field, but soon rallied, and inquired how things went.

On receiving the answer, 'All is well,' the gallant soldier replied, 'Then I am well also,' and instantly expired.

When King William heard of his death, he said, 'Then the war in Scotland is over.'

Surely never was countenance more indicative of the inner man than the comely face with which we are so familiar in the portraits of John Graham of Claverhouse. The faultless features, the fair complexion, the profusion of silken hair, and the slight moustache, convey an idea of refinement and delicacy, we should almost say gentleness. But a glance at the dark hazel eyes, full of latent fire, and (even plainer reading to a physiognomist) the determined lines of the exquisitely curved lip, bring us face to face with the obdurate, and (the true word must be spoken) cruel man of blood. He was verily 'an eagle at assault and a maiden in the bower,' and there have been few characters that inspired such extremes of love and hatred.

He was idolised by his soldiers, whose hardships he gladly shared in times of privation, often sending, to the sick and wounded among his troops, the dainties which had been provided for himself. Yet so strict was he as a disciplinarian, that for an officer at least, there seemed no slighter punishment for any military fault than death; and indeed he said all other punishment, in his opinion, disgraced a gentleman.

A striking anecdote is told, characteristic of the man himself, and of his system, and worthy of the days of Sparta: A young gentleman was observed by the General to fly in his first action. He had compassion on the boy, and pretended that he himself had sent him to the rear, but alas! on the next occasion the young soldier was again found wanting in courage, and Claverhouse, calling him to the front of the army, shot him with his own pistol, being loath, he said, 'to let a youth of gentle blood fall by the hand of a common executioner.'

Walter Scott tells us another anecdote, of a less tragic nature, although he does not vouch for its authenticity. The story goes that the gallant Claverhouse had heard of the fame of a certain Lady Elphinstone, aged upwards of a century, and was very desirous to see her. Now the centenarian was a staunch Whig, and required some persuasion to induce her to receive the enemy of her party, but she, perhaps, had some feminine grain of curiosity in her composition, and was tempted by the notion of seeing the far-famed captivating monster.

In the course of conversation the soldier remarked that the lady, having lived so long, must have witnessed many wonderful changes. 'Hout na, sir,' answered the stout-hearted old Whigamore; 'the warld is just wi' me where it began. When I was entering life, there was ane Knox deaving[1] us a' wi' his *clavers*,[2] and noo I am ganging out, there is ane *Claver'se* deaving us wi' his knocks.'

There can be little doubt the old lady's courage and humour were equally appreciated by the General.

Lord Dundee married Jane, youngest daughter of Lord Cochrane, and (as before mentioned) granddaughter of the first Earl of Dundonald, by whom he had an only son, James, who succeeded to his father's titles, but died a few months after.

No. 138.

FREDERICK, KING OF BOHEMIA.

Profile. Oval. Armour. White Collar, blue Ribbon and Order.

No. 139.

LADY ESSEX RICH, COUNTESS OF NOTTINGHAM.

BY SIR PETER LELY.

Seated. Light blue dress. White sleeves.

SHE was the daughter, and one of the co-heirs of Robert Earl of Warwick. She married (as his first wife) Daniel Finch, second Earl of Nottingham, who afterwards succeeded his father (the famous Chancellor) as Earl of Winchilsea. Lady Essex Rich had one daughter, married to the Marquis of Halifax.

[1] *Deaving*, *i.e.* deafening. [2] *Clavers*, idle chattering.

No. 140.

FIRST VISCOUNT WEYMOUTH.

DIED 1714.

Black dress. Embroidered collar. Long hair. White sleeves.

No. 141.

MR. KELIFET.

Dressed in black. Ruff. Pointed beard. Arms of Kelifet in corner of picture.

THIS portrait is supposed to be that of Richard Kelifet, Esq. of 'The Place,' Egham, county Surrey.

He was chief groom of Queen Elizabeth's removing wardrobe, and yeoman of Her Majesty's standing wardrobe, and a most faithful servant of Her Majesty, according to an inscription on his monument in Egham Church. His daughter Cicely married Sir John Denham, Baron of the Exchequer, to whom she brought 'The Place,' at Egham, as her dower.

In 1673 this house was occupied by a connection of the Longleat family, John Thynne, Esq., when (we are told) 'it contained many valuable and curious pictures.' This circumstance may possibly be a clew to the fact that the portrait above-named finds a place in the collection of the Marquis of Bath.

No. 142.
HENRY LORD BEAUCHAMP.
By Sir Peter Lely.
BORN 1628, DIED 1656.

Brown coat. White sleeves. Red mantle.

E was the eldest son of William, second Duke of Somerset, by his second wife, Lady Frances Devereux, eldest daughter of the Earl of Essex. He married Mary, daughter of Lord Capel, by whom he had one son, William, (who succeeded his grandfather as Duke of Somerset,) and three daughters. Two died in infancy, and the third married Thomas Lord Bruce, afterwards Earl of Ailesbury.

Lord Beauchamp died *vita patris*.

No. 143.
THE HONOURABLE LEOPOLD FINCH.
DIED IN 1689.

In black, with white band.

IFTH son of Heneage Finch, second Earl of Winchilsea, by Lady Mary Seymour, daughter of William Duke of Somerset.

He was Warden of All Souls, Oxford. Married Lucy, daughter and co-heir of John Davie, of Ruxford, in the county of Devon, and died without children.

No. 144.

THE HONOURABLE LADY SAVILE.

Blue mantle.   White dress.   Ringlets.   Leaning against a tree.

DAUGHTER of Lord Keeper Coventry, married first Sir William Savile, and afterwards Sir Thomas Chicheley of Wimpole, Cambridgeshire.

No. 145.

DON FERDINAND, CARDINAL INFANT OF SPAIN.

AFTER RUBENS.

BORN 1609, DIED 1641.

Scarlet robes and cap.

WAS the son of Philip III., King of Spain, by Margaret, daughter of Charles Archduke of Austria, and born at the Escurial.

When only ten years old he was created Cardinal Archbishop of Toledo, and other dignities were conferred on him, which brought in enormous revenues. His father on his deathbed sent for the little ecclesiastic, and admonished him on the sacred nature of his duties. Ferdinand was remarkable as a warrior, a politician, a connoisseur of art, a man of pleasure, and much given to hospitality. He kept open house at his country palace near Madrid, where he instituted a species of dramatic performance, half-pageant, half-operatic, which took the name of the Zarzuelas, from the country house in question.

He studied foreign languages, mathematics, philosophy, and strategics; loved books and literary society, patronised the arts, studied painting himself under Vincenzo and Carducho, and sat for his portrait both to Vandyck and Rubens.

But the career in which he distinguished himself most was that of arms. He was an enthusiastic soldier and an able general, and did good service for Spain in the field, especially at the battle of Nordlingen, against the Imperialists. Upon the death of the Archduchess Clara Eugenia, Ferdinand Cardinal Infant succeeded to the government of the Low Countries, and continued his military career with honour and success. A parallel has been drawn between him and the Cardinal Ippolito de Medici, natural son to Julian of that house :—Both ecclesiastics by profession, and soldiers by choice; both remarkable for personal beauty, for accomplishments as well as learning, fond of the fine arts, of society and splendid living; both sat for their portraits in most unclerical costumes,—Ippolito to Titian in the dress of a Hungarian noble,—see the superb picture at Florence; the other to Rubens,—armed and mounted on his charger, ready for the field. It was his boast, among other successes, that he obliged the army of the Prince of Orange twice to raise the siege of Guelders. He died the 6th of November 1641, when his loving countrymen erected a gorgeous monument to his memory in the cathedral at Toledo, seventy feet high, the work of Lorenzo Fernandez de Salazar, with eulogistic inscriptions in various languages. The funeral was conducted with great pomp. Canon Antonio Calderon pronounced the funeral oration, speaking of him as one of Spain's greatest men,—a hero, a skilful general, a virtuous citizen. Nor did the preacher forget to remind all good Catholics that the scene of Ferdinand's most celebrated victory was Nordlingen, where 'the heretic Luther had preached his most pestilent doctrines.'

No. 146.

ROBERT HARLEY, EARL OF OXFORD.

By Sir Godfrey Kneller.

BORN 1661, DIED 1724.

Seated. Black coat and breeches. Wig. Star and ribbon of Garter. Holding his wand of office. Left arm akimbo. Hat on table.

STUDIED under the famous Dr. Birch, who boasted of the number of statesmen he had educated; showed great promise. In 1688 he raised a troop of horse for the service of William of Orange, whom he joined, but who showed him no particular favour. Harley sat in Parliament, but waited for office till 1704, when Queen Anne gave him a seat in the Council, and made him Secretary of State. He was much opposed to Godolphin and Marlborough, and made common cause with the Queen's new favourite, Mrs. Masham, to overthrow the power of the Whigs.

The Ministers insisted on his dismissal, but the Queen stood by him as long as she could. When Harley was compelled to resign, the Queen said to him: 'You see the unfortunate condition of monarchs,—they are obliged to give up their friends to please their enemies;' but so good was Anne's opinion of Harley, that she constantly consulted him on public affairs, even when out of office.

On the downfall of the Whig Administration, he was made Chancellor of the Exchequer, and Treasurer.

He was much censured, even by his own party, for some of his financial measures, by which however he enriched the royal coffers. In March 1711 an event happened which made a great noise, and rendered Harley the hero of the day. A French adventurer called Bourlie, or the Marquis de Guiscard, was a shifty individual, who acted first as a spy of England against France, and then of France against England, being in the pay of both. His intrigues were discovered, and he was brought before the Privy Council. Believing that Harley had been instrumental in his detection, he resolved to be revenged. While waiting his turn for examination, he found means to secrete about his person a penknife which was lying on the table, among some papers. No sooner was he brought forward, than he rushed in a fury upon Harley and stabbed him several times, the Minister falling senseless on the ground, covered with blood. A scene of confusion ensued, and the Duke of Buckingham, drawing his sword, wounded the assassin, who was conveyed to Newgate, where he died in a few days, either from the effect of the sword-thrusts or by his own hand.

The event seemed to have revived Harley's popularity; both Houses presented an address to the Queen, assuring her that Harley's loyalty had brought this attack upon him, etc. etc., and when he reappeared in the House, a brilliant reception awaited him, and a Bill was passed making an attempt on the life of a Privy Councillor a felony, which deprived the offender of benefit of clergy. In the same year, Robert Harley, being then Lord High Treasurer, was created Baron Wigmore, and Earl of Oxford and Mortimer, and next year he received the Garter, and became Prime Minister of England.

Lords Oxford and Bolingbroke at first worked together to withstand the power of the opposition, and to bring about the pacification of Europe, and the Peace of Utrecht added to the popularity of the ministerial party; but dissensions arose between Bolingbroke and the Premier, and recriminations and fresh intrigues, in which Mrs. Masham was implicated, all of which belongs to England's political history.

Oxford was deprived of all his offices, and accused of plotting in favour of the Pretender. The Queen died, and in 1715 he was sent to the Tower, on an accusation of high treason. He was imprisoned for two years, and on his release gave himself up to the enjoyment of art and literature. He formed a magnificent library, which cost him a fortune, not only from the splendour of the works themselves, but on account of their sumptuous binding. His collection of MSS., called after him the Harleian MSS., which was afterwards greatly increased by his son, is now one of the glories of the British Museum, purchased by the Government after the second Lord Oxford's death.

Few men have been more eulogised on the one hand and reviled on the other, but he has been unanimously described as a kind patron of men of letters.

It was Harley who brought into operation the measure known to posterity as 'The South Sea Bubble,' which entailed ruin on numbers, and in spite of much opposition he established State lotteries.

Lord Oxford was twice married, first to Elizabeth, daughter of Thomas Foley of Whitley Court, county Worcester, by whom he had one son, and two daughters; and, secondly, to Sarah, daughter of Thomas Myddleton, Esq., who was childless.

No. 147.

LORD JOHN RUSSELL, AFTERWARDS EARL RUSSELL, K.G.

BORN 1792, DIED 1878.

As a young man. Resting his hand on the inner frame of the picture.

HE youngest son of Lord John Russell, afterwards sixth Duke of Bedford, by the Hon. Georgiana Elizabeth Byng. Born in the very crisis of the French Revolution, his uncle (the reigning Duke) was the champion of French ideas, and having been carried far beyond the opinions of his family, which for more than a century had been zealously Whig, both he and his brother, young Russell's father, settled that on John's leaving Westminster, he should go to the University of Edinburgh, Oxford and Cambridge being too Tory in their proclivities to suit the family traditions. By the time (we quote an able article in the *Times* of 1878) the youth left College, his political faith had crystallised into something very like that in which he consistently lived, laboured, and died. A visit to the Peninsula, however, where the star of Wellington was then in the ascendant, modified his French ideas and inspired him with such an admiration for the hero, that ever afterwards, in the fiercest political struggle, John Russell maintained towards the Duke the attitude and language of profound respect, almost amounting to veneration. On his return to England, while still under age, he sat for Tavistock, and threw himself heart and soul into the Parliamentary fray at one of the most eventful periods of the history, not only of England, but of Europe, and of that history John Russell's career forms a most important feature. But our limited space will only allow us to glance at the prominent events of his life. He was a zealous advocate for Catholic Emancipation, and all Liberal measures, and from the very first threw in his lot with those who demanded Parliamentary reform, in which cause he was the primary mover, and the draught for the first Bill of which was drawn up by his own hand. To his early efforts in this cause Macaulay refers with his usual eloquence, saying : 'Those were proud and happy days, when amid the applause and blessings of millions, my noble friend led us on in the struggle for the Reform Bill; when hundreds waited round our doors till sunrise, to hear how well we had sped; when the great cities of the North poured forth their populations on the highway to meet the mails which brought tidings from the capital, whether the battle of the people had been lost or won,' etc. etc. Lord John Russell sat for Tavistock, Hunts, Bandon, etc.; and was a member of the Lower House for forty-seven years, during many of which he was the leader of the Opposition. He filled at various times many of the highest offices of State, Home, Foreign, Colonial, Lord President of the Council, Commissioner to the Congress at Vienna, and First Lord of the Treasury from 1846 to 1852. Once more Foreign Secretary in 1859, and again at the head of the Government in 1865, he retired in 1866, having been raised to the Peerage as Earl Russell and Viscount Amberley in 1861, and receiving the Garter in 1862. He married, first, (in 1835,) Adelaide, daughter of Thomas Lister, of Armitage Park, widow of the second Lord Ribblesdale; she died in 1838, leaving two daughters. His second wife was Lady Frances Elliot, daughter of Gilbert, second Earl of Minto, by whom he had three sons and a daughter. Besides a drama, 'Don Carlos,' written in his youth, Lord Russell was the author of several literary works, political, historical, etc. etc. He died at Pembroke Lodge in 1878. His latter years had been much embittered by the premature death of his eldest son, Lord Amberley, and his wife (a daughter of Lord Stanley of Alderley), within a few months of each other. They left two little children, of whom one is the present Earl Russell.

No. 148.

A LADY.

Seated. In a rich dress.

DOUBTFUL. Called the Countess of Stamford. Possibly Lady Ogle, married to Thomas Thynne of Ten Thousand.

No. 149.

THOMAS THYNNE, Esq.

By Sir Godfrey Kneller.

Light brown coat. Long fair hair. Arm akimbo.

FATHER of the second Lord Weymouth.

No. 150.

MR. CONINGSBY, USHER OF THE BLACK ROD.

Red cloak. Black skull-cap. Embroidered vest and gauntlets. Gold chain and medal. Ruff. Holding a wand. In the background is the coat of arms of the Coningsby family.

No. 151.

ELIZABETH, MARCHIONESS OF BATH.

HEAD BY SALISBURY.

BORN 1735, DIED 1825.

White lace cap.

HE was the eldest daughter of the Duke of Portland by Lady Margaret Harley. In 1754 she married Thomas Thynne, first Marquis of Bath, by whom she had a very large family. She survived her husband many years.

No. 152.

MR. COLE, HOUSE STEWARD.

UNCERTAIN.

Brown coat. White wig. Writing. A seal lying on a book on the table.

No. 153.

PORTRAIT UNKNOWN.

No. 154.
ANNE BRUDENELL, COUNTESS OF SHREWSBURY.
BY WISSING.

BORN 1621, DIED 1702.

Brown dress. White sleeves. Blue mantle.

THE daughter of Robert Brudenell, second Earl of Cardigan, by Anne, daughter of Viscount Savage. She married Francis, eleventh Earl of Shrewsbury, as his second wife.

De Grammont, in describing the beauties of the Court of the new Queen, Catherine of Braganza, mentions Lady Shrewsbury in the first flight. She seems to have surpassed most of the members of the royal circle in vice and effrontery, and a long list is given by the author above quoted of those who did not sigh in vain, but De Grammont says she was even more remarkable for the misfortunes she brought on those with whom she had to deal than for her conquests. The well-known wit and courtier, Thomas Killigrew, after her desertion of him for the Duke of Buckingham, amused himself by writing lampoons and speaking of her in a most unrestrained manner. He had been admonished that such a proceeding would prove dangerous, but persisted in his invectives. He was attacked one evening on his return from the Duke of York's at St. James's by some assassins, who made several sword-thrusts through his chair, one of which pierced his arm. After this narrow escape he bridled his tongue and pen, but sought for no redress, well aware the attempt would be fruitless.

Pepys tells us the Duke of Buckingham took Lady Shrewsbury to his house, whereupon the Duchess, usually very sparing of her reproaches, remarked it was not fit for her and the other to remain together under the same roof, to which the Duke agreed, adding, 'I have therefore, Madam, ordered your coach to take you to your father's;'—a speech which honest Pepys designates as 'devilish.'

Evelyn, in his account of his visits to Newmarket, 'where was racing, revelling, and feasting with jolly blades' during the King's residence there, mentions the Duke of Buckingham with that abandoned woman, Shrewsbury, with fiddlers, and the like, 'all of which,' he said, 'did ill become a Christian court.'

Her lover also installed her in his beautiful country house on the banks of the Thames, to which Pope alludes—

'Cliveden's proud alcove,
The bower of wanton Shrewsbury, and love.'

But the incident by which she is best remembered is the famous duel, which ended so fatally. Whether Buckingham's boasts were too loud, when he expatiated on the constancy and devotion of the hitherto fickle beauty, or from some other cause, the patient husband's indignation was at length roused, and he sent a challenge to the Duke. We subjoin Pepys's account: 'Much discourse of the duel between the Duke of Buckingham, Holmes, and one Jenkins on one side, and my Lord of Shrewsbury, Sir John Talbot, and one Bernard Howard, on the other. It was all about my Lady Shrewsbury, who is, and hath been for a long time, mistress to the Duke of Buckingham. The husband challenged him, and they met yesterday, January the 16th, 1667, in a close, near Barne Elmes, and Lord Shrewsbury is wounded, run through the body from the right breast, through the shoulder, and Sir John, all along one of his arms, and Jenkins is killed, and the rest all in a measure wounded.' Pepys makes a sapient remark on the subject: 'This will make the world think that the King has some good councillors about him, when the Duke, the greatest man, is a fellow of no more sobriety than to fight a duel about a mistress.' He tells us that the King, having got wind of the matter, had sent a message by the Duke of Albemarle to Buckingham, forbidding him to fight, which message, like many others, was never delivered. 'There was great talk of the business, and Lord Shrewsbury's case was considered very bad, and if he should die, it might make it worse for the Duke of Buckingham, and I shall not be much sorry for it, as we may have some more sober man in his place, to assist in the Government.'

On the 16th of the ensuing March, Lord Shrewsbury died of his wounds. There is a story currently believed, that his shameless wife held her lover's horse, during the duel, in the disguise of a page.

The Queen put herself at the head of a party that declaimed against the Duke and his wicked transactions; but she was soon silenced, and the whole matter hushed up.

Lady Shrewsbury lived to find a man adventurous enough to marry her, in the person of the son of Sir Thomas Brydges of Keynsham, county Somerset. She died at the age of eighty-one.

No. 155.
DOROTHY PERCY, COUNTESS OF LEICESTER.
AFTER THE VANDYCK AT PETWORTH.
DIED 1659.

Seated. White satin gown. Blue mantle. Pearl ornaments.

HE was the eldest daughter of Henry Percy, ninth Earl of Northumberland, by Dorothy, daughter of Walter, first Earl of Essex, of the Devereux family. She married in 1618 Robert Sidney, Earl of Leicester.

Of her affection for her husband let her own letter speak, written eighteen years after their marriage, when Lord Leicester was Ambassador in Paris. She says, if she were not bound to entertain his messenger a little, 'I would bestowe one side of this paper in making love to you, and since I maie with modestie expres it, I will saie that if it be love to think of you sleeping and waking, to discourse of nothing with pleasure, but what concerns you, to wishe myselfe everie hower with you, and to praie for you with as much devotion as for mie owne sowle, then sertainlie it maie be said that I am in love.'

Dorothy was indeed of a gentle and loving disposition, and of a character in all respects strongly opposed to that of her sister, the Countess of Carlisle, whom Sir Philip Warwick designates as 'that busy stateswoman,' with other observations by no means flattering. Dorothy's tastes were of a more domestic kind, and her temper amiable and peaceable. She could not, however, prevent a dissension which arose between her brother Algernon Earl of Northumberland and her Lord, when the latter was in Holstein. A letter addressed by Lord Leicester to his brother-in-law shows plainly that he was not the implacable one in this matter. After many assurances of friendship he goes on to say: 'I present a request to your Lordship, that you will make a visit to your sister, my dear wife, if she be at Penshurst. That poor place has not offended, that it should be forbidden the honour to receive you. She hath not offended, that she should be deprived of the consolation and delight that your Lordship's company ever brings her;' many more arguments and conciliatory expressions going to prove that Leicester, at least, desired to be reconciled; but Northumberland remained irate. We may gather this from another letter, from 'Dorothy to her husband. 'I have not yet seen my brother,' she writes, 'he being full of the King's business, as he pretends, neither have I perceived any inclination to drawe me from the solitarines I suffer in this place; for though I expressed a willingnesse to go to him, yet have I received no manner of invitation, which I take a little unkindlie. But I thanke God and you, mie dearest harte, that the obligations I have received from frendes have been small, and I hope mie necessities of the times maie not be encreased. But of this coldnesse in my brother I will take little notice, and content myself the best I can, with this lonelie life, without enveing others their greatnesse, their plenty, or their jollitie. . . . My best and most earnest praiers shall be offered for you, and with your owne, which I believe are better than mine, I hope the blessinges shall be obtained, which shall make us happy.' We hear of her afterwards visiting her husband in Paris, when the Queen of France presented my Lady Leicester with a costly diamond.

During the civil war Lord Leicester's well-known loyalty made him obnoxious to the Parliament, and his estates were sequestered. But the Countess drew up what Lodge designates as 'a bold and dignified memorial,' and which perhaps tended to the removal of the sequestration which followed shortly afterwards, enhanced, **as it was, by the combined** influence of her brother and her son.

Lord Northumberland, now partially reconciled to his sister, had been coquetting for a long time with the Royalist and the Roundhead parties, and was therefore thought worth winning over by both, while the young heir of Penshurst, Lord L'Isle, was very popular with the powers that were **then** in the ascendant, on account of his republican tendencies. So Lord and Lady Leicester were left in peaceful possession of their beautiful home, the 'Arcadia' of the Sidneys.

On the death of King Charles I., the care of the younger children, the Princess Elizabeth and the Duke of Gloucester, devolved on the Countess, and we **cannot** doubt her guardianship was tender, though Lord Clarendon, who did not much affect the **Lord** and Lady of Penshurst, speaks **rather slight**ingly on the subject. But the reduced allowance, the lessening of respect, the omission of titles, and the like, were not to be laid to the charge of the royal children's guardians, but to that of the Government then in power. At all events, Princess Elizabeth evinced her affection for Lady Leicester by bequeathing to her a jewel of much value, on her death, at Carisbrook in the Isle of Wight, where she had been removed from the shades of Penshurst. This token of gratitude and friendship was grudged by the Parliament, who, questioning the validity of the will, instituted a suit against the Earl of Leicester, and after some litigation, (as might have been expected,) gained possession of this bone of contention.

Lady Leicester did not long survive her young ward. There is a letter extant, addressed by her husband, on her death, to her unkind brother, Lord Northumberland, which we do not transcribe, as the cringing, courtier-like style does not take our fancy, although speaking with much affection of the wife whose loss he no doubt so deeply mourned.

They had four sons and eight daughters.

CARDINAL RICHELIEU.

BORN 1585, DIED 1642.

Red dress and cap of Cardinal. Ribbon and Order.

RMAND, the son of Francis Duplessis Richelieu, who was Captain of the Guard to Henry IV. of France. The family was originally of Poitou. Born at Paris, educated at the Sorbonne. Evinced great talent at an early age. Went to Rome, where he was elected Bishop of Luchon when only twenty-two. It is said that he gave himself out for two years older to Paul V., who, on discovering the deceit that had been practised, observed, 'Ce jeune évêque a de l'esprit, mais ce sera un jour un grand fourbe.'

On Richelieu's return to France, his insinuating manners and agreeable conversation, combined with more solid qualities, made him very welcome at the Court of the Queen-Mother, Mary of Medicis, Regent of the kingdom. The newly-made bishop was chosen as her Grand Almoner, and afterwards made Secretary of State. But the Queen fell into disgrace both with her son and the Government, and was exiled to Blois, where Richelieu followed her. He paved the way to his own aggrandisement by effecting a reconciliation between the young King and his mother, for which he was rewarded with the red hat of a Cardinal.

Louis XIII. in these early days disliked Richelieu, who stood so high in the Regent's favour, and warned her: 'Il est d'une ambition démesurée.'

This was his estimate of the man in whose hands he became later but a mere puppet.

The rise of Cardinal Richelieu to the zenith of power, and his administration as Prime Minister, the manner in which he fell and rose alternately, in the confidence of the Regent and the King, forms one of the most important pages in the history of France. He always knew how to right himself in an emergency, and as far as public affairs were concerned he advanced the power of France in a most eminent degree, and in so doing gratified his own personal ambition. He was one of the many who did not scruple to throw down the ladder on which he had risen, and that in several instances. He hated the Huguenots, and worked against them, but he hated Austria still more, and, to humble her power, he assisted the Protestant leaders in Germany, during the Thirty Years' War, with supplies. He also loved to take down the pride of the French aristocracy, and no consideration of mercy or rectitude arrested him in his course, particularly where his own personal animosity urged him forward. He showed remarkable aptitude for military affairs, and beneath his rule, as we have said before, the glory of the French arms was much advanced. He also patronised the arts of peace, founded institutions, erected many splendid edifices, and built for himself a magnificent dwelling in Paris, which he called 'Le Palais du Cardinal,' now the Palais Royal, which he bequeathed to Louis XIII. Richelieu loved literature, and left numerous writings.

His cruel sentence in respect to Cinq Mars, and De Thou, accused of conspiracy, is a well-known episode in the life of this Minister. He did not long survive his victims, but died, after great suffering, with courage and firmness, protesting solemnly in his last hour that his whole aim in life had been the welfare of his king and country.

He was a man of gallantry, and was said to have presumed so far as to raise his eyes to the reigning Queen, Anne of Austria, who, however, much disliked him, and opposed him whenever it was in her power to do so.

PORTRAITS NOT PLACED.

PORTRAITS NOT PLACED.

No. 157.

CHARLES BRANDON, DUKE OF SUFFOLK.

After Holbein.

BORN 1504, DIED 1545.

Black and red dress. Black cap. Seated. Escutcheon of arms in the corner.

E was the son of Sir William Brandon, by Elizabeth, daughter and co-heir of Sir Henry Bruyn, and widow of one Mallory. Sir William had been a zealous adherent of Henry Earl of Richmond, afterwards Henry VII., one of the first assertors of that Prince's right to the throne of England, and so much attached to his person, that he forfeited a good fortune to join his royal friend in Brittany. Brandon returned in Henry's suite to England, and sealed his fidelity with his life-blood, dying on the field of Bosworth by the hand of Richard III. himself. The favour which could not be awarded to the father was extended to the son, and King Henry became friend and guardian to the young orphan, who was bred up at Court, and made the companion and playfellow of the royal Henry, afterwards the eighth of that name, on whose accession to the throne Charles Brandon was appointed Esquire of the body, and Chamberlain of the Principality of Wales.

2 X

In 1513 Lord Herbert thus makes mention of him :—
'The gallants of the Court, finding the King's favour shine manifestly on Cardinal Wolsey, applied themselves much to him, and Charles Brandon especially, who for his goodly person, courage, and conformity of disposition, was noted to be most acceptable to Henry in all his exercises and pastimes.'

In these pursuits indeed he rivalled his royal master.

The year in which he attracted the notice of Lord Herbert, Brandon first served with distinction, in an engagement with a French squadron, off Brest. On his return he was raised to the Peerage by the title of Viscount L'Isle.

Later on, Lord L'Isle made the French campaign with the King, and fought at the battle of the Spurs, the siege of Terouenne, etc. etc., holding a high command in the English army. Thence they marched into Flanders, reduced Tournay, and were received with splendour and sumptuously entertained by the Emperor Maximilian. The goodly person and other noble gifts of Charles Brandon appear to have made an impression on the heart of the Archduchess Margaret, the Emperor's daughter. Herbert says: 'Find some overtures of a match between Lord L'Isle and the Princess Margaret, which, though they took no effect, were not yet without much demonstration of outward grace and favour on her part.'

But Brandon was reserved for a still happier fate. In the early part of the year 1514, having been created Duke of Suffolk, he formed one of the band of noble 'jousters' who graced the nuptials of Mary Princess of England, (the King's sister,) with Louis XII. of France. Historians differ as to the time at which the germ of a deep attachment sprang up in the heart of Princess Mary for the captivating young noble. By some it is maintained that before political considerations had compelled her to consummate a union with the already aged and feeble King, she had nourished a tender feeling for her brother's early playmate; while others affirm that it was on the occasion of her ill-assorted marriage that the courage, skill, and grace which he displayed in the chivalrous exercises, to which we have alluded, captivated her fancy. Be this as it may, the French King only survived his marriage a few months, and a day or two after his death the young widow secretly espoused the man she dearly loved. We have again recourse to Lord Herbert's testimony. Speaking of the treaty of peace then pending with France, he says :—' Together with the proposing of this treaty, our King sent a letter to the Queen, his sister, desiring to know how she stood affected as to her return to England, and desiring her not to match without his consent. She, on the other hand, who had privately engaged her affections to Suffolk, made no difficulty to discover herself to both Kings, (her brother Henry, and Francis I., who had succeeded her late husband as King of France,) entreating the latter to mediate the marriage, and our King to approve it, unto which Francis easily agreed. But our King, for the conservation of his dignity, held off a little ; however, he had long designed her for Suffolk,' the Queen observing, 'that if the King would have her married in any place but where her heart was, she would shut herself up in a religious house.' And no wonder she should so speak, being in fact already the wife of Charles Brandon. Mary took all the blame of this step on herself, striving to shield her beloved from Henry's displeasure, who, with the good offices of Francis, soon restored the pair to his favour. Wolsey also stood their friend with the King, observing how much better it was that the Queen had not bestowed her hand on some Frenchman of quality.

They were publicly married, first at Calais, and afterwards at Greenwich in May 1515. Mary brought her husband enormous wealth. In addition to her other gifts, of birth and nature, her jointure was 60,000 crowns annually, besides personal property brought from France, estimated at 200,000, with a diamond of enormous price, entitled 'Le Miroir de Naples.'

A disagreement shortly afterwards arose between Suffolk and Cardinal Wolsey, which caused the Duke to retire for a while into the country, whence Henry, who could not brook the loss of his society, soon recalled him. Suffolk reappeared at Court, and accompanied his august brother-in-law to France, where he was present at the world-famed interview between the French and English Kings, entitled 'The Field of the Cloth of Gold.' Some years later, Suffolk went again to France in command of an invading force, where, in spite of the successes which his courage and military skill insured to the English arms, he was compelled to retreat in consequence of the scanty manner in which his troops were provisioned, those being days when the commissariat department was little understood. This step was blamed by Henry, and it was some time ere the royal anger could be appeased.

In 1529 Suffolk was a witness in the inquiry on which Henry founded his plea for the desired divorce from Catherine of Arragon, was one of the peers who subscribed the declaration to the Pope, threatening the abolition of the Holy See, should Clement refuse to annul the marriage, and was also a party to the accusations preferred against Cardinal Wolsey. For these too ready proofs of his subservience to Henry's wishes the Duke was rewarded by considerable grants of Church lands. He was again called into active service, in order to quell some disturbances in Lincolnshire and Yorkshire, and in 1544 made his last campaign in France, reducing the town of Boulogne, after a siege which lasted six weeks. Previous to his departure from England he made his will, containing some curious bequests; amongst others, desiring that a cup of gold should be formed out of his Collar of the Garter, and given to the King. He ordered that his funeral should be conducted 'without outward pomp or pride of the world,' and that his body should be interred in the Collegiate Church of Tattershall, in Lincolnshire. But the King's special commands overruled his last wishes, and Charles Brandon, Duke of Suffolk, was buried with unusual magnificence in St. George's Chapel, Windsor. He was 'Justice in Eyre' of all the King's forests, and Great Master or Steward of the royal household.

Charles Brandon was four times married. From his first wife, Margaret, daughter of John Melville, Marquis Montague, and widow of Sir John Mortimer, he was divorced at her suit, in consequence of his having previously signed a contract of marriage with Anne, daughter of Sir Anthony Browne, Lieutenant of Calais. This lady became his second wife, and by her he had two daughters, who married Lords Powis and Monteagle. The Queen-Dowager of France brought him a son, created Earl of Lincoln, who died young, and two daughters, the eldest married to Henry Clifford, Earl of Cumberland, and the younger, first to Henry Grey, Duke of Suffolk, and afterwards to Adrian Stokes. His fourth wife was Catherine, daughter and heir of William Lord Willoughby d'Eresby, by whom he had two sons, who both died on the same day, shortly after their father, of the sweating-sickness, at the Episcopal Palace of Buckden, county Hunts.

No. 158.

LORD KEEPER WILLIAMS.

PAINTER UNKNOWN.

BORN 1582, DIED 1650.

Painted on wood. Black eyes, moustaches, and beard. Low-crowned broad-brimmed hat. Left hand rests on the case of the Great Seal. In the corner a shield, with many quarterings, surmounted by a mitre. Inscription: 'Lord Keeper Williams, Archbishop of York, 1625.'

JOHN, son of Edmund Williams, by Anne Wynne, (both names that testify to true Cambrian descent,) born at Aberconway, county Carnarvon, educated at a Grammar School, where it was said of him, 'that he was a proficient in Greek, and Latin, but had little Sassenach.' He then went to Cambridge, where all the Welshmen were proud of their countryman's talents, although his accent and pronunciation caused an occasional laugh at his expense. He accepted a small living in Norfolk, and a better one in Northamptonshire, but still continued to reside for some time at the University. Lord Chancellor Ellesmere was so taken by his preaching and his good character that he appointed Williams his private chaplain, took him into his confidence, and made him his inseparable companion. Even in the Courts of Chancery and the Star Chamber the young man sat beside his patron, and as an earnest listener did the future Lord Keeper begin his legal education. He had the chief command of the Chancellor's ecclesiastical patronage, which he dispensed with judgment, never losing sight for a moment of his own interests. He became a large pluralist, had two good livings, and stalls in four cathedrals, while a sermon he preached at Court, on the divine right of kings, insured him the favour of James I. Prince Henry also admired his preaching, and said he was 'an honour to the Principality.'

Lord Ellesmere was now growing old, and made use of his chaplain in all his business transactions with the King, a fortunate circumstance for Williams, as James took a great liking for him. When the Chancellor was dying, he offered his chaplain a reward for his services. 'I wish for nothing at your hands,' was the reply, 'you have filled my cup so full. Give me directions how to live in the world, if I survive you.' 'You are an expert workman,' said the dying man; 'take these tools, they are the best I have,' at the same time giving him his own four treatises, on the manner of conducting business in the Courts of Chancery, Parliament, the Star Chamber, and Council.

Lord Bacon, on succeeding to the Woolsack, offered to continue Williams as his chaplain, but he chose rather to go to his living, and work there as parish priest, Justice of the Peace, etc. etc., with occasional visits to London to preach at Court, and keep up his interest there. Watching passing events, he soon made up his mind, that it was impossible to rise without the help of the all-powerful Buckingham. Fortunately for our wary Welshman, an opportunity soon offered to ingratiate himself into the Duke's good books. The handsome courtier was a suitor for the hand of the beautiful heiress, Lady Catherine Manners, but her father, the Earl of Rutland, considered Buckingham 'an upstart,' and the lady was a strict Roman Catholic, and moreover much scandalised by her lover's reputation as a man of gallantry. Williams lived near Belvoir, where he was a frequent and welcome visitor, and Buckingham asked his mediation. So successfully did he conduct matters, that ere long all scruples were overcome on the part of father and daughter, and the latter converted to the Protestant faith, according to the tenets of which Williams married the couple, having first himself drawn up the marriage settlements. He used to say, with reason, that this affair was the keystone in the arch of his fortune.

As a recompence, he demanded and obtained the Deanery of Westminster. When the cry was raised against Lord Bacon, Williams took part with his enemies, at first secretly. When the Great Seal was taken from Bacon, and put into commission for a time, Williams, after some delay, carried off the prize in spite of numerous competitors,—the King and Buckingham being both in favour of this most unpopular choice. The lawyers were irate, that one who had never run in the race should win the garland! His installation was delayed, and he now set to work to educate himself for the post he had already attained, studying day and night, and scarcely allowing time for food or sleep. Indeed we are told that through life he never slept more than three hours at a time. He had not, said his Secretary, 'one drop of lazy blood in his veins.' He was raised to the See of Lincoln, and on becoming Lord Keeper, retained all his ecclesiastical preferment. 'He had a whole diocese in his person,—Bishop, Dean, Prebendary, Parson, and Priest.'

Verily the Lord Keeper had feathered his nest! In his legal capacity he worked strenuously, and chose his advisers well, although at times an error in technical terms caused a titter in Court. There is a good story of a certain lawyer attempting a joke at the Lord Keeper's expense, by making a sham motion, which was crammed like a grenade with obsolete words, of far-fetched antiquity, thinking to keep the new Judge in the dark, and take him at a disadvantage. But we are told it is dangerous to play with edged tools. The Lord Keeper discovered the plot, and rising, answered his antagonist in a long speech, in which the words categorematical and syncategorematical were among the shortest and simplest of his polysyllables. The laugh, and the tables, were turned in an instant. So zealous and skilful was he in the prosecution of his new duties, that few complaints were heard; but Buckingham and Laud were both jealous of his growing power, and preferred charges against him, the latter especially, for betraying 'the secrets of the Council.' He was moreover in bad odour at this time, for the violent part he took against Abbot, Archbishop of Canterbury, who had accidentally shot Lord Zouche's gamekeeper, instead of a deer at which he was aiming. There were whispers that Williams would not have disliked the post of Primate, but nothing came of it.

Buckingham returned about this time from Spain, and accused the Lord Keeper of having plotted against him during his absence. Williams humbled himself before the great man, who said, 'I will not seek your ruin, though I shall cease to study your fortune.'

When King James lay on his deathbed, Williams ministered to him, closed his eyes, and preached his funeral sermon. Charles, on his accession, confirmed him in all his offices, but was soon persuaded by Buckingham to deprive him of the Great Seal. Williams therefore retired to his palace at Buckden, which, being in a dilapidated condition, he restored, and lived there in much state.

But he could not place a guard over the door of his lips, and he who had been accused of employing spies himself, seems to have been surrounded by them. It was reported at Court, how disrespectfully Williams spoke of high personages and their doings, and he was forbidden to appear at the forthcoming Coronation. Many slights and indignities were put upon him, but for all that, he kept his place on the bench of Bishops, and supported the popular cause, more especially the famous Petition of Right. He was now attacked on all sides, and grave charges were made against him, so that he was dismissed from his seat at the Council Board, and then brought to trial. Found guilty of manifold crimes and misdemeanours, he was sentenced to be fined, suspended, and imprisoned. Accordingly he was arrested and sent to the Tower. Before he was released, fresh accusations were brought against him, and the fines upon him were increased; Laud being always foremost in the rank of his adversaries, for he had no reason to love Williams. It was now proposed to the prisoner, voluntarily to resign all his offices, including his bishopric, and to accept an Irish See, but this offer he stoutly refused. Williams was at length released by the Long Parliament, and all proceedings against him cancelled. On his appearance at Court, he was received with open arms, and raised to the Archbishopric of York. Although professing to disapprove of the attainder of Strafford, he advised the King most cruelly, and Clarendon says was instrumental in Strafford's death. He opposed the Bill for excluding the Bishops from the House of Lords, and took so active a part that he was once more sent to the Tower for a short time. During his second imprisonment, (Laud being then under the same gloomy roof,) the two Archbishops met, and were reconciled. On his release, Williams entered on a new career, that of arms, joining the Royal cause with all his heart, and working strenuously to advance it in Wales. He had a design of fortifying Carwood Castle in his See, but found the place untenable, being almost a ruin; and he was obliged to fly in the dead of night, on the approach of 'those two traitors, Sir John Hotham and his son,' with scarcely a change of raiment, without provisions, and not a coin in his purse. The next day, meeting his royal master by the way, this loyal subject gave up the best of the horsemen who rode with him, and proceeded to his native town, which he had left as a mere stripling, about fifty years before. The Archbishop continued to preach religion, morality, and loyalty among the Welsh, and repaired and fortified Conway Castle, for which good service King Charles (whom he joined at Oxford for a time) appointed him Governor of the same. This displeased Prince Rupert, who hated Churchmen, and he caused Williams to be superseded,—a circumstance which rankled deeply in the warlike prelate's bosom.

He remained for a time inactive, but falling in with a Parliamentary force, the desire of revenge got the better of his loyalty, and he was persuaded by the General to assist him in the attack on Conway, still under the command of his successor. The assault succeeded, and Williams was once more for a short period installed in Conway Castle. Soon after this he retired to the house of his kinswoman, Lady Mostyn, where he remained till his death. He was horrified when he heard the King had left Oxford. 'What!' he said, 'take the advice of a stranger, and trust the Scots! then all is lost.' On being told of Charles's execution, he fainted away, and said he would never take comfort more. He survived about a year, but spent most of his time in bed, rising at midnight to pray, 'as that was the hour at which Christ would come to judge the quick and dead.' He died on his sixty-eighth birthday, his last words being 'Lord Jesus, come quickly,' for he had long wished for death. His temper was fiery, owing, said his Secretary, to his Welsh blood. He was hospitable and charitable, had a great taste for building, and restored Westminster at his own expense, besides many munificent grants to both Universities. He gave much offence to the Puritans by his love of dramatic performances. One Sunday, the very day of an Episcopal ordination, he caused the 'Midsummer Night's Dream' to be represented, (on a stage erected in Buckden Palace,) for the edification of the young priests.

In person he was handsome; his countenance comely, his complexion fair, his gait stately. He was merry, and even facetious, until the time of the King's death, after which he seldom opened his lips, except to call down vengeance on Cromwell and the Regicides.

He repurchased his family estate, and bequeathed it to his heir. He left several theological writings. Lord Keeper Williams, Archbishop of York, lies buried in a small church near Penrhyn, in Wales.

No. 159.

SIR THEODORE MAYERNE.

PAINTER UNKNOWN.

BORN 1572-3, DIED 1656-7.

Seated in an arm-chair. Dressed in a black gown. White collar and cuffs. Black skull-cap. Grey beard and whiskers. His hand resting on a bust of Hippocrates. A large clasped book on the table, inscribed 'Hermes.' The painting is on wood.

THEODORE TURQUET, Sieur de Mayerne, Baron D'Aumont, born at Geneva. His father was an author of no very great repute. Theodore was Physician-in-Ordinary to Henry IV. of France, and after his death, came to England, and occupied the same post at the courts of James I., Charles I. and his Queen, and Charles II. His name is specially remembered in connection with that of Henry, Prince of Wales, whose last illness was so sudden, but it was not for some days after the attack that Mayerne was called in to consult with Henry's own medical adviser. There were rumours afloat that the hope of the nation, the darling of his father's people, was the victim of poison, administered by Lord Rochester, the King's favourite, through jealousy of the Prince's supposed admiration for the beautiful but abandoned Countess of Essex, but Mayerne refuted the accusation, in an elaborate account of Henry's illness, (which he published in English, French, and Latin,) proving that the Prince's death was occasioned by natural causes.

He disagreed with the other physicians as to the treatment of the patient, and the King gave him a certificate, and the Lords in Council and the gentlemen of the Prince's household expressed their entire satisfaction with the manner in which this able man had conducted the case.

Theodore Mayerne, Baron D'Aumont, received the honour of Knighthood from the hands of Charles I. His death was caused by drinking (though moderately) of bad wine when dining with a few friends at a tavern in the Strand. Bad wine is usually a slow poison, but in Sir Theodore's case, advanced age, and consequent weakness, quickened the result. He foretold to his companions the exact hour at which death would ensue, and the prediction proved but too true. Mayerne had the credit of inventing many valuable medicines, and left behind him many receipts that were much esteemed. He was an excellent Latin scholar, and wrote several medical works in that language. He was moreover an admirable chemist, and Walpole tells us that the celebrated miniature painter Petitot owed the perfection of his colouring in enamel to some chemical secret imparted to him by the Court physician.

Sir Theodore was buried in the old church of St. Martin's in the Fields. He had an only daughter, married to the Marquis de Cugnac, who died when only twenty. She was buried at Chelsea.

No. 160.

SIR THOMAS CHICHELEY.

Black dress.

E have not been able to gain much information respecting him, but the fact that Lady Savile married him as her second husband will sufficiently account for his portrait being here. We believe him to have been a staunch Royalist, which may have recommended him in the lady's eyes, though it is curious that her biographer, Dr. Barwick, makes no mention of this marriage, or, if at all, only in a scanty note. We find in Collins's *Baronetage,* that Thomas Chicheley of Wimpole, county Cambridge, was recommended as qualified to be made a Knight of the Royal Oak, in 1660, and that Sir Thomas Chicheley was Master of the Ordnance to King Charles II. He sold the estate of Wimpole, in 1686, to Sir John Cutler.

INDEX OF PORTRAITS.

INDEX OF PORTRAITS.

The first page mentioned indicates the notice of the Life.

	PAGE
ALBEMARLE, GEORGE MONCK, DUKE OF,	231
... ELIZABETH, DUCHESS OF,	137
ARLINGTON, HENRY BENNET, EARL OF,	234
ARUNDEL, HENRY FITZALAN, EARL OF,	167
BATH, FIRST MARQUIS OF,	70
... FIRST MARCHIONESS OF,	76, 336
SECOND MARQUIS OF,	57, 249
SECOND MARCHIONESS OF,	134
... FOURTH MARQUIS OF,	79, 133
... FOURTH MARCHIONESS OF,	58
BEAUCHAMP, LORD,	327
BEDFORD, JOHN RUSSELL, SIXTH DUKE OF,	250
BOHEMIA, KING OF,	281, 325
... QUEEN OF,	268

Index of Portraits.

	PAGE
BUCKINGHAM, EDWARD STAFFORD, DUKE OF,	226
... GEORGE VILLIERS, SECOND DUKE OF,	145
CARNARVON, EARL AND COUNTESS OF,	130
CATHERINE OF BRAGANZA, QUEEN OF ENGLAND,	160
CAVENDISH, ADMIRAL, THE CIRCUMNAVIGATOR,	315
CHARLES, PRINCE OF WALES,	225
... THE FIRST, KING OF ENGLAND,	218, 303
... THE SECOND,	160
CHARTRES, VIDÂME DE,	122
CHICHELEY, SIR THOMAS,	360
CHILDREN OF CHARLES THE FIRST,	219
... OF SIR JOHN THYNNE THE BUILDER,	199
COLE, MR.,	336
COLIGNY, ADMIRAL DE,	96
CONDÉ, PRINCE DE,	120
CONINGSBY, MR.,	335
COVENTRY, THE HONOURABLE HENRY,	72
... SIR JOHN,	64
... THE LORD KEEPER,	79, 30
... SIR WILLIAM,	82
COVERT, SIR WALTER,	94
... LADY,	95
DEVEREUX, THE LADIES,	115

Index of Portraits.

	PAGE
DIGBY, SIR KENELM,	250
DORSET, EDWARD SACKVILLE, FOURTH EARL OF,	31
DUNDEE, JOHN GRAHAME OF CLAVERHOUSE, VISCOUNT,	319
ELEANOR OF AUSTRIA,	200, 202
ESSEX, ROBERT DEVEREUX, EARL OF,	102
FALKLAND, LUCIUS CAREY, SECOND VISCOUNT,	27
FERDINAND, DON, CARDINAL, INFANT OF SPAIN,	328
FINCH, THE HONOURABLE LEOPOLD,	327
FISHER, BISHOP OF ROCHESTER,	166
GEORGE THE FIRST, KING OF ENGLAND,	134
GRANVILLE, GRACE CARTERET, COUNTESS,	116
GRESHAM, SIR RICHARD,	171
GUSTAVUS ADOLPHUS, KING OF SWEDEN,	108
HAMILTON, WILLIAM, SECOND DUKE OF,	220
HARLEY, LADY MARGARET,	318
HENRIETTA MARIA, QUEEN OF ENGLAND,	219
HENRY THE EIGHTH, KING OF ENGLAND,	36
HENRY THE FOURTH, KING OF FRANCE AND NAVARRE,	225
HENRY, PRINCE OF WALES,	307
HERTFORD, EARL OF, AFTERWARDS DUKE OF SOMERSET,	111

Index of Portraits.

	PAGE
HOLLAND, HENRY RICH, EARL OF,	34
INNOCENT THE ELEVENTH, POPE,	139
JERSEY, EDWARD VILLIERS, FIRST EARL OF,	117
JUXON, ARCHBISHOP,	257
KELIFET, MR.,	326
KEN, BISHOP,	5
LANSDOWNE, GEORGE LORD,	45
LADY,[1]	110, 78
LAUD, WILLIAM, ARCHBISHOP OF CANTERBURY,	261
LEICESTER, ROBERT DUDLEY, EARL OF,	191
... DOROTHY SIDNEY, COUNTESS OF,	340
LONSDALE, JOHN LOWTHER, VISCOUNT,	302
... VISCOUNTESS,	303
LUTHER, MARTIN,	224
LYNCH, SIR WILLIAM,	256
MACCLESFIELD, CHARLES GERARD, EARL OF,	286
MARY, QUEEN OF ENGLAND,	129
MAXIMILIAN, EMPEROR OF GERMANY,	203
MAYERNE, SIR THEODORE,	358
NEWCASTLE, WILLIAM CAVENDISH, FIRST DUKE OF, AND HIS DUCHESS,	239

[1] By inadvertence, Lady Lansdowne has been called 'Viscountess' in the text of the book.

Index of Portraits.

	PAGE
NORTHUMBERLAND, ALGERNON PERCY, EARL OF,	286
NOTT, LADY,	190
NOTTINGHAM, HENEAGE FINCH, EARL OF,	227
... CATHERINE CAREY, COUNTESS OF,	150
... ESSEX RICH, COUNTESS OF,	325
OVERBURY, SIR THOMAS,	244
OXFORD, ROBERT HARLEY, EARL OF,	330
PEMBROKE, PHILIP HERBERT, EARL OF,	265
RALEIGH, SIR WALTER,	155
RICHELIEU, CARDINAL,	343
RICHMOND AND LENNOX, FRANCES HOWARD, DUCHESS OF,	53
ROSAMOND, FAIR,	129
RUBENS, PETER PAUL, WIFE AND CHILD,	167
RUSSELL, LORD JOHN, AFTERWARDS EARL RUSSELL, K.G.,	333
SAVILE, THE HONOURABLE LADY,	118, 328
SEYMOUR, ELIZABETH, AFTERWARDS COUNTESS OF AILESBURY,	302
SHAFTESBURY, ANTHONY ASHLEY COOPER, FIRST EARL OF,	11
SHREWSBURY, ELIZABETH BRUDENELL, COUNTESS OF,	337

Index of Portraits.

	PAGE
SIDNEY, SIR HENRY,	153
SOMERSET, DUKE OF, PROTECTOR,	21
... WILLIAM, DUKE OF,—A Boy,	304
SOUTHAMPTON, THOMAS WRIOTHESLEY, EARL OF,	42
STRAFFORD, THOMAS WENTWORTH, EARL OF,	209
ST. ALBANS, FRANCIS BACON, VISCOUNT,	276
STUART, LADY ARABELLA,	172, 116
SUDELEY, THOMAS LORD SEYMOUR OF,	36
SUFFOLK, CHARLES BRANDON, DUKE OF,	347
THURLOW, EDWARD, FIRST LORD,	47

THE THYNNE FAMILY—

THYNNE, SIR EGREMONT,	68
... SIR HENRY FREDERICK,	45, 77
... HIS WIFE,	94, 315
... THE HONOURABLE HENRY,	238
... THE HONOURABLE JAMES,	195
... JAMES, Esq.,	98
... SIR JAMES,	121, 73
... LADY ISABELLA, HIS WIFE,	89, 78
... SIR JOHN, THE BUILDER OF LONGLEAT,	66
... THE SECOND SIR JOHN,	115
... HIS WIFE,	114
... SIR THOMAS, OF RICHMOND,	71

	PAGE
THYNNE, SIR THOMAS, OF LONGLEAT,	122
... HIS FIRST WIFE,	87
... HIS SECOND WIFE,	88
... THOMAS, FATHER OF SECOND VISCOUNT WEYMOUTH,	83, 335
... TOM O' TEN THOUSAND,	73, 95
TINTORETTO, GIACOMO ROBUSTI,	133
TÖCKOLI, HELENA, COUNTESS,	290
... COUNT EMERIC,	296
TORRINGTON, GEORGE, FOURTH VISCOUNT,	77
... VISCOUNTESS,	109
WEYMOUTH, FIRST VISCOUNT,	63, 5, 326
... HIS WIFE,	61
... SECOND VISCOUNT,	62, 110
... HIS FIRST WIFE,	61
... HIS SECOND WIFE,	70, 110
WILLIAMS, LORD KEEPER,	352
YORK, JAMES DUKE OF,	190

ERRATA.

Page 290 and 296, *for* (Emperor of) Austria *read* Germany.

,, 331, *insert* Langallerie *after* Marquis de Guiscard.

,, 344, *for* Palais Royal *read* Bibliothèque du Roi.

www.ingramcontent.com/pod-product-compliance
Lightning Source LLC
Chambersburg PA
CBHW030404230426
43664CB00007BB/738